SUNNY JIM YOUNG

Celtic Legend

SUNNY JIM YOUNG

Celtic Legend

David Potter

This edition published in Great Britain in 2013 by DB Publishing, an imprint of JMD Media.

Copyright © David Potter

ISBN 9781780913124

Printed and bound by Copytech (UK) Limited, Peterborough.

CONTENTS

ACKNOWLEDGEMENTS   7

CHAPTER ONE   THE PRE-CELTIC YEARS   8

CHAPTER TWO   ARRIVAL   16

CHAPTER THREE   FORMATION OF THE TROIKA

                   AND THE SCOTTISH CUP   28

CHAPTER FOUR   GLORY, GLORY, GLORY   54

CHAPTER FIVE   THE GREATEST SHOW ON EARTH   81

CHAPTER SIX   TRANSITION AND CAPTAINCY   112

CHAPTER SEVEN   1913–1914   139

CHAPTER EIGHT   THE WAR YEARS AT PARKHEAD   157

CHAPTER NINE   1916 – 1922   183

STATISTICS   201

ACKNOWLEDGEMENTS

I am grateful to many people for their help in producing this book, and I apologise to anyone I may have omitted. Andrew Blue was very helpful in the ancestry research part of the book; Phil Yelland and Mike Gardner gave me valuable information about Barrow, as Mike Jay and Stephen Byrne did about Bristol Rovers. The Celtic Graves Society, paticularly Jamie Fox and John McLauchlan, were very helpful and encouraging as were George Sheridan and Tom Campbell. Jim Scullion gave me permission to use his painting, and I was always met with unfailing courtesy and helpfulness by the staff at the Mitchell Library, Glasgow, the National Library of Scotland, Edinburgh and the Wellgate Library, Dundee.

CHAPTER ONE

THE PRE-CELTIC YEARS

James Young was born in the early hours of the morning at 15 Kirktonholme Street, Kilmarnock on 10 January 1882 to William and Annie Young. Anne's maiden surname was Gilmour, and sometimes Jimmy would sign official documents as James Gilmour Young, but his Birth Certificate definitely says that his name is James Young. His father William had a good job on the railway as a Goods Porter, and he was literate, for he was able to sign the Birth Certificate. In 1882 literacy could not always be guaranteed, although following the Education Act of 1872, it was becoming more likely than not. The couple had married in Loudoun on 15 July 1864.

No certain trace of the family can be found in Kilmarnock in the 1881 census, so it is likely that they had just recently moved into the town, but by 1891 when James was nine years old, the family had moved to 7 Nursery Street, Kilmarnock where we find that William was now a Warehouseman rather than a Goods Porter and that the William and Annie now had eight children still living with them, of whom James was the second youngest. In order they were William jr, Anne, Sarah, Jeannie, Maggie, John, James and Nancy. The eldest five were working but John, James and Nancy were described as "scholars".

Kilmarnock is in East Ayrshire, and like most places, was small and insignificant, built round a Church, until the Industrial Revolution of the early 19th century when miscellaneous industries sprung up. But Robert Burns from nearby Alloway had already immortalised the place. In 1786, the first edition of Burns poetry *"Poems, Chiefly in the Scottish Dialect"* was published there by John Wilson, and this work has become known to posterity as *"The Kilmarnock Edition"*. Moreover, Kilmarnock is mentioned several times in Burns poetry, notably in the *Elegy of Tam Samson*.

Has auld Kilmarnock seen the deil?
Or great Mackinlay thrawn his heel?
Or Robertson again grown weel,
To preach an' read
"Na, waur than a'!" cries ilka chiel
"Tam Samson's dead!"

Kilmarnock lang may grunt an' grane
An' sigh, an' sab, an' greet her lane,
An' cleed her bairns, man, wife an' wean,
In mourning weed;
To death, she's dearly paid the kane,
"Tam Samson's dead!"

but the news turns out to be false!

Go, Fame, an' canter like a filly
Thro' a' the streets an' neuks o' Killie,
Tell ev'ry social honest billie
To cease his grievin',
For yet, unskaith'd by Death's gleg gullie,
Tam Samson's livin'!

What usually determined the progress and growth or otherwise of a town in the nineteenth century was the arrival of the railway. Not only did the railway itself provide employment to people (like William Young) and encourage them to settle in the town, but it meant that local industry could thrive, knowing that goods could be readily transported to potential markets. It also meant that people could choose to live in a town and not necessarily work there, and the town could provide a "dormitory" facility. Moreover, there was a feeling of well-being, civic awareness and prosperity associated with having the railway in town!

Kilmarnock did well from the railway. A line opened to Troon in 1812 (even before the arrival of steam locomotion, so horse power was required) for the transport of both goods and passengers, but the real boost came in 1843 when the Glasgow, Paisley, Kilmarnock and Ayr Railway was opened. Such was the success of this company that three years later in 1846 a bigger and better station was opened, and this station still exists to serve Kilmarnock today.

Lines would open to Dumfries and the South in due course, (a massive railway viaduct, still in existence, being built for this purpose) but it was the link to Glasgow and the Clyde that was the important one. Glasgow would soon become the "Second City of the Empire", and the whole Clyde valley area would be described as "the crucible of the British Empire". In truth, west central Scotland was as busy a part of the world as any, with people flocking to Glasgow, Lanarkshire, Renfrewshire, Ayrshire and Dunbartonshire in a way that was totally amazing to the rest of the country and the world. The Irish potato famine sent many Irish men and women, (something that had a huge impact, of course, on the genesis of Celtic Football Club), the Highland Clearances brought in the Highlanders, and various others from diverse parts of Scotland and England came to this part of Scotland to find work.

Kilmarnock was on the periphery of this huge expansion, close enough for people to travel to Glasgow but with some country and green fields between Kilmarnock and the huge metropolis that was Glasgow. Kilmarnock was fortunate in that it was not over-dependent on any one industry in the way that Motherwell, for example, was always associated with steel or Dundee with jute. Textiles, heavy engineering, carpets and shoes were all made there, with iron turners being particularly required by the form of Andrew Barclay and Sons for the making of locomotives. *The Titanic*, apparently, went to the bottom of the Atlantic in 1912 with carpets made by Stoddart Carpets of Kilmarnock.

Sport had started early in Kilmarnock. Organised team games only really began in Great Britain in the early part of the 19th century, but Kilmarnock Cricket Club was founded as early as 1852 (making it one of the oldest in the country) and Kilmarnock Football Club was founded in 1869, making Kilmarnock Scotland's second oldest football club (of those who are still with us) with only Queen's Park in 1867 claiming a longer history. There was thus in the town of Kilmarnock loads of opportunity for a young man to play sport.

Another stimulus for the development of sport was of course the proximity to Ayr and the inevitable struggle for local supremacy. Rivalry can of course be a very good thing, but this particular rivalry was not always friendly. From an early stage, we hear of fights between youths of Kilmarnock and Ayr at cricket matches, on one occasion the constable being compelled to use his "cudgel of office" to restore order, and several times Kilmarnock Cricket Club had to put an advertisement in the local paper to discourage youths from attending.

There is of course nothing new or unusual about thick-headed youths fighting each other. Such tribal behaviour is endemic, particularly with the added spice of sport and local rivalry as there undeniably was in Ayrshire between Ayr and Kilmarnock, or as they would have been pronounced them "Err" and "Kullie". It was a by-product of the Industrial Revolution. The town, perhaps, had replaced the tribe or the clan as the focus of where one belonged.

By 1901, the Young family had moved to 1 McLelland Drive and James had followed his elder brother John into the Iron Turner trade. But James now 19 was like most Scottish boys of that age, utterly obsessed with football. Unlike most however, he was good at it, (*The Bible* perhaps would put it "many are called, but few are chosen") and he cut his teeth with quite a few of the juvenile and junior football teams which abounded in the locality. He played for Lilliemount Juveniles, Dean Park, Kilmarnock Rugby XI, then, hoping to turn professional, he had an unsuccessful trial for Kilmarnock FC, before playing for Stewarton and Shawbank.

In February 1902, he felt that he should move on, leave the area and perhaps turn professional in England. It was of course a huge leap in the dark to become a professional footballer. It was not guaranteed that a living could be made from it, and it was undeniably a short life with no professional footballer likely to be plying his trade beyond the age of 35, and of course, injury could cut it shorter than that. But it was what he wanted to do. He tried his luck for a short spell in early 1902 with Barrow, and I am grateful to Phil Yelland and Mike Gardner for their help.

It is of course possible that his motive for moving to Barrow-in-Furness was to ply his trade as an iron turner, and that football was an added extra. There would certainly have been a job for him there, because Barrow in 1902 was a hive of industry, specialising in steel and shipbuilding. Sometimes called the "English Chicago" because of its rapid growth, its metamorphosis in the 19th century was truly phenomenal. There are Scottish parallels in places like Coatbridge and Airdrie which barely existed in 1800, yet were bustling, thriving hives of industry by a hundred years later.

Henry Schneider's discovery of hematite steel and the Furness Railway led to Barrow developing quickly on a grid plan – one of the largest planned towns in the British Isles. By 1901, there was a population of over 67,000 when a hundred years previously, there had been less than 2,000 living in the town at the end of the Furness peninsula, sometimes called the "longest cul-de-sac in Britain".

Barrow were a very young team, founded only the previous year in 1901 and played at a ground with the unlikely name of "The Strawberry". In 1902 they played in the Lancashire League, and Young joined them in time to play six League games and two friendlies at least (possibly another one against the Edinburgh side St Bernard's) between February and the end of the season. The League games were against Stalybridge, Workington, St Helens, Darwen, Wigan United and Southport, and the friendlies were against Workington Black Diamonds and Bolton Wanderers. He was clearly good enough to attract the attention of Bristol Rovers.

It was midsummer 1902 (8 July to be precise) when James Young joined Bristol Rovers. He was 20. 1902 was of course the end of the Boer War and the summer of the Coronation of King Edward VII. The Coronation itself had to be postponed from June until August because of the King's health and his being obliged to undergo the then very dangerous operation for appendicitis. Back in Scotland, although Young would then have had only a passing interest in such things, Celtic won the British League Cup (sometimes called the Coronation Cup) by beating Rangers 3–2 after extra-time with a young fellow called Jimmy Quinn scoring a hat-trick. Football of course had been rocked by the Ibrox Disaster on 5 April 1902. Over 20 people had been killed when a stand collapsed at the Scotland v England game, as people swayed from one side to another (so it was claimed) to see Kilmarnock man Bobby Templeton run up the wing.

Bristol was a huge city in 1902, although the feeling persisted that Bristol had perhaps passed its peak. If Glasgow was the "Second City of the British

Empire" in the late nineteenth and early twentieth century, Bristol had had that role in the eighteenth century, being the chief city and port for the Americas and, in particular, the West Indies. It was a sad and uncomfortable fact that a large part of Bristol's wealth and glory had derived from the slave trade, but slavery had been abolished for almost a hundred years now thanks to the strenuous efforts of William Wilberforce and others, and it was only the slightly more respectable trade of tobacco that held sway now.

The railways had made a great difference to Bristol as well. The GWR (the Great Western Railway, or as it was more commonly referred to, "God's Wonderful Railway") had opened up the south-west for Londoners, who were thus able to establish business contacts and enjoy holidays in the beautiful countryside of Gloucestershire, Somerset, Devon and Cornwall. The famous engineeer Isambard Kingdom Brunel had also built in Bristol the Clifton Suspension Bridge, a remarkable feat of Victorian engineering, and to this day a scary-looking walk and drive across.

But Bristol never has been a great footballing city. Rugby was strong there even as early as 1902, and cricket in the summer, but even so, the records of the two teams Bristol City and Bristol Rovers have never really made as big an impact on English football as their population and fan base might have led us to expect. Birmingham is another under-performing footballing city, but Aston Villa, for example, have had their moments. In comparison with Liverpool and Manchester (and Newcastle long ago) Bristol has been a sad disappointment with the FA Cup and and English League Championship Trophy yet to make an appearance in the great city of the south-west, although City came close in 1907 and 1909.

A visit to Bristol on a match day can be a disappointing experience. There is little sign that there is a game on, few supporters' scarves or colours, no excited animation of anyone asking whether injuries have healed up or whether the team will be third in the League by tonight. Asking a passer-by for details of the way to the game can see one being directed, politely and courteously, to the wrong ground! This is in total contrast to a city like Newcastle for example. Similar prolonged and chronic under-achievement have not led to similar apathy there. Black and white scarves are ubiquitous, enthusiasm is prevalent – and how one wishes that they had a worthy team to support! But Bristol is different. It is not, by nature, a footballing city, and probably was the same in 1902 when Young arrived.

Bristol Rovers, founded in 1883, is the more senior football team in the city, but they were not known as Bristol Rovers until 1898, having previously been known as the Black Arabs, Eastville Rovers and Bristol Eastville Rovers. Their nickname is "the Pirates", for no other reason than the seafaring connections of Bristol, but they have also been known as "the Gas" because of a gasworks near their Eastville ground. They joined the Southern League in 1899 having played in the Bristol and District League, which became known as the Western League. In season 1902–03 they wore a black and white vertical strip, and would do so until 1919. They joined the Football League in 1920, the major moment of triumph in the Southern League coming in 1905 when they won it. (I am grateful to Mike Jay and Stephen Byrne, two Bristol Rovers historians, for supplying this information).

The manager of Bristol Rovers was a man called Alf Homer. He had been in position since 1899 and would stay in some capacity until 1928. Rovers owe a great deal to him. He was welcoming and encouraging to Young, and like most English teams of the day, Bristol Rovers employed many Scotsmen, so Young did not exactly feel lonely, even though he would not have been human if he had not been a little homesick. Bristol was a long way away from Kilmarnock.

The big sporting interest of that summer in Bristol was of course the Ashes between England and Australia. It was one of the epic series won 2–1 by Australia as Joe Darling and Victor Trumper took on Archie McLaren, Wilfred Rhodes and Ranjitsinghi. Gloucestershire's moment of glory came in the Fifth Test when their local hero Gilbert Jessop "the croucher" hit a century in 85 minutes to help England to a famous victory at the Oval. It was the day when the two Yorkshiremen George Hirst and Wilfred Rhodes, England's last two at the crease, edged home to win by one wicket. According to legend (but almost certainly without foundation) Hirst said to Rhodes "we'll get 'em in singles, Wilfred".

On that particular day (13 August 1902), Young made his home debut at right-half at Eastville as Cartlidge, Dunn and Griffiths; Young, McLean and Lyon; Muir, Howie, Corbett, Wilcox and Marriot beat Watford 5–1 in the First Division of the Southern League, with Fred Wilcox scoring a hat-trick before 5,000 spectators. It was a good start to the season, for the previous week, they had beaten Northampton Town 2–1 at Northampton.

The Southern League contained teams like Tottenham Hotspur, West Ham United and Queen's Park Rangers, and although it was still probably considered inferior to the Football League, the fact that Tottenham Hotspur had won the FA Cup in 1901 and Southampton had reached the final in 1900 and 1902 showed that the standard of football played in the Southern League was quite high.

Tottenham Hotspur were the biggest team in terms of support, (110,280 had attended the first game of the 1901 FA Cup Final at Crystal Palace between them and Sheffield United) and Young celebrated (if that is the right word!) his 21st birthday on 10 January 1903 at White Hart Lane on the wrong end of a 0–3 defeat before a crowd of 12,000. Southampton won the Southern League in 1903. Young was out of the team on 29 November 1902 when Southampton beat Rovers 3–1 at the Dell, but he played a creditable part when Southampton came to Eastville on 14 March 1903 and were, by all accounts, lucky to get away with a 1–1 draw.

The FA Cup campaign lasted no longer than one round, as far as Bristol Rovers were concerned, in season 1902–03. Yet it took Millwall three games to get the better of the Pirates. A 2–2 draw at Eastville on 13 December was followed by a trip to London to play a 0–0 draw at North Greenwich (the Den would not be opened until 1910) on the following Thursday afternoon, and the tie was finally resolved on Monday 22 December at the neutral venue of Villa Park, Birmingham when the Pirates went down 0–2 before a minuscule crowd. Young played in all three games. The Cup was won by Bury that year, beating Derby County by the record score of 60 in the final before 63,102 fans at the Crystal Palace.

Young played a total of 19 League games that season, in all three half-back positions, although mainly as a right-half. He was more of an asset than a debit however, in his 19 games, he won 9, drew 5 and lost 5. His final League game for the club was against Kettering Town on 4 April 1903. But in spite of having met and courted a young Bristolian lady, Young was wanting home to Scotland.

CHAPTER TWO

ARRIVAL

Celtic in **1903** were not doing at all well. They were well aware that if you discounted the one-off British League Cup (or Coronation Cup as some called it) in 1902, Celtic had won nothing since 1900, and it was hard to resist the conclusion that hegemony was passing (indeed possibly had already passed) across the city to Rangers who had won the Scottish League from 1899 until 1902. This year they had lost that particular crown to Edinburgh, to Hibs, but had more than made up for it by landing the Scottish Cup by beating Hearts at Celtic Park 3–0 after a replay. No-one knew it at the time, but it would be 25 years before the Ibrox men would repeat that feat.

It is important to realise that at the time that Jimmy Young, a non-Catholic, joined Celtic in 1903, there was as yet no huge issue of sectarianism in Scottish football. It did exist, of course, with Celtic being seen as the "Irish" team of Glasgow, so that those of other persuasions might tend to drift to the "non-Irish" team which was rising in the west of the city. But there was nothing hard and fast about it, and the driving force behind the rivalry was of course money. Some would say, that even in the 1920s when Rangers unashamedly identified themselves with Protestantism and Orangeism, the driving force was still money! But until the end of the Great War in 1918, sectarianism was not a major issue in Scottish football. Alec Bennett and Willie Kivlichan played for both teams before the Great War. Indeed, even when it did become enshrined in the rivalry between the clubs, the problem tended to exist mainly in the minds of supporters, even though Rangers did not help matters by their "no Catholics" policy of the 1920s which pandered to the bigotry in the minds of their less clear seeing supporters.

Celtic had been woefully inconsistent in 1902–03 in the League and finished up a distant fifth, and had gone out of both Cup competitions to 0–3 defeats. The Glasgow Cup Final in October 1902 had seen them go down 0–3 to a very fine Third Lanark side, but quite a few of the Celtic fans in the 20,000 crowd had been distressed by Celtic's lack of fight; the exit from the Scottish Cup had been even worse. 40,000 had been at Parkhead to see Rangers score three first half goals and stay on top in the second half with old warriors like Sandy McMahon and Barney Battles clearly outplayed by a younger and more determined Rangers team.

This is a wonderful collage of the early Celts, produced by kind permission of the artist Jim Scullion. Sunny Jim is appropriately in the middle above the old pavilion

Maley, now coming up for six years as manager, knew that sooner or later he would have to bite the bullet and go for younger players. Some of the booing from his own supporters had not been pleasant for anyone to listen to, and Maley's feelings were of anger at the ingratitude shown to the great Sandy McMahon for example by the disgruntled fans. Yet in his heart of hearts, Maley knew that Sandy was going to have to go, as indeed would Johnny Campbell. Young Quinn, Maley was reluctant to drop, for he was strong, and Maley always felt that if only the fragile young Crojan could close his ears to the barracking of the impatient, he might make something of him yet. Like most boys from mining villages, Quinn was socially inept in the big city and needed careful and tactful handling.

There was some talent in that young McMenemy and his friend Bennett as well, but there were still too many players in that team who were not of real Celtic class. But Maley, who had suffered some dreadful knocks in his private life, and who was already aware that he was a great deal fonder of the Celtic than he should be – a paid employee should not be as obsessed with his firm as he was! – decided that 1903 was going to be the year that things were to change. Already, with the backing of the Board, he had decided to change the format of the strips – still green and white, but horizontal rather than vertical – from the start of next season and he would like to think that there would be a permanent change in the team's fortunes as well. More players would be required.

Jimmy Young's arrival at Celtic Park was fortuitous, to put it mildly. Maley had heard good reports of an ex-Clyde and Kilmarnock right-winger called Bobby Muir, currently playing for Bristol Rovers. Muir was apparently homesick and wanted to return to Scotland, and he was good enough for Celtic to become interested. Accordingly, committee man Mick Dunbar was despatched south to have a look at him and to offer Muir at least a trial for Celtic, if he was interested.

Sometime in late April, Dunbar was successful in persuading Muir to come north, having agreed it all apparently over lunch at the Black Swan Hotel near Eastville, the home of Bristol Rovers. But there were another two players there as well at that lunch, both also from Kilmarnock, an inside-right called John Graham and a centre-half called James Young. Dunbar was impressed by their sincerity – Young in particular saying that he wanted to try again in Scotland as he did not really fit in at Bristol Rovers, and he felt he would like to play for a Scottish team with a large support. He was honest enough not to utter specious nonsense that "Celtic were the only team he ever wanted to play for" – because that would have been blatantly untrue – and said he was a professional footballer, and now suspecting that he would soon have a wife and child to support, he needed money.

All four men enjoyed their lunch that day, and Dunbar, apparently acting on his own initiative, (for in 1903, in the absence of mobile phones and texts, it would not have been easy to establish instant contact with Glasgow), decided that he would take all three of them to Glasgow, but in the case of Young and Graham, without making any promises. He sent a telegram to Maley. Maley might well have chuckled at the thought of these two youngsters being brought along as an afterthought, for was not that the way that he himself had joined the Celtic 15 years ago? The committee men in 1888 had been interested in his brother Tom, but then one of them had said "Why don't you come along as well?".

Both Muir and Young (Graham's chance would come later) were given a fairly immediate opportunity on Monday 27 April 1903. Celtic had arranged a friendly with Manchester City, both managers of course being the brothers Maley – Willie of Celtic and Tom of Manchester City. It was a poor game on an end-of-season bumpy pitch before a meagre crowd of 2,000, not helped by the weather breaking an hour before kick-off, and it ended in a goalless draw. Young played at centre-half under the pseudonym of "Smith" whereas Muir was "Jackson" for the purpose of this exercise with *The Evening Times* predicting that "Celtic will try out a few new recruits tonight". The team was McPherson; Watson and Battles; Loney, Smith and Weir; Jackson, McMenemy, McLeod, Somers and Thomson.

The game may have been a poor one, (it is hardly mentioned in the press which is far more bothered about the imminent visit of King Edward VII to Scotland in a few weeks time) but Maley was impressed by his centre-half James Young. He made a few mistakes, but his attitude was first class and he radiated command of the situation, not being afraid to shout at men like Barney Battles when he felt he was a little slow in getting to the ball. Willie Maley talked to his brother Tom at the post-match dinner, and Tom agreed that Young was worth persevering with – "Efter a', even wi' Meredith playing, we didnae score!". This was a reference to the great Billy Meredith of Manchester City and Wales, and arguably, the best played in Britain. Some of Tom Maley's contacts in Bristol had also talked highly of him.

Young may have tamed Billy Meredith but he was still technically a Bristol Rovers player, and immediately after this game, all three aspirant Celts had to return to Bristol to play in the Gloucestershire Cup Final against city rivals Bristol City at St John's Lane, then the home of City. This took place on

Wednesday 29 April. It was the third game, the other two having been drawn, but on this occasion, Rovers made no mistake, winning 4–2 and the three Scotsmen earned themselves a medal each with Young having an outstanding game at centre-half.

The medal whetted Young's appetite. He was a professional football player and needed more money, for he intended to marry Florence Coombs, who was now beginning to suspect that she was "expecting" a baby. She said she would be happy to go to Scotland with him. He still wanted to return to Scotland, and after winning the Gloucestershire Cup did just that. He talked to Maley again. Maley offered all three men from Bristol terms. They accepted happily, on a part-time basis initially, and this suited Young, for he would be able to resume his trade as an Iron Turner in Kilmarnock, just in case his footballing career did not work out.

Young promised Maley that he would work on his football, because "I want tae win medals, just like the Gloucestershire Cup one"."That's the spirit", thought Maley, "I can go places with young men like that!". Maley then asked what his plans were about houses etc., offered his help if necessary, and hoped that he would have a long and bright future at Celtic Park. Both men shook hands, but neither of them quite realised how long and how bright it was going to be.

"Man In The Know" in *The Glasgow Observer* of 9 May is distinctly unimpressed by all this. "I don't think much of Celtic's English captures. These three Bristol men – Muir, Graham and Young were reputed to be clean done (sic) before they left Scotland...I really fear that unless the Parkhead managers have a few better arrows in their quivers, there will be another season of disappointment for Celtic supporters." He was however impressed by Bennett from Rutherglen and "Allan McLeod, the Dunfermline youth", but it is clear that "Man In The Know" is going through an unhappy phase of his life, for he says that the season just ending has been a "beastly bore" and then goes on to state that supporters "wear a depressed air of chronic sadness born out of the conviction that only through sheer force of habit are they wasting an afternoon in watching fifth rate football".

It is of course not uncommon for supporters of teams who have had an unsuccessful season to complain about the general standard, and one feels that "Man In The Know" pessimistic outlook on life has a great deal to do with the poor performances of his beloved Celtic, rather than the standard of football in Scotland as a whole. As to who "Man In The Know" was in this rabid Roman Catholic newspaper which talked about Celtic most of the time and the other teams as a sort of afterthought, no-one knows.Some thought it was Tom Maley, Willie's elder brother; others thought it was the rising Labout politician John Wheatley. The truth was possibly that it was simply the Oberver news staff getting together and concocting a piece.

A fine view of the old pavilion with its cycling embankment taken during the Celtic Sports

The next few days after Young signed for Celtic were spent in arranging the "flitting" – a complicated business from Bristol to Kilmarnock (he had decided to stay in his home town, rather than Glasgow) and also training hard. His next game was also a friendly at Ayr on the night of Wednesday 13 May when all Scotland was thrilled about the Royal Visit to Glasgow and elsewhere of King Edward VII and Queen Alexandra. A great deal less prestigious was the 2–2 draw at Ayr in which Young actually scored what may well have been his first senior goal. A centre-half scoring was of course quite common in Edwardian football, for he was expected to go "up" whenever he had the opportunity as an extra forward and leave the defending to the full-backs and the half-backs.

Young was then delighted to find that his name was on the team sheet for the Glasgow Charity Cup game against Hibs against Parkhead. (The Glasgow Charity Cup had been expanded this season and included quite a few non-Glasgow teams with the laudable intention of raising more money for the victims and their relatives of last year's Ibrox disaster fund, when a stand had collapsed at the Scotland v England game). Thus it was that Young found himself playing his first competitive game for Celtic against this year's Scottish League Champions and winners of last year's Scottish Cup – Hibs.

The relationship between Celtic and Hibs was complex. Hibs were looked upon as the "parent club" from which Celtic had sprung. They had won the Scottish Cup in the February of the year (1887) that Celtic had been born, and there seems to be little doubt that that was what put the idea into the head of Brother Walfrid and others that for the purpose of feeding poor children in Glasgow's east end, a football team might be a good idea.

But Hibs had hit bad times in the early 1890s and Celtic had taken a few of their players, causing resentment in the Edinburgh Irish, who even saw the Glasgow side taking away some of their supporters as well. Celtic had of course done well in the 1890s, winning Scottish Cups and Scottish Leagues, but Hibs had fought back in the last year or so, delighting their supporters when they beat Celtic 1–0 to lift the Scottish Cup in 1902, and now winning the Scottish League. On 2 January 1903, Hibs had hammered Celtic 4–0 at Celtic Park, a defeat that hurt Maley and the supporters particularly hard, for the struggle to be the flag bearers and the rallying point for the Irish in Scotland was a real one.

One of the points at issue between them was of course how far the "Irish" sides should sign Protestants and non-Irish. Celtic were of course far more visionary than Hibs in this respect, realising that Irish roots were significant, but the Scottish side of the club was far more so. Part of Hibs' problems of the early 1890s had been caused by their exclusive sectarianism, whereas Celtic, Maley in particular, were always prepared to play players of non-Irish descent. Several motions had been put forward at Celtic's AGMs in the 1890s suggesting that there should be a limit on Protestants signed, but the motions had always been rejected. Young, of course, with no obvious Irish connections was an excellent example of non-sectarianism, but the same man was not unaware of the undercurrents present whenever Celtic played Hibs.

On Saturday 16 May Jimmy Young made his official debut before a disappointing crowd of 2,000 (something that perhaps said a little about Celtic's poor season) in the Glasgow Charity Cup against Hibs. The team was McPherson; Watson and Battles; Moir, Young and Orr; Loney, McMenemy, Bennett, Somers and Quinn. Quite a few of the great team to come in the next few years were in place, although not in the position we would expect them to be. The two inside men Jimmy McMenemy and Peter Somers were where they would become immortal. Young was at centre-half, and Willie Loney who would become the centre-half was played on the right wing where he was "a galaxy of tricks and dodges" as *The Glasgow Observer* put it. The curmudgeonly "Man In The Know" however remains melancholic. He accuses both teams of "rough and shady play" and says "I was not very highly impressed with the play of Young, the Celts' Bristol capture at centre-half-back. He seems a very common player", and by "common", we assume he means "ordinary".

Given the foul weather and the unsatisfactory nature of the Cathkin pitch (neutral venue was used because Celtic Park had already been booked for a cycling event, while the other semi-final between St Mirren and Rangers was played at Ibrox), Young felt that he did well. After all, a goalless draw is a good result for a centre-half and he was told by Maley that he would be in for Thursday night's replay at the same venue.

Loney didn't play in that game – injured presumably and his place in the replay went to Willie Grassam – but it was a totally different game with Jimmy Quinn hitting four goals and Jimmy McMenemy scoring one. Quinn's second goal was a brilliant individual goal, much appreciated by the 4,000 crowd, the larger attendance reflecting the fine weather. At the back, Young was outstanding, being singled out for praise for his "splendid tackling". Maley was jubilant, making a point of congratulating the two Jimmys (or as he kept calling them "Jamies"), Quinn and Young. Indeed Maley felt a tingle for the approaching Glasgow Charity Cup Final on Saturday that he had not felt for a long time.

This game in many ways defined Celtic of this time. It was the last time that the team would play officially in the green and white vertical stripes; it was the first official trophy won since the Scottish Cup of 1900; and it was the harbinger of really great things for Celtic with several players, not least Jimmy Young, making their first mark on the Scottish game.

The opponents were St Mirren, another non-Glasgow team invited to take part in view of the money required for the Ibrox Disaster Fund, and there was a certain amount of "history" between the teams that season, for Celtic had removed them from the Scottish Cup at the third attempt, and there had been a distinct "over-familiarisation" between certain players and a few vendettas being played off. It would be the first time that the Buddies would see James Young, though.

The weather was splendid with loads of sun on 23 May, and a huge crowd of 15,000 turned up, something that was far too much for the inadequate pay-boxes at Cathkin. "A few scoundrels managed to enter without parting with their sixpence" said the Press, and *The Glasgow Observer* talks about the huge crowds along Batson Street, Cathcart Road and Allison Street. The takings were a healthy £500, however, for the Charity Cup committee to "disburse as they thought fit".

The teams were:
Celtic: McPherson, Battles and Watson; Moir, Young and Orr; Loney, McMenemy, Bennett, Somers and Quinn.
St Mirren: Rae, Jackson and Cameron; Greenlees, Bruce and McAvoy; Lindsay, Hamilton, Reid, Wilson and Robertson.
Referee; T. Robertson, Queen's Park.

There is some dubiety about the Celtic team selection and the newspapers disagree. *The Evening Times* and *Daily Record and Mail*'s accounts of the game give Muir (Bristol Rovers), as if he had not yet signed for Celtic and was currently on loan. *The Glasgow Herald* and *The Glasgow Observer*, on the other hand say that Willie Loney is on the right wing, whereas the right-half is Jimmy Moir who has indeed played there for a considerable part of the season. Loney is an unlikely right-winger, but he was also said to have played there in the 0–0 draw against Hibs, and it is unlikely that Jimmy Moir would be dropped in a Cup Final in favour of a man on loan. We shall never know, of course, but the confusion, presumably, arose from the similarity of the names and the traditional and notorious bad spelling and writing of Edwardian journalists. Indeed there was no such thing as a football correspondent in many cases.

An exception however was "Man In The Know", but he was not really a correspondent, more a "fan with a pen", and like quite a few fans, was fickle and changeable. He certainly underwent a sea change in his attitude to James Young after this game. "After his two latest displays, I am inclined to revise my first impression of Young, the Celts' Bristol capture, who now bids to prove a good deal better than a "common player". He uses his head in more ways than one and his judicious placing and feeding have had a good deal to so with the recent successes of the Celtic forwards..."

Young was indeed impressive. He had an outstanding game being described as a "glutton for work" and being part of a defence which was " a safe division" of the team, according to *The Glasgow Herald* which also praises the forward line, although there are reservations that the forwards may be too light for a whole season. St Mirren scored first from a corner kick which goalkeeper McPherson did not deal with, but then Celtic took a grip of the game with goals from Alec Bennett, Jimmy Quinn and Alec Bennett again, before a collision between Alec Bennett and St Mirren goalkeeper Louis Rae saw Rae taken off with what looked like a broken leg. In the second half Willie Loney scored with a header, before Alec Bennett attained his hat-trick as the ten-man St Mirren side began to fade, nevertheless scoring a consolation goal at the end.

It was a great Celtic performance. "Man In The Know", so down in the dumps a week ago, cannot contain his enthusiasm. Celtic "simply staggered their opponents and the spectators by the splendour of their form, which recalled that of Aston Villa or the old North End", – the two teams who in England the previous century had won the League and Cup double. It was a "brilliantly successful close to the season", and the support now had something to look forward to over the summer.

There was however a down side to this game, and it lay in the behaviour of some of the crowd. Whether they were day-trippers from Paisley or Glasgow youths who simply did not like Celtic, their activities involved "the necessity of deploying the constabulary" on one occasion in particular when Maley, acting as linesman (there were no neutral linesmen appointed for the Charity

Cup) gave a throw-in to Celtic "contrary to the opinions of the mob" and was pelted with missiles for so doing.

But they were a minority. Young was taken aback at the sheer enthusiasm of the Celtic crowd, some of whom invaded the field at the end. He was an instant hero of the fans, and was presented with a lovely gold medal at the end to add to the Gloucestershire Cup one that he had won less than a month ago. Maley the manager congratulated his players, who, he felt (correctly) could now go on to better things, and said that he was looking forward to seeing them for the start of the season. Young smiled and was happy with the way that his footballing career had gone. He had clearly done the right thing in coming back to Scotland, but there was something that needed attending to in Bristol.

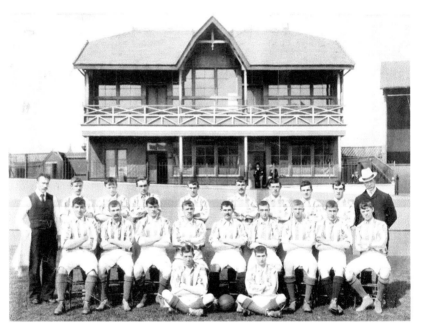

Possibly the last picture to be taken of Celtic with their vertical stripes in 1903. Sunny is third from the right in the front row. In the back row in the middle on his own is the brooding figure of Jimmy Quinn and to the right of the back row are the great Alec Bennett and Jimmy McMenemy standing beside the dapper manager Willie Maley

There was the girl he had left behind him, Florence Coombs. As both of them suspected when he left Bristol to come to Scotland, she was indeed pregnant. There was a mild scandal and embarrassment about this but "mild" was the word. It was hardly unusual to be caught "firing before the twelfth" (a metaphor from the Scottish grouse season which always started on 12 August) in Edwardian Britain, but the couple were in love and Jimmy would certainly do the decent thing and marry her, which he duly did in Bristol in June 1903.

Mr and Mrs Young then moved to take up residence at no 14 Barbadoes Road, Kilmarnock, and Jimmy took up a job as an Iron Turner (he had now served his apprenticeship) while keeping up his training and playing for Celtic on a part-time basis when the season started again in August. He did of course hope to get a full-time contract, and would do so in due course. The Scottish League winners in 1903 were Hibs, and the Scottish Cup winners were Rangers. Young was determined to play his part in changing that.

CHAPTER THREE

FORMATION OF THE TROIKA AND THE SCOTTISH CUP

1904

McPherson; Battles and Strang; Moir, Young and Hay; Muir, Somers, Bennett, McMenemy and Quinn were the first men to wear the green and white horizontal stripes, now called the hoops, in what is generally agreed to be the most famous and best loved strip in the world. Some supporters feel cheated when they travel for miles to see a team running out with some kind of yellow or black strip, all for the sake of television, sponsorship, advertising (so that the bogus strip gets some kind of viewing), and they are entitled to feel "done". Celtic means green and white hoops.

Funnily enough the word "hoops" is a fairly modern one in this context. Until the 1990s, the strip was called the green and white "stripes", although one must admit that "hoops" is technically a better description in that it can only mean horizontal stripes whereas "stripes" tends to be vertical. Vertical stripes were indeed worn by the team until that day at the start of the 1903–04 season against Partick Thistle on 15 August when Maley decided that a new strip was appropriate for what was a new, young team. *The Glasgow Observer* said that it gave them "a youthful appearance". The change of strip was meant to symbolise the start of a new era. Maley, although technically a Secretary/Manager with no official authority over the selection of the team, was now "the Boss" and would stay in charge for the best part of the next forty years.

The Roman writer Pliny the Younger in the 2nd century AD does not like chariot racing. He moans about the crowd, their bad language, their excitement, the fact that there is nothing varied about chariot racing and is further upset by the fact that the fans do not really like the race itself but they are cheering on their team and they love the colour.

"Si tamen aut velocitate equorum aut hominum arte traherentur, esset ratio nonnulla; nunc favent panno, pannum amant, et si in ipso cursu medioque certamine hic color illuc, ille huc transferatur, studium favorque transibit, et repente agitatores illos, equos illos, quos procul noscitant, quorum clamitant nomina, relinquent."

"If they were attracted however by the speed of the horses or the skill of the men, there would be some sense to it; as it is, they support the colour, they love the colour, and if in the race itself and the middle of the competition, the colours were to be transferred from one to the other, the passion and the support would go as well, and suddenly they would abandon those drivers, those horses whom they recognise from afar and whose names they shout out"

Celtic supporters a couple of millenia later would have to admit that the sententious, priggish and occasionally somewhat boring Pliny may well have a point here. We do love the team's colours and the green and white hoops, as evidenced by the amount of supporters seen wearing the strip even on the coldest of days in winter! Rightly do we feel cheated when a team appears in an away fixture wearing black or yellow, and claiming to be Celtic! In the pre-Stein days, Celtic sometimes took the field in a strip of white and green sleeves, (rather like Hibs but in reverse), and Stein tended to deploy an all-green strip. On one occasion in a Scottish Cup semi-final aginst Morton in 1969, Celtic ran out first in all-white, something which confused the fans who, from the top of the terracing, thought for a moment that they were Morton! We want the green and white hoops. Maley did indeed start something in 1903!

The spectacle of the appearance for the first time of the green and white hoops paled into insignificance in comparison with the recent coronation of Pope Pius X which was of course duly reported in detail in *The Glasgow Observer*. The new Celtic look was somewhat spoiled by the torrential rain which put the match in a little danger for a spell. Even so about 5,000 appeared for the game which Celtic won 2–1 with Alec Bennett scoring early on, then Campbell of Partick Thistle scoring just on half-time following an error from McPherson before the brilliant young McMenemy scored in the very last minute. (*The Glasgow Herald* says it was Jimmy Quinn). Celtic should have killed the game earlier, but Barney Battles missed a penalty-kick. Jimmy Young at centre-half had a good game, radiating command when the spirited Partick Thistle team piled on the pressure in the second half.

The Glasgow Observer is far from happy with this performance. It exempts from criticism the newcomers – Strang, Hay, Young and Muir – but castigates the Celtic forwards for not killing the game when they could. "It would have been the price of them" it says, if Thistle had run up the field and scored, but fortunately McMenemy saved the day at the end in a way that reminded the scribe of a "sort of deathbed confession" like Roman Emperors of old who persecuted the early Christians but then decided to get baptised at the end "just in case". That was fine imagery, but that Young made an instant impact on the Celtic crowd was obvious from the game at St Mirren the following week on 22 August. This was the game in which he earned his nickname "Sunny Jim". *The Kilmarnock Standard* in its tribute to Young the week after his death in 1922, tells the story, attributed to Young himself, of how a supporter "of the leather-lunged variety" whose voice could be heard "almost from Parkhead to Paisley" kept on cheering the team (they won 1–0 that day with a goal from Peter Somers) and having exhausted all the names of the players suddenly remembered the name of a well advertised product and shouted "Come Away, Sunny Jim!". Young had a good game that day – "a hardy strong fellow who never admits defeat" said *The Glasgow Observer.*

Young was referred to by that name, even in the Press, from then and forever after. By the following week, in a dismal 1–3 defeat by Third Lanark at Parkhead, he was commonly known as "Sunny Jim". And very soon a song was heard on the terraces along the lines of:

Oh, Sunny, Sunny Jim!
Oh how we love him!

So who was the original "Sunny Jim"? From 1900 onwards there had been advertisements in Glasgow newspapers trying to persuade people that they should eat "Force" cereal for their breakfast. In these poverty-stricken, hunger-haunted days (the Boer War recruiting campaign of a few years previously had foundered because so many young men in big cities like Glasgow and Liverpool were malnourished and unfit for military service!) Force needed an advertising campaign to persuade people that their product would make them healthy. Not only that, but it would make them cheerful as well in the metamorphosis that changed Jim Dumps (as in "down in the dumps", presumably) to "Sunny" Jim.

Jim Dumps was a most unfriendly man
Who lived his life on the hermit plain
In his gloomy way he had gone through life
And made the most of woe and strife
Till Force was one day served to him
Since then they've called him Sunny Jim!

Sunny Jim was portrayed as striding along, or jumping over a fence

High o'er the fence leaps Sunny Jim
"Force" is the "force" that makes him!

To what extent, "Sunny Jim" helped the sale of Force cereal among Celtic supporters over the next 20 years is not certain, but Force of course still exists today, and there could hardly be a more appropriate nickname for the young, strapping, genial, hard-working and totally dedicated man from Ayrshire who became a Parkhead hero in astonishingly quick time!

But hero though Sunny was, Maley was very aware that there were some parts of his play that needed attention, and Maley used him sparingly in the first half of the season as he tried to find the best combination. The best team in Scotland in autumn 1903 was Third Lanark who, having defeated Celtic at Parkhead, proceeded to do the same at Cathkin on the Holiday Monday in late September, winning 3–1 and repeating the score of Parkhead a month earlier. They would win the Scottish League for the first and only time in 1904.

Young had a poor game that day against the fine Thirds' side now managed by a man with the unlikely name of Frank Heaven, and containing ex-Celtic Johnny Campbell who had a point to prove against what he may have seen as a premature departure form Parkhead. Maley decided that perhaps Young was due a rest after his good start, for he wanted to see how Willie Loney might fare in the centre-half spot. So Young now disappeared for a spell from the Celtic team. In any case he had a domestic matter to attend to.

Early in the morning of 3 November 1903 at 14 Barbadoes Road, Kilmarnock, Florence gave birth to a baby girl to be called Alice Maud Young. The Birth Certificate is interesting in two ways. One is that Sunny is called James Gilmore Young, (whereas his own Birth Certificate of 1882 merely says James Young) and he signs himself James G. Young, and the other thing is that he is described as an Iron Turner (Journeyman) rather than Professional Footballer – something that makes one think that at this stage of his career at least, he was still playing part-time football for Celtic, probably training at Kilmarnock and going to Glasgow only on a Saturday and match days. On the other hand, very few football players would want to be described as a "Professional Footballer" on an official document – there still remained, as a relic from the Victorian age, a strong horror of professional sport in polite society – and would described themselves as something else, as if playing football professionally was only a temporary thing – as indeed it was.

Four days after Alice was born, Sunny played for Celtic in the Glasgow Cup semi-final against Clyde in an impressive 2–0 victory, but it was the only game that he would play for a spell. He played that day only because of an injury to Willie Loney, whom Maley now seemed to think was a better centre-half than Jimmy Young. Young thus missed playing in the first ever game at New Hampden (on 31 October 1903) and also both the Glasgow Cup Final and its replay against Third Lanark. In the replay the very fine Third Lanark side, the "sodgers" (as they were called, because they were the Third Lanark Rifle Volunteers originally) edged home with a shot from Johnny Campbell which squeezed under goalkeeper Davie Adams' gloves on the wet ground. Adams then in desperation joined the attack as Celtic pressed for an equalizer, but Thirds held out to win the Glasgow Cup to the despair of the huge Celtic crowd at Ibrox, and of Young who was sitting powerless in the stand.

He had rather hoped to get the nod for this important game (the Glasgow Cup was a mighty tournament in those days) but accepted his disappointment with equanimity when Maley patted him on the back and told him that "your day will come". Indeed, Maley was in a quandry. Young was too good a player to leave out. He was hard-working, earnest and, importantly for Maley, genial and cheerful without in any way diminishing his will to win. He was also, Maley noticed, a great team man, the broad Ayrshire accent being heard from the stand roaring on the team when he wasn't playing. Other players took the huff when they were dropped and secretly hoped that the team would lose, but Sunny was always seen talking to supporters and speaking about little other than Celtic's chances of winning the game.

Sunny played two games in early December, both of them impressive wins against Morton and Airdrie, but then Loney returned and played so well that he could not be dropped. New Year 1904 arrived with Maley reasonably happy about the form of his side. There were inconsistent performances but that is always likely to happen with a raw "developing" (as Maley kept saying) side. He was also faced with the difficult problem of keeping so many talented young men happy. There were simply so many good youngsters around at that time – in particular he had two centre-halves of immense talent in Willie Loney and Jimmy Young. He hated disappointing one of them (as he had to do every week) but 1904 was to bring the solution to this problem which would also re-establish Celtic as undeniably the greatest team in Scotland and possibly the greatest on earth.

Centre-half is a position that has changed over the years. Now there is possibly not such a thing a centre-half, for he is usually one of two in the back four called a "central-defender". In the 1950s and 1960s he was very definitely a defender who would come up for a corner kick often with devastating effect (Billy McNeill was an excellent example of that!) but before that he was possibly even more of an attacker and in his frequent forays upfield, the two wing-halves would be expected to cover for his absence. Maley's philosophy for Celtic was one of attacking, fast football with everyone able to pass to each other and if possible to interchange with each other. He certainly expected his five forwards to do that and he would expect his centre-half and centre- forward to do that on occasion as well.

None of this really solved his conundrum of what to do with Jimmy Young and Willie Loney. In the event it was a combination of injuries, whims and sudden impulses, which released on Scottish football the mightiest half-back line with the key factor possibly being Maley's conversion to the idea that he should play his best players regardless and allow abstract ideas about team formation to take second place.

Young did not play in the New Year Day fixture against Rangers, a 2–2 draw in which a late lapse of concentration in the Celtic defence allowed Rangers an undeserved equalizer. Willie Orr who had played right-half that day was given a rest the next day, 2 January for the friendly against Corinthians, the London amateur club who usually played their Scottish counterparts Queen's Park on New Year's Day. Sunny Jim was brought in at centre-half and Willie Loney moved to right-half, so that the half-back line read Loney, Young and Hay. On a frosty day, Celtic had few problems with the hard pitch and defeated the Corinthians 5–0.

Then on Wednesday 6 January in a friendly against Clyde (which Celtic won 2–1) with Loney given a rest, a fellow called Thomson was given a game at centre-half and Sunny Jim moved to right-half. He impressed there, but Thomson apparently didn't and in any case, Loney was available again, and thus it was that on 9 January 1904, Young, Loney and Hay took their place for the first time in a competitive match against Airdrie in what was Celtic's first ever visit to Broomfield.

It would be nice to say that this was a total success, but unfortunately it wasn't – but no blame can be attached to the three young half-backs. Games against Airdrie, even "friendly" ones, had often been rough with the added ingredient of religious bigotry thrown in, in the shape of a remark, often a ludicrous one. Thus a god-fearing Presbyterian who just happened to play for Celtic might be called a "Fenian" or a "Popehead". But then again religious bigotry, by definition almost, owes little to logic or even common sense! We have stated that Rangers had not as yet risen (or sunk!) to the bigotry that was to foul their existence, and ultimately perhaps over a century later lead to their downfall, but anti-Catholic prejudice was by no means absent at places like Airdrie, St Mirren or Motherwell.

This game turned out to be as rough as they come. Right-back Hugh Watson, a good player, had his leg broken as early as the fifth minute and thus the half-back line was broken up for Sunny was compelled to defend in the right-back position. (This was, of course, a good sixty years before the legalisation of substitutes.) The game was thrilling for the spectators but brutal for the players, and Celtic ended up on the wrong end of a 4–3 defeat following a late Airdrie onslaught. Sunny Jim played well but was unfortunate to concede a penalty-kick when he brought down Collins inside "the penalty line" and a penalty was awarded by the referee Mr Jackson of Rangers (sic!). It would be a defeat that would cost Celtic dear in their quest for the League Championship. It is difficult however to resist the conclusion that had Celtic played the whole game with eleven men, they might well have won.

Young was restored to centre-half for the next few games because of various injuries to other players, notably Loney and held his place until the end of January for good victories against Motherwell and Morton, then an unlucky defeat against Dundee at Dens Park, which even *The Dundee Courier* concedes that "It was a great game and with a spice of luck, the Celts would have drawn… so class was the football shown that each team deserved a point. There was not a dull moment all the time…" Loney returned in February, and this meant a back seat for Young, until a replayed Scottish Cup quarter-final at Dens Park (again) when Young, Loney and Hay took the field with captain Willie Orr who had been at right-back now in the left-back position in which he was to excel. At right-back Donnie "Slasher" McLeod took the place of the now ageing Barney Battles. The main thing, however, was that the penny had dropped with Maley that it might be an idea to see how Young and Loney got on together, even though it meant playing the ever willing Young out of what he then thought to be his better position.

This game on 27 February 1904, so pivotal to Celtic history, very nearly did not take place for a severe snowfall in Dundee and Angus meant that the ground was covered in snow. It was however wet, melting snow and a telegram was despatched to Glasgow assuring Celtic that the game would be on. Instead of simply allowing the snow to melt however Dundee made the mistake of trying to shovel it off as well, and the result was that the pitch, although just playable, was a sea of mud in the middle of the field. A huge crowd of 20,000 (including many who had travelled through from Glasgow as well as Celtic's sizeable local support) saw a goalless draw in which Dundee might have sneaked it, had it not been for the efforts of goalkeeper Davie Adams. *The Dundee Courier* however makes a snide remark about how "Dundee were drawing in the shekels" as a result of drawn cup-ties,but also praises Adams for his "application".

Adams of course came from the small Angus village of Oathlaw and was well known in the locality, but Celtic in 1904 (and for many decades afterwards) had a huge support in Dundee, drawn basically from the Dundee Irish who worked in the jute mills from the 1860s and 1870s onwards. Sociologically, it is interesting to note that the Dundee Irish remained loyal to Celtic, even though a Dundee Irish team called Dundee Hibs (later Dundee United) was formed in 1909. This would be the case until the rise and promotion to the old First Division of Dundee United in the late 1950s and early 1960s, and it is no accident that Dundee United's rise and growth of support occurred at a time when Celtic were going through a prolonged poor spell.

Maley made two correct decisions after the game. One was that he called correctly in the toss of the coin so that the second replay was at Parkhead the following Saturday (5 March) and the second decision was that the half-back line should stay as Young, Loney and Hay. In addition he had a word with Sunny, encouraging him to go forward, to take a grip of the game and not to be afraid to "get stuck in" if necessary. This was the Scottish Cup, said Maley, already won three times by Celtic, and as Third Lanark were going to win the League if they won their backlog of fixtures, there was only really the Scottish Cup left for Celtic.

As if sensing something in the air a big crowd of 35,000 came to Celtic Park to see the decisive game against Dundee. This game, in some ways marking the birth of Maley's great side, was played in splendid spring conditions, although there was a breeze blowing from the west. Celtic, represented by Adams; McLeod and Orr; Young, Loney and Hay; Muir, McMenemy, Bennett, Quinn and Hamilton, played with the wind in the first-half, took an immediate command of the game and by half-time Muir, Bennett and Quinn (from an impossibly tight angle) had scored to make it 3–0. Even against the wind, Celtic kept control over a dispirited Dundee side and goals from Muir and McMenemy saw Celtic home by a 5–0 win, and their supporters waiting for their horse-drawn trams to take them back to the city centre were in high spirits, as were those who walked back along London Road and the Gallowgate.

The discerning supporters however were able to point to the real success of the side. The forwards had all done well, but it was the half-back line with their control, ball-winning, distribution and spraying of passes which was the key to the success. "Man In The Know" is in no doubt about why the team played well. It lay in "the improvement of their defenders who gave a display far in advance of that shown in the other games". Sunny Jim had been a revelation in his new role as a wing-half, and hopes were now expressed that the Scottish Cup could be landed for the first time since that windy day at Ibrox four years ago in 1900 when they beat Queen's Park.

The Dundee Courier while expressing sympathy with the Dundee supporters, about 1,000 strong, who returned to Dundee West Station at about 11.00 pm with "drooping plumes and sore hearts", recognises that a change is in the air at Celtic Park. "Like the Heathen Chinese, the ways of the Celts are peculiar" it says with a touch of racial superiority, but pays tribute to Celtic's "sterling halves" who sent over a whole series of "high swinging passes" for the forward to capitalise on.

Celtic now with their support galvanised into action would have liked the semi-final against Third Lanark to be played the next Saturday, but this was not possible because Scotland were playing Wales in an International at Dens Park (then considered to be one of the best grounds in Scotland). In the event, Willie Orr and Alec Bennett played for Scotland in a 1–1 draw while Celtic beat St Mirren 3–1 in a League match before a "reasonable attendance"

So it was 19 March which saw the semi-final at Celtic Park (neutral venues were not used for semi-finals until 1912) and a huge crowd of near 40,000 (according to *The Glasgow Herald*) turned up to see a match between the thrilling young Celtic team and the team who had already won the Glasgow Cup, looked likely to win the Scottish League this year and who had been Celtic's bogey team in the autumn, Third Lanark.

The weather was good, although the ground was a bit soft after a fair amount of rain during the week, and the game, "without reaching the dizzy heights of Olympus or Everest", was an excellent example of the new professionalism and never-say-die spirit of the Celtic, who were, it was believed, on a bonus of £10 per man to win. The gate was £998, so £110 was a fair fraction of

Celtic's share of their revenue, but such was the determination of everyone at Celtic to get to the final where Rangers and a huge crowd awaited them at the impressive new Hampden stadium.

The semi-final was an excellent example of the value of a good half-back line in a situation where the teams were of roughly equal ability. It was also an example of the toughness of this new Celtic team who were able to grind out a victory without necessarily playing any spectacular football. Third Lanark scored early on through McKenzie when Celtic were temporarily down to ten men with McLeod off injured, and really should have scored more by half-time but were thwarted by some fine Celtic defensive work.

In the second half, however, Celtic slowly gained the ascendancy and, beginning to pass brilliantly to each other, forced Thirds on the defensive. With fifteen minutes remaining, Bobby Muir equalized. The roars of delight on the terracings were then repeated when Jimmy Quinn ran on to a through ball from Young to score the winner. *The Glasgow Observer*, blatantly pro-Celtic as ever, chortles that, "Young supplied the power, the thrust and the drive, McMenemy the trickery and the wizardry". It was indeed a great triumph for Maley's young side.

This game now saw Celtic into the Scottish Cup Final, and the atmosphere was tangible around Parkhead. Young's fine performance in this game – the word "outstanding" was used in several newspapers – also had another effect in that he was granted International recognition when he was chosen to play for the Scottish League against the English League (or as they called themselves, arrogantly, the Football League) at Bank Street, Manchester, the home of Manchester United on Monday 4 April 1904.

The League Internationals, sadly no longer played, were very important in those days, for they were looked upon as a spring board for a full International cap. Sunny had only really played as a regular right-half since the end of February on that quagmire of a pitch at Dens Park, and here he was playing for the Scottish League at the beginning of April! Admittedly, he was not the first choice and only came in at the last minute, but nevertheless the opportunity to play against Bob Crompton and Steve Bloomer in front of a 40,000 crowd was an exciting one for the ambitious Sunny. Jimmy Quinn was also chosen for the left-wing spot.

Chapter Three

It was a fine day at Clayton (as Bank Street was sometimes called) and the holiday crowd enjoyed a good game in which the wind played a fairly significant part as the Scottish League were winning at half-time when they had the wind behind them, but lost out 1–2. This was of course no disgrace to lose by this narrow margin, and *The Glasgow Herald* says that Young "acquitted himself creditably".

As important as anything else in these games was the social side of things. There was always a post-match dinner (sometimes called grandiloquently a "banquet") and Young, sociable as always, sought out the England players like Bloomer, Greenhaugh and Baddeley, some of whom remembered him vaguely from his Bristol Rovers days, talked to them about the game, picked up a few tips, exchanged opinions, but told them that something was soon going to happen in Glasgow and that was the arrival of the Celtic to become the best team on earth. Pointing to the shy, introverted Jimmy Quinn, he said that this man was going to score all the goals. Everyone laughed good naturedly at such banter while the Englishmen began to boast about Blackburn Rovers, Manchester City or Bolton Wanderers as appropriate.

It is probably true to say that in 1904 what really mattered to all of Scotland was the full International against England. It would be talked about and anticipated with enthusiasm from soon after the New Year. It was more important than club games in that it attracted bigger attendances from all over the country, including a few who would claim to have arrived by that modern invention "the motor car". Sometimes simply called "the International", it was scheduled for Celtic Park this year and was to be played on Saturday 9 April, only a few days after the League International which was in some ways looked upon as the trial match for the big game. The ever optimistic Sunny Jim might well have hoped for a call up to this match as well, but the right-half place went to Andy Aitken of Newcastle United, commonly known as "the Daddler". Aitken stayed uninjured in the few days before the game, so Sunny watched the game from the gallery of the Parkhead pavilion beside other Celtic players and all the dignitaries like the Lord Provost of Glasgow, Sir John Ure Primrose, much fawned upon sycophantically by the Celtic Directors in spite of his Rangers connections.

Ironically for the game being played at Celtic Park, there was not a single Celtic player in the team, but there was a huge crowd with the police and ambulancemen on a high state of alert following what had happened at Ibrox two years ago. Fortunately nothing untoward happened in front of a slightly disappointing crowd of only 45,000 (foul weather and the genuine fear of another disaster in the big crowd keeping the attendance lower than expected) but all of Scotland was distressed when England won 1–0 thanks to a goal from Steve Bloomer of Derby County, sometimes called "the ghost" because of his pale face.

That was a disappointment, but Sunny and the rest of the Celtic team knew that next Saturday was what really mattered to them and the Celtic fans. It was the Scottish Cup Final between themselves and the well-supported team from the west of the city called Rangers. As we have said, at this stage of footballing history, there was no great sectarianism or bigotry from Rangers or even their supporters. They were however the main rivals to Celtic in terms of support and the size of their stadium, and therein lay the real rivalry. Queen's Park, who had rigidly refused to turn professional had perhaps had their day, and Third Lanark were at the moment enjoying a brief moment of ascendancy, but it was Rangers who were always likely to be the main rivals. Since they had won the Scottish League four years in a row from 1899 until 1902, there was an arrogance about them, a feeling that they were the team that was "meant" to win honours, and they certainly had the wealth and the support to do so.

Another factor that added spice to the 1904 Scottish Cup Final was that it was to be played at New Hampden Park, the massive stadium erected by Queen's Park and opened in a game against Celtic last Hallowe'en. There was little doubt that the purpose of building this stadium was to outdo Celtic Park and Ibrox and to host the biennial Scotland v England International and Scottish Cup Finals, but it was an indication of the continually growing interest in football in Glasgow that the city now had three stadia capable of hosting big crowds, even though it would be some time before Ibrox could be used again for this purpose. Great stress was laid on safety at Hampden in a fairly obvious dig at Rangers after their disaster, and a subtle reminder of the dangerous overcrowding that had been obvious at Celtic Park in 1896.

The New Hampden was rumoured to be capable of holding 80,000 at least and plans were in place to extend it so that a six figure crowd could attend the Scotland v England International of 1906 and so that it could be even bigger and more commodious than the famous Crystal Palace of London. It had been built just a little too late to be given the Scotland v England International of 1904, which, as we saw, went to Celtic Park, but as it turned out, the newly-built Hampden was the ideal neutral setting for the meeting of the Glasgow giants on 16 April 1904.

We have said that sectarianism was not yet the poisonous issue that it was to become in later years. Nevertheless, loyalties did create a problem in the week before the Cup Final, concerning Celtic's centre-forward (although most supporters thought he would be a better right-winger) Alec Bennett. Alec, like Sunny Jim and a few others in the team, was a non-Catholic. This was emphatically not an issue at Celtic Park, but it seems to have been in the mind of Bennett and perhaps a few of his family who were putting pressure on him to join Rangers. Rangers themselves, it was believed, had also approached him (there was nothing illegal about this in 1904) with a view to him joining them next year, something that he had so far steadfastly refused to do out of his innate goodness and loyalty to his current employers.

Yet Bennett was unhappy and upset about all this, and although Sunny Jim and his good friend Jimmy McMenemy tried to laugh him out of his depression and uncertainty, Maley eventually decided, very reluctantly, to drop Bennett from the Cup Final team. Bennett was a great player and would be missed, but there was an alternative strategy. This way he could bring in Davy Hamilton to play on the left-wing and allow Jimmy Quinn to come into the centre while retaining Bobby Muir on the right wing. Jimmy McMenemy and Peter Somers then filled the inside-forward positions. Diplomatically, the Press were told that Bennett had "flu". *The Glasgow Herald* which may or may not have known the truth, uses the word "indisposed", a delightfully vague word which can mean "ill", but can also mean "not willing". In any case, it was Bennett's loss and certainly Quinn's gain. *The Dundee Courier* describes Bennett's absence and Quinn's triumph as a "lucky accident".

The half-back line chose itself. Since they had come together, the form of the team, previously fitful and unpredictable, was now impressive and commanding with Young in particular acting as if he had all the experience and know-how in the world. He had just turned 22, had played less than 20 games for the club, yet one got the impression that he had been there for years and that he was going to drive the others to greater things. "Face the ball, Celts!" was already his warcry, and his stentorian, loud, rasping Ayrshire accent was heard all over the ground. There was an affiliation and identity with the support that was difficult to parallel in other players. Maley would chuckle to himself when he heard all the talk about religion. There was no problem there with Sunny Jim, but then again perhaps it was football (and football played in the Celtic way) that was the real religion of Sunny Jim Young.

Davie Adams was in the goal, a huge figure of a man, and at full-back were Donnie McLeod and captain Willie Orr, a man who had now been ousted from the half-back line, but was possibly, in any case a better full-back. Barney Battles, that most loyal and gentle of Celts, had now disappeared from the scene and would move to Kilmarnock before the start of the next season. Man for man, Maley believed that Celtic were a better side than Rangers, but he also knew that it was a Cup Final and anything could happen.

The weather was fine "the very antithesis of last week" as a huge crowd of 64,323, by some distance a record for a club game in Scotland, although the Crystal Palace had on occasion held more for the English Cup Final and indeed Celtic Park probably held more in the 1896 Scotland v England International. The Press is delighted to report that there was no crushing or swaying in the vast crowd which was well housed, and although there was some overcrowding at the turnstiles, this was more because of ignorance of where the turnstiles actually were and of the layout of the splendid new ground. In addition, with a sigh of relief, the Glasgow Police were pleased to remark that everyone behaved!

The size of the crowd was definitely helped by the price for admission which was sixpence. Often in the past it had been double that amount at one shilling, and on occasion two shillings for Internationals and Cup Finals. More and more, football was becoming a working man's game. Twenty years ago, it was undeniably middle class, but now with professionalism legalised for the past ten years, it was the new opium of the masses who were more than willing to pay their "tanner" or their "sickie" (sixpence) to see the game.

It was clear too that the crowd, even for two Glasgow teams, did not come exclusively from Glasgow. That had been obvious at the railway stations that morning, and although both teams had their own committed band of supporters, both sets of fans mingled happily together, exchanging gentle banter without any real hint of nastiness. A large amount of fans, "with a strong female element not absent" particularly those from out of town, seemed to decide at the last moment who they were going to support and bought for a penny a rosette, of either green or blue, from the many vendors outside the ground. This was long before the days that every supporter committed himself uncompromisingly to one team. People simply loved football, this game which had simply taken over Scottish life for the past twenty years or more.

The Glasgow Observer is impressed by the size of the crowd which, "submerged the landscape of Mount Florida", and says that "Numerically, the Rangers supporters held sway but for enthusiasm and confidence, the Celtic contingent was an easy first". There were at least two "unhappy happenings" among the crowd on their way to the match. Alexander Cowie aged 21 was caught in the rush between the carriage and the platform as the crowd invaded the train at Glasgow Central Station, and a 66-year-old man called John Cunningham had his leg broken when he was knocked down by a horse and cab, the cabman being arrested and detained for "careless driving". The referee was Tom Robertson of Queen's Park, and the teams were;

Celtic: Adams, McLeod and Orr; Young, Loney and Hay; Muir, McMenemy, Quinn, Somers and Hamilton.
Rangers: Watson, N. Smith and Drummond; Henderson, Stark and Robertson; Walker, Speedie, Mackie, Donnachie and A. Smith.

Celtic had not won the Scottish Cup since 1900 and had lost two desperately unlucky finals in 1901 and 1902 to the Edinburgh duo of Hearts and Hibs. The League had not been won for even longer than that because 1898 was the last year of Celtic being champions, and the Glasgow Charity Cup of 1903 was the only domestic Scottish trophy Celtic had won since 1900, if one excludes the British League Cup (sometimes called the Glasgow Exhibition Cup or even the Coronation Cup of 1902). But supporters now felt that with this developing team, the trophy drought might well be coming to an end. Rangers had had a bad season. Their four League Championships in a row (1899–1902) side had clearly faded, and although they had won the Scottish Cup in 1903, their League form this year had been dismally unproductive.

Disaster seemed to be looming for Celtic after only ten minutes were played. Against the run of play, Rangers were two ahead, both goals scored by their excellent inside-forward Finlay Speedie. The first was a header, which goalkeeper Davie Adams gathered but not cleanly, and as he collided with a post, the ball trickled into the net. It was an extraordinary goalkeeping error, and things became a lot worse a minute later when the same Speedie took a snap shot at goal from the edge of the penalty box. It missed everyone and the ball entered the net past a bewildered Davie Adams, who had clearly lost confidence and judgement.

The Rangers players and their fans could hardly believe their luck. Celtic supporters were despondent, but told themselves that there was still a long time to go and this young team of theirs was resilient and could yet fight back. Indeed the key thing about them was their youth. They were also determined that they could yet do it, and knew that a goal would bring them back into it. Poor Davie Adams, jeered by both friend and foe in the crowd, reckoned that things could not get any worse and wondered what people would think of him for his dreadful mistake in New Hampden's first Scottish Cup Final. Fortunately for the amiable Angus man, someone else would appear as the eponymous hero of the 1904 Scottish Cup Final.

Celtic now concentrated on their two triangles. On the right were Young, Muir and McMenemy who could interchange passes, and on the left were Hay, Somers and Hamilton who could do similarly, while in the middle Quinn and Loney (an attacking centre-half) were beginning to alarm the Rangers defence with their "strength in the barging," as *The Glasgow Observer* put it.

Half-time was approaching when Celtic's hard work paid off. But it was all due to one man – the unpredictable, brooding, shy, not always confident Jimmy Quinn. He picked up a ball in the middle of the Rangers half and charged at goal using his speed to swerve and avoid some challenges and using also his sheer brute strength to brush others out of the way before he arrived inside the penalty box and lashed a shot past Watson. *The Glasgow Observer* turns alliterative when it says that Quinn survived "bumps, bangs and bashes from all quarters". It was, certainly, a great solo goal, much applauded by the large crowd, and the writer of *The Scotsman* even saw some supporters with blue rosettes "applauding vigorously and sportingly". That would be an unlikely scenario in 2013.

And then just before Mr Robertson "called for half-time", Celtic and Quinn had scored again. This time credit must be given to right-winger Bobby Muir, (Sunny's old friend from his Bristol Rovers days) who, in what would become known as a trademark Scottish goal, picked up a ball from Sunny Jim on the right, "skinned" the Rangers defence at full speed, hit the by-line, crossed low and hard and there was Quinn to bang the ball first time into the net. There was seldom anything complicated about Quinn. He would never dribble in the penalty area, but believed that the ball was there to be hit once – hard and accurately.

Thus half-time saw Celtic in better spirits than Rangers, for they were the team who had come back and were now on level terms. It would be a prolonged half-time interval for a collection was being taken for the families of the victims of a crowd disaster at a Scottish cricket match! This was the Perthshire v. Forfarshire game at the North Inch, Perth last summer when a temporary stand had collapsed injuring many people, some of whom were permanently maimed and therefore unable, in those pre-Welfare State days, to support their family. The huge crowd contributed generously, throwing coins into sheets which volunteers walked round the running track with.

In the Celtic dressing room, Maley came in, said they were doing well and wished them all the best in the second half. He then, as was his wont, went off to have a cup of tea with the Rangers manager, his good friend William Wilton, leaving the players to talk among themselves. The very experienced Willie Orr was of course the captain and he said his piece but it was then that Sunny Jim went around everyone cheering them up. Davie Adams tried to apologise for his howlers, but was told by Sunny to "F***in' shut up aboot it, Davie. Show us what ye can do in the second half!", Jimmy McMenemy was told to keep up the good stuff, Davie Hamilton, a shy retiring kind of man on the left-wing was given a word of encouragement, and then the other shy man in the team, Jimmy Quinn, was pointed to by Young who proclaimed prophetically, "This is the man who will do it for us". Then another early example of his famous war cry "Face the ball, Celts!"

The second half opened with Rangers on top, but that was only a temporary phenomenon as the Celtic midfield once again rallied and took control. Playing towards the as yet incomplete East Terracing (which in years to come would house huge Celtic crowds), Celtic charged forward, with everything done in their triangles of Young, Muir and McMenemy on the right side of midfield, Hay, Hamilton and Somers on the left "passing prettily", and a vice like grip in the centre of the midfield with Young, Loney and Hay in total command. Yet the Rangers defence held out, and a replay looked the most likely outcome, until Jimmy Quinn, already a hero, became immortal and ensured that his name will be mentioned whenever anyone talks about Celtic and football.

The winning goal had some similarities to his first goal, but this time it came from a visionary pass from captain James "Dun" Hay. Quinn was on his way to goal when he was tackled fiercely by the fair haired Nick Smith. It was brutal and might have floored lesser men, but this was Jimmy Quinn! He stumbled, but picked himself up, gathered the ball and slid the ball past the advancing goalkeeper. As Hampden erupted in applause, Jimmy merely turned round and walked back to the centre circle looking as "cool as Hell" in the unlikely simile of *The Glasgow Observer,* as his team mates went berserk all around him. Another newspaper talked more graphically about "The Croy Express being almost dismembered by his teammates". But Jimmy was not too given to such shows of emotion. "The game's no' finished yet", he muttered with grim determination as he marched back purposefully, head down and eyes set, to the centre line and Sunny Jim was seen with clenched fists, telling the players the same message.

Indeed there were ten minutes to go, but Rangers were a well beaten team. As full-time approached, so too did the volume of applause and cheering rise around Hampden with green and white favours now prominent. Full-time came when Mr Robertson blew and pointed to the pavilion. Sunny Jim jumped up and clapped both hands above his head, then shook hands with his Rangers opponents before joining in the general mayhem of this young and enthusiastic Celtic side. Celtic had won their fourth Scottish Cup, now level with Rangers and one ahead of Hearts, although still some way behind the ten of Queen's Park. There was dancing in the streets of the Gorbals that night.

The Dundee Courier, which, in its desire to appease the Dundee Irish of Lochee and Hawkhill, tended to support Celtic unless they were playing against Dundee, naturally is in ecstacy about the performance of Jimmy Quinn, but also has this to say about Sunny Jim..." Young, who though sometimes inclined to methods not permitted by the laws of the game, was about the best half on the field". Then as an afterthought "Lonie (sic) and Hay were also good". The "methods not permitted by the laws of the game" would appear to be a reference to Sunny's inclination to dish out a little raw meat, now and again, and to deliver a few robust challenges, when the occasion demanded.

The Glasgow Observer reluctantly agreed about Sunny's over-motivation. Although enthusiastic about his "length of limb", it says that "Young wasn't uniformly safe in his tackling and at times he failed to control his temper." This was however only a small point in its glowing praise of Celtic's performance. It cannot have helped the cause of Celtic's increasing desire to be integrated into Scottish society when it talks about an "Irish Football Triumph" – a somewhat ludicrous headline when one considers that all eleven of the Celtic team were born in Scotland, and that a handful of them were from a Protestant background.

The real significance of this game, much talked about even in England in the context of "hat-trick Quinn", however, lay in what happened next. The Cup Final immortalised by Jimmy Quinn was the springboard for the team that would go on to dominate Edwardian Scotland and become, without any great doubt, the greatest team on earth, winning six League titles in a row. There is indeed a very strong parallel with what happened 61 years later in 1965. The epic Scottish Cup win against Dunfermline Athletic (two goals from Bertie Auld and Billy McNeill's late headed winner) opened the doors for the glory that was to come. That team of the late 1960s would also be the greatest team on earth, but, as everyone admitted, it might not have happened but for that Scottish Cup Final of 1965. For 1965, read 1904 and one will get an idea of how significant it was.

The mighty troika of Young, Loney and Hay

For Young, 1904 was a dream come true. A year previously he had still been in Bristol with his career going nowhere, the only bright spot being the Bristol lady that he had met called Florence Coombs. Now he was married, had a lovely baby daughter, lived in the town of his birth, not far from his parents and family who were thrilled that he was playing for the great Glasgow Celtic. And this was the team that he had already fallen in love with and which had a huge support, who had clearly fallen in love with him as well. He had a Glasgow Charity Cup medal and now, pride of place, a Scottish Cup medal. Not only that, but he got on with his manager, who described him as "a man and a half".

But there was more to that, mused Sunny as he boarded his train for Kilmarnock late that Saturday night after the post-match dinner. He had had a few to drink of course, as Maley smiled tolerantly, and he had been surrounded on his way to Central Station by loads of well wishers and was particularly struck by the sight of the barefooted urchins with a smile on their faces. Manager Maley had told him about 1892 when they first won the Scottish Cup, and how he, Maley, had been deeply affected by the happiness that he had brought to so many people who had little enough else going for them. Twelve years later, this was still true. There was an incredible amount of poverty and misery in Glasgow, and Sunny began to think that perhaps Keir Hardie and Ramsay MacDonald had a point about the necessity for society to change.

But there was also the future. With a team like that, the possibilities were endless. He loved the fact that the Press already talked about Celtic's "three musketeers" in Young, Loney and Hay, (one newspaper talked about a "troika" which after some diligent enquiries he discovered was a Russian wagon, particularly useful in the snow, with three horses for the transport of "Czar Nick" and other dignitaries) and what a player that McMenemy was! And Jimmy Quinn, the hat-trick hero! Difficult man to get through to, but, thought Sunny, I'll do it! A few dirty jokes and impressions of Maley (Sunny and other comedians like Peter Somers had already perfected Maley's slight slur and his manner of holding his head when he was being pompous) talking about "the honour and privilege to play for THE Celtic" had made the introverted Quinn laugh before the Third Lanark semi-final and on the train down to Manchester for the League International. Yes, thought Sunny, I'll do all that, and I'll make Celtic the greatest team on earth!

But 1904 still had a bit to go yet. There was a tour of Europe apart from anything else! But before that there was a lot going on at Parkhead. In the first place there was the Alec Bennett problem. Maley realised that Bennett was far too good a player to be allowed to go to Rangers, and employed all his resources to keep him, including the persuasive tongue of Sunny Jim who, of course, was also a nominal Protestant, but now as much a Celt as anyone. It is possible, indeed likely, that Sunny "had a word" with the reluctant Bennett, stressing that this Celtic team was going to be the best team on earth, and that he would be better off "steyin' wi' us". Bennett stayed for another four years and earned the nickname "the artful dodger" for his brilliant right wing play. By the time of Celtic's tour of the Highlands in early May, the immortal forward line of Bennett, McMenemy, Quinn, Somers and Hamilton was in place.

On that tour of Aberdeen, Dundee and Inverness the social skills of Young came to the fore. It was the custom of Maley to organise soirees by the team at the hotel in which they were staying to which the other guests of the hotel and the management were invited. Middle class ladies were charmed by these well dressed young men and their genial, urbane manager. This was a part of what Maley saw as his social mission to spread the word "Celtic". (It also meant that Maley could keep an eye on any players who might have been inclined to overindulge in alcoholic refreshment! As far as alcohol was concerned, Maley perhaps lacked the obsessive, prohibitionist zeal that Stein possessed, but he was always keen to make sure that Celtic players behaved in public). Young, being a natural extrovert, was always well to the fore in such things. Being an Ayrshireman he was expected to do something on Robbie Burns which he did brilliantly, singing, reciting or simply talking about the Bard. He did a great "Tam O'Shanter", it was said.

But not everything was sweetness and light at Celtic Park. Shortly after Celtic beat Queen's Park 2–1 in the semi-final of the Glasgow Charity Cup on Monday 9 May, an unfortunate fire burned down the grandstand on the North side of the ground at Celtic Park. It was probably not an "insurance job" as was widely believed at the time, and it was a blow for the club, but worse was to come on the following Saturday in a very unpleasant encounter with Rangers in the Glasgow Charity Cup Final.

28,000 attended Hampden and a sum of more than £1,000 was raised for charity, but that was about the only good news for Celtic that day. *The Glasgow Herald* is tactful (some would say that it is deliberately failing to tell the truth) when it says that "ere the game was many minutes old, Quin (sic) their clever centre...met with a severe accident by coming in contact with Nick Smith and was unable to resume". In fact, Quinn was felled and had his thigh (!) split open by a challenge from Smith that was virtually an assault. Smith was not even spoken to by the referee, Quinn was carried off and Rangers had their revenge already for the Scottish Cup Final. A hundred years later it would have been an instant red card and a lengthy suspension. It would be a tackle that would be remembered and related in vivid detail by all who saw it, all their lives, and it was never likely to be forgiven, even when Smith himself died, unforgiven by the Celtic community, of enteric fever the following winter. Quinn himself was on crutches for three months and missed the European tour... but his day would come again.

The young Celtic team were of course upset by all this and never recovered, losing three goals before a brief revival in which they pulled two back before finding that the numerical disadvantage was too much. Young had allowed himself to get upset at the sight of the smirks of some Rangers players when Quinn was carried off, and did not play well, finding himself described as "inexperienced", as *The Glasgow Herald* added that "tempers were not kept in such control as might be expected in a Charity tie". Young however realised that revenge "a dish to be served cold" would be better delivered to Rangers on the football field itself by beating them time and time again. He would go on to do just that.

Rangers eventually won this travesty of a tie 5–2. It was a chastening experience for Sunny Jim who thus realised that there was an unpleasant side to Scottish football as well. Still, Celtic had won the main prize, the Scottish Cup, and in any case, there was no time to brood on things, for on the Monday afterwards, they were off to Europe on a tour of the Austro-Hungarian Empire. For the still immature and "gallus" Sunny Jim, there was a salutary lesson.

Mention has been made of Maley's desire to bring to the fore the "missionary" aspect of Celtic. He had already this year taken them to the north of Scotland and to England. This one was slightly further afield, and he was already eyeing the possibility of a tour to the new world of Canada and the USA. Austro-Hungary had of course only 15 years to live before it brought about its own destruction, but in 1904 it was opulent, effete, decadent and appallingly ill-divided with the ruling class dreadfully out of touch with its peasants and working classes. There was, as in Russia, a revolution waiting to happen. Football was in its infancy in Europe but all football people there were thrilled at the prospect of the famous Scottish team coming to play a few games against their teams in their cities of Vienna and Prague.

Celtic sailed on Monday 16 May, and by the following day the party reached Frankfurt. The players had been travelling for over 24 hours and were glad of a chance to stretch their legs around the station, where they had to change trains for Vienna. Then something strange happened, and we will never know the exact truth, but it appeared that Maley called the players together and told them to get on the train in five minutes. Stations are noisy places and Sunny Jim thought that Maley had said 25, so went off on his own for another wander, this time outside the station, and missed the connection.

There are at least two strange aspects to this story – one was why no one went with him (had he fallen out with some of them?) and the other was why he didn't notice that he was on his own. Maley must accept some of the blame for not ensuring that everyone was on the train, but there exists a small possibility that Young deliberately got lost, perhaps feeling ill in the intense heat and unable to face more of the train journey, perhaps having quarrelled with Maley and wanting to make his own way home. The most likely explanation, however, was that he simply was a young Scottish lad, overwhelmed by his first trip abroad and fascinated by the sight of Frankfurt.

In any case, the Celtic party on the train were well out of Frankfurt before someone said "Where's Sunny?" Panic ensued for there was no way of getting in touch with the wayward Young who had now reappeared at Frankfurt Station and discovered that the train had gone. Not only that, but there wasn't another train direct to Vienna until 4.00 pm the next day, although he could take a less direct route at 6.00 pm that evening. And Young was a "gallus" Kilmarnock boy with no real experience of the ways of the world.

A helpful stranger who spoke some English enabled Young, however, to send a telegram to the hotel which he knew Celtic would be staying at in Vienna, and thus anxiety was eased somewhat, but Young didn't rejoin the Celtic party until the Thursday when Jimmy Hay found him looking lost in Vienna. There was a certain amount of ribbing and one assumes a severe dressing down from Maley. Some thought that he had been waylaid by the attractions of a German fraulein; others thought that he had had too much German beer, but Maley, although angry and upset, nevertheless had sufficient regard for Young that he insisted that the affair remained confidential. It was years later before the truth was released, although stories reached the Scottish Press about "a Celtic player" getting lost.

Young himself may have been upset about the incident, but he did not let it bother him, telling everyone that, "If it hadnae been for my command o' languages...". In fact he only ever spoke broad Ayrshire and could hardly be understood in Bristol, let alone Frankfurt or Vienna! He thus missed the game on Wednesday 18 May when Celtic beat Wien AFC 4–2 in Vienna's Athletiksportsplatz. Maley was able to indulge himself in this game by taking Sunny's place at right-half. Maley was still only 36 and still reasonably fit, and his own position had been right-half but he changed his position to left-half in the second half so that he would be playing in the shade! He was after all "the Boss"!

The errant Young played in the next game against a Vienna Select team on Sunday 22 May. Celtic won very comfortably 6–1. Then after a few jokes about putting a rope round Sunny and dragging him along so that they wouldn't lose him again, the team went on to Prague where they beat SK Slavia 4–1 on 25 May and "a German club" 3–0 on 29 May. It was light-hearted none-too-serious stuff and went a long way to building the rapport and team spirit which would characterise the Celtic team of the next few years.

CHAPTER FOUR

GLORY, GLORY, GLORY

1904–1907

Sunny could hardly wait for the start of the new season. He trained hard in his determination to be as fit as possible, for he knew that in Scottish football there was nothing easy. There was no such thing as an easy game or an easy team. He was also aware that Celtic were one of the teams that everyone else wanted to beat. Third Lanark, of course, were the League Champions, and Rangers were the biggest rivals in terms of support, but a strong challenge could also be expected from the two Edinburgh teams, and further afield, from Dundee. As it turned out, Airdrie would also be a good team this year.

Various friendlies and benefit matches were arranged, but the League season opened on 20 August 1904 in glorious weather at Meadowside the home of Partick Thistle. To Sunny Jim went the honour of scoring the first goal of the season in ten minutes from a free-kick, and Celtic remained on top for the whole game, even without Jimmy Quinn who was used sparingly in his recovery from his horrendous injury of last May.

Young himself picked up an injury in a benefit match against Rangers in midweek and missed the next two League games, the capable Willie Black filling in for him at Clune Park, Port Glasgow in an easy win and in a less pleasant game, the visit of Hearts to Parkhead. Sunny was badly missed as Hearts were allowed a late and undeserved equalizer. The appearance of Parkhead was odd, for there was now no stand on the North side of the ground after the fire of May 1904 and although Celtic wanted to build a new enclosure, they were held up until 1907 by the bureaucracy of Glasgow Corporation.

Hearts gave Celtic a certain amount of trouble in autumn 1904, for they beat them at Tynecastle on the Edinburgh Holiday Monday of 19 September as well, and this time Sunny was playing. It was one of the those days when Celtic played as well as Hearts did, but it was the Tynecastle men who got the goals. Curiously, on that same Holiday Monday, Rangers also travelled to Edinburgh to play Hibs, with both sets of fans apparently mingling harmoniously on the trains! It is difficult to imagine that scenario today!

But there was no real doubt that the competition that was exercising the minds of the Glasgow population in autumn 1904 was the Glasgow Cup, then competed for with much intensity and excitement between the six teams of Glasgow – Celtic, Rangers, Partick Thistle, Third Lanark, Clyde and Queen's Park, and the final normally held on the weekend of the Glasgow Autumn Holiday. The format was of "two ties and two byes" and Celtic were not lucky enough to get a bye in the first round and had to entertain Queen's Park, with an Englishman, one John Lewis from Blackburn Rovers, invited to referee, lest there might be accusations of bias about Scottish referees!

The weather was beautiful on 10 September at Celtic Park, and Celtic, with Young, Loney and Hay in commanding form in midfield, won comfortably 3–0 in front of a good crowd of 21,000. Two weeks later the weather was a lot less hospitable and the crowd correspondingly smaller at Parkhead as Celtic took on Partick Thistle in the semi-final. Only 6,000 were there, a larger attendance being seen at Ibrox to see Rangers take on the League champions, Third Lanark. *The Glasgow Herald* claims (improbably) that, "Thistle were easily the better team" but it was Celtic who got the goals through Peter Somers and Willie Black, and thus, as Rangers beat Third Lanark in the other game, New Hampden would stage its third "Old Firm" (as Celtic and Rangers were now called because of their ability to make money) Cup Final of 1904. Celtic had won the Scottish Cup, and Rangers the Glasgow Charity Cup last year. This would be the decider, as it were, and some reports say that 65,000 (more than the Scottish Cup Final) were there to see it. 31 turnstiles were now in operation at Hampden Park, and the ambitious claim was made that nine hundred could be admitted every minute!

The consensus of opinion, however, seems to indicate that the attendance was 55,000, and they saw the following teams take the field on Saturday 8 October. Celtic, having beaten Queen's Park in the Scottish League the week before with Young being singled out "as the best of the winners" in *The Daily Record and Mail* were confident of a victory, although the Press tended to think that Rangers were marginally better.

The teams were;

Celtic: Adams, McLeod and Orr; Young, Loney and Hay; Bennett, McMenemy, Quinn, Somers and Hamilton.

Rangers: Allan, N. Smith and Fraser; May, Speedie and Robertson; Mackie, Kyle, Hamilton, McColl and A. Smith.

Referee: T. Robertson, Queen's Park.

The weather was ideal, and the turf in perfect condition. In spite of the early loss of a goal, Celtic came really good in this game, as the Rangers attack "died away". Sunny Jim, having mastered the dangerous Bob Hamilton, took control of the midfield, spraying passes, shouting, cajoling, winning balls and feeding Bennett and McMenemy. Quinn (some say Bennett) soon equalised and then in the second half, Alec Bennett (who, it will be remembered did not play in the Scottish Cup Final because his loyalty could not be depended upon!) scored the winner off a rebound after Davie "the Dancer" Hamilton hit the bar.("The air was vocal with Celtic jubilation" says *The Glasgow Observer.*) Rangers then renewed their efforts for an equaliser, but Celtic defended well with goalkeeper Davie Adams playing "out of his shell" in the last desperate ten minutes. But Celtic held out for a narrow but deserved win, until "Tom Robertson's bugle sang truce" in the poetic words of the triumphant *Glasgow Observer*.

"The Celts now romped off the field" winners of the first Cup of the season. It was totally deserved on the run of play. It was (amazingly) their first win in this competition since season 1895–96 and Sunny Jim now had won in less than eighteen months a winner's medal in four different Cup competitions – the Gloucestershire Cup, the Glasgow Charity Cup, the Scottish Cup and the Glasgow Cup. And he was still only 22!

"Bedouin" in *The Daily Record and Mail* sums up this game by saying that, "By an all round exhibition of pluck and determined play, the side least expected to win rose to the occasion against an eleven reputedly more clever in attack, and gained the Glasgow Cup in a manner that left no dubiety in the minds of the vast throng as to which was the most deserving side on the run of the game". *The Evening Times* credits the Celtic defence for the victory, and in a classic piece of Edwardian prose says that "Hay and Young were largely responsible for the spoliation of Rangers deadliness forward".

The Glasgow Observer is in gloating mood. It puts its opinions into the mouth of a fictitious character called Riley who talks about "...the teetotal (sic) failure of the Rangers forwards. For two months now the country has rung with the praises of the Ibrox front line. Their skill was poetic, miraculous. It hasn't taken Sunny Jim long to burst that bubble... the halves (Young, Loney and Hay) are guilty of a sort of athletic gluttony. They monopolise the play".

The Glasgow Cup, being held in October, was like the Scottish League Cup in the 1950s and 1960s when it was normally done and dusted at that sensible time of the year. The winners had a sense of achievement that stayed with them for the rest of the season. It was a great encouragement. Flushed with this success, Young stepped up his game. A Scottish League medal was still missing, and Sunny was determined to get the full Scottish set.

As luck would have it, the next game was against Rangers at Parkhead. It was a full-blooded encounter, ending 2–2, but then Celtic laid down a marker for themselves by beating Third Lanark 2–1 before 12,000 fans at Cathkin. It was a game not without incident and Sunny Jim was the unwitting catalyst of it all. Celtic were leading 2–0 at half-time with two Jimmy Quinn goals, and early in the second half Sunny Jim cleared the ball and hit the referee, Mr Murray of Stenhousemuir, in the mouth. His whistle was at his lips and the result was a dreadful mess of the man's mouth with five teeth subsequently having to be removed. Sunny was naturally quite upset about all this, apologised profusely and helped to carry Mr Murray off.

This might have meant the abandonment of the match, but it so happened that this match had been allocated neutral linesmen (this did not always happen in 1904 and on occasion clubs had to provide their own linesman) and one of the linesmen, Mr Miller of Motherwell prepared to take over. Willie Maley then said he would do the linesman's job (he usually did so with the utmost integrity) but Third Lanark objected, not so much to Maley officiating, but to the fact that Mr Miller who had already had words with their centre-half Sloan, would become referee. Thirds wanted the other linesman to do the job, but Mr Miller insisted he was refereeing, threatening to abandon the game and award the points to Celtic if they did not agree.

For a long time there was a stand-off with Sunny himself at one point offering jokingly to referee "Efter a', it wis me that caused it", until Third Lanark eventually agreed, under protest, to play under Mr Miller. Their misgivings about Mr Miller proved unjustified, and indeed Thirds scored late in the game, until the Celtic defence took charge once again and Celtic held out for a 2-1 win. Maley on the line was even suspected of bending over backwards to Thirds and awarding a few debatable throws (or "shies" or "flings" as they were known) to Thirds.

Following a successful November, Sunny would have less happy relations with a referee on 17 December. By this time, Celtic's consistent performances had seen them to the top of the League but this match at Parkhead against Partick Thistle (a 2–2 draw) was described as "wild". The time the referee was Mr Deans of Dalkeith. In addition to the normal, full-blooded but healthy Glasgow rivalry, the weather was poor with persistent drizzle in the midwinter darkness, and the pitch was very soft and slippery with players inevitably following through with their tackles and hitting the man as well as the ball. Celtic had gone ahead, but then Thistle had scored twice before Jimmy Hay playing left-back and deputising as captain for the injured Willie Orr, equalized with a penalty-kick which Thistle had disputed. Shortly after that Willie Black playing at left-half to release Hay to the left-back position was carried off injured after a nasty challenge from Thistle forward Jimmy Sommen.

Sunny, who had been having a poor game ("Young was led a sorry dance by the Partick Thistle left-wingers, Wilkie and Gray" according to *The Daily Record and Mail)* then targeted Sommen for a few tackles. In the aftermath of one of them as time was running out, Sommen remonstrated and Sunny was seen to aim a kick at him and Sommen went down. Mr Deans had little option to order Young from the field as Sommen was stretchered off. Celtic thus finished the game with nine men as Black was unable to resume.

The Daily Record and Mail describes things thus, "The game was also marred by a good deal of hacking and foul kicking, and the most glaring instance occurred just on time when Young made a flying rush at Sommen, who dropped and had to be carried off. As Young had previously been cautioned, Referee Deans made him accompany his victim to the pavilion". Clearly Sunny was not immune to what is now called "the red mist", something that is by no means uncommon among highly charged, highly committed, emotional young men.

The Glasgow Observer, unsurprisingly, is not without sympathies for Sunny Jim. "Riley" says, "Poor Black the quietest man of the twenty-two got the shipyard twist (sic) and was borne groaning to the pavilion. Sommen tried to send Sunny Jim high o'er the fence by a liberal use of "Force". Next minute Sommen himself went soaring heavenward on the toe of Young's boot. The Celt walked straight into the pavilion without waiting for the referee's notice to quit, and Sommen followed Black into the ambulance ward". Although there was little doubt that Sommen deserved all that he got, a lengthy suspension awaited Young in the New Year.

Celtic finished 1904 clear of Rangers at the top of the Scottish League, but January 1905 was to be a difficult month for the club. It started with an aborted New Year Day game at Ibrox which had to be abandoned because of continual crowd encroachment caused by enthusiasm and a genuine fear of being crushed to death rather than any hostile intent. This game was followed by a rare defeat for Celtic against Airdrie at Parkhead where a crucial penalty miss by Jimmy Hay was followed almost immediately by Airdrie's winner in a 3–2 defeat. Airdrie's victory was commented upon in Scottish society as much as was the other piece of news in early 1905 when in Manchuria in the Russo-Japanese war (an incredibly bloodthirsty affair by all accounts which Britain did well to avoid) the garrison of Port Arthur fell to the Japanese after a prolonged struggle and with an appalling loss of life.

A win followed over Port Glasgow, but then Celtic went down again this time to one of their bogey teams, Dundee at Dens Park. It was quite simply a poor performance on a bone hard pitch on a cold frosty day. Celtic made the mistake of taking the field in rubber soles, but discovered that this particular pitch demanded boots with studs. Referee Kirkham of Preston, generally regarded as the best referee in Great Britain and who was given a lot of difficult Scottish games to do, refused to stop the game so that Celtic could change back into studded football boots, and so the players had to take it in turns, one by one, to leave the field and change their boots. This rather disrupted things, and Dundee scored twice while this was going on. Celtic pulled one back but to no avail.

Celtic then beat Hibs at Parkhead and progressed to the next round of the Scottish Cup by beating Dumfries (not the team that we now know as Queen of the South), but then Sunny Jim on 31 January at 6 Carlton Place, the Headquarters of the SFA got the news that he had been dreading – namely that he had been suspended for a month for his violent conduct against Jimmy Sommen of Partick Thistle. Mr Deans the referee said (with a hint of exaggeration, one feels) that it, "was the most brutal he had ever witnessed" but when Young pleaded, "excessive provocation" in extenuation, the referee admitted that Young had a point. An SFA member suggested two weeks suspension, another said two months, but the disciplinary committee compromised and decided that Sunny Jim should be suspended for a month, effectively all of February.

This to Young seemed draconian. It was a first offence, and not for the first or the last time, a trace of anti-Celtic bias was smelt here in some quarters. (Jimmy Quinn would discover that in two high profile incidents – one later in 1905 and another in 1907). Nevertheless, Sunny accepted it, and had no choice but to continue his job as an Iron Turner for a month, and attend Celtic Park only as a spectator. It was agony for him, but he was pleased to see that the team did well in his absence! His loud raucous Ayrshire voice was heard once or twice from the players section of the old Celtic Park balcony.

That winter saw two deaths of football players which affected Young deeply, albeit in different ways. One was that of Rangers player and fellow Ayrshireman Nick Smith who died in early January of enteric fever, a disease that had ravaged Ayrshire that year. While upset at his death, Young could not forget nor forgive the brutal assault on Jimmy Quinn in last year's Charity Cup Final. Indeed, Smith might well have been on Young's "list".

He felt differently about Barney Battles who died of flu in February. Battles, now playing for Kilmarnock, had been a great, if occasionally controversial Celt, but he was famously a great hearted fellow whose sociability off the field was in direct proportion to his aggression on it. Sunny and Barney were not close (although Young's name is mentioned among the mourners in the newspapers, he was not one of the pall bearers) but Sunny modelled himself on Barney as far as attitude was concerned. Barney, in spite of his infamous "falling out" with the Celtic establishment in 1896, was a great lover of the

Celtic club. That was in fact the way that Young was going to be as well. He could not ever exclude the possibility of a disagreement with Maley or anyone else, but he would always love the club.

Young trained hard while under suspension. Celtic were now in the semi-final of the Scottish Cup against Rangers, and had finished their League programme. They had played their 26 games and had amassed 41 points (2 points for a win), but they could still be equalled by Rangers if Rangers won their three games in hand. The end of the season promised to be very exciting.

Young was due back on 11 March, and was expecting to play in a friendly between Celtic and Kilmarnock with the proceeds to go to the widow of Barney Battles (she was pregnant with Barney Battles junior who would play for Hearts in future years), when he was unexpectedly chosen to play for the Scottish League against the English League at Hampden. Donnie McLeod, Alec Bennett and Jimmy Quinn also played in this game which attracted 30,000 to Hampden, but the Englishmen won 3–2 and Young, apparently, did not play well enough to earn a place in the full International the following week at Parkhead against Ireland. Nevertheless he was now proud of his two Scottish League International caps.

It was the game on 25 March at Parkhead, against Rangers in the Scottish Cup semi-final which caused serious ructions. Rangers were 2–0 up late in the second half when there occurred the incident which became the talking point of Edwardian Scotland for a few years. It happened when Jimmy Quinn was ordered off by referee Tom Robertson of Queen's Park for seeming to aim a kick at the head of Rangers Irish defender Alec Craig as he lay on the ground. What actually happened, as was agreed by all the participants, was that Craig fell on the wet ground and in so doing grabbed Quinn's leg to break his fall. Quinn then shook his leg to free it of Craig's hand, and it looked to Mr Robertson that he was aiming a kick. In spite of protests and appeals, not least from the honourable Ulsterman Alec Craig himself who would later testify at Quinn's hearing, Quinn was sent off.

All hell now broke loose as Quinn walked to the pavilion on the north-west corner of the ground. Some hotheads invaded the field and Mr Robertson had to be escorted to the pavilion by the police while Celtic fans actually carried some of their men off! Sunny Jim, although incensed by the injustice done to his friend, appealed for calm, as did manager Maley. After ten minutes, the pitch was cleared and an attempt made to restart the game. A further pitch invasion, however, curtailed proceedings, and Celtic conceded the tie which the SFA in any case awarded to Rangers. In truth Celtic 0–2 down and now without Quinn would probably have had no chance of righting matters. It was a sad end, however, to a Scottish Cup campaign, and Sunny had every right to feel sore at what had happened.

What was going on in the League in the meantime? Celtic, as we said, had finished their League programme in Young's enforced absence in February. Rangers frustratingly kept winning their League games (although they lost the Scottish Cup Final to Third Lanark), while Celtic played meaningless friendlies and games in the Glasgow League (a little valued competition played when there were no other games to play!) until Rangers finally caught up with them on 29 April when they beat Morton 2-0 at Cappielow. Both teams had 26 games played and 41 points won, but Rangers would have won the title on goal average or goal difference, for they had scored 83 and conceded 28, while Celtic had scored 68 and conceded 31. Would the Scottish League decide to employ either of these expedients? Or would they simply share the title, as had happened in 1891, the very first year of the League's existence when Rangers shared with Dumbarton?

There was a way round this problem. The two clubs were scheduled to play each other in the Glasgow League on 6 May. The Glasgow League, as we have said, was little valued and clubs would often play their fringe players or trialists for this competition which was soon to come to an end in any case, when the Scottish League was expanded to allow more teams. The Scottish League decided to hijack this fixture, move it to Hampden, and make it the League decider. Rangers, who would have been the beneficiaries if they hadn't done that, didn't seem to mind or object, the pill sweetened, no doubt, by the prospect of a 30,000 crowd. Annoyingly for Sunny, he seems to have picked up an injury in a Glasgow League match the previous Monday, and was unavailable for this game. He thus sat in the stand and watched his team mates win 2–1, with Alec McNair at right-half, and thus Celtic gained their first League title since 1898.

Sunny had of course played in enough games to win a League medal, and there was more good news for him before the end of the season. He won his second Glasgow Charity Cup medal. Having defeated Queen's Park with a degree of confidence on 17 May in the semi-final, Celtic played Partick Thistle in the final at Ibrox some ten days later.

The teams were;
Celtic: Adams, Watson and Orr; Young, Loney and Hay; W. McNair, McMenemy, Quinn, Somers and Hamilton.
Partick Thistle: Howden, Harvey and McKenzie; Walker, Melville and Wilson; Laurie, Gray, Kennedy, Gilchrist and Sommen.
Referee: Mr J. Baillie, St Bernard's.

15,000 appeared for this game, thereby contributing a goodly amount to worthy Glasgow charities, but there was also a certain amount of "history" about this fixture, particularly between Sunny Jim and James Sommen who had, of course, been responsible for Sunny's lengthy suspension in February. But the match, played in intermittent showers, was well controlled by the referee Mr Baillie of Edinburgh, and Sunny played Sommen fairly, never allowed himself to be riled by provocative remarks and hurt Sommen more by his fine play than he would have if he had allowed himself to get angry. It was a mature response to a potentially dangerous situation.

Celtic scored in the first half through Davie Hamilton and Jimmy McMenemy or "the Dancer" and "Napoleon" as they were commonly known, and thereafter, Young, Loney and Hay took a vice-like grip on proceedings. Celtic might have scored more in the second half but the score remained Celtic 2 Partick Thistle 0. *The Glasgow Herald* states laconically, "Celtic were always the better team". Sunny even felt magnanimous enough to shake the hand of Jimmy Summen at the end. The handshake was returned, "but none too cordially", and Celtic had now won three of the four available trophies in season 1904–05.

Celtic fans were now, in 1905, neither, "to haud nor to bind" (meaning they were not to be tied down in their exuberant celebrations). After a few years of under-achievement, a new young team was assembling, and the great thing was that they knew that there was more to come. Indeed there was, and it was round about now that stories and a culture grew up about the great Jimmy

Quinn and the three musketeers behind him. A middle aged lady rejected a proposal of marriage because she wanted somebody "young". "Sorry, he's already meeriet wi a bairn and bides in Kilmarnock. But there's Loney, if ye want or Hay..." A Celtic supporter went into a bar and asked for three whiskies. "Young, Loney and Hay". "Pardon" said the bemused barman. "Ye heard me, ah want three halves of the best!".

Young kept a low profile in the close season, seldom venturing far from Kilmarnock. He would of course be instantly recognised by his large frame, fair hair and athletic build, something unusual in these poverty and disease ridden days. He would be seen around the town, but he was a man whom one heard before one saw, talking to everyone, asking about people who were ill, offering his opinion on what the Russians were going to do now that they had lost the war to Japan, discussing the progress of the local cricket team, the need to get rid of the Conservative government of the disliked Arthur Balfour, and of course the Celtic team of which he was such a proud part, with even a mention of his old friends at Bristol Rovers who had won the Southern League in 1905. "It was me that made them, ye ken!" He also talked proudly about his beloved Flora (as he called her) and his beautiful daughter Maud, now a toddler. Like so many other great Celtic players, before and since, he was disarmingly, "just like an ordinary man".

Celtic opened the 1905–06 season with ten straight wins and a draw (against Hearts, a team who would also have a great season and would give Celtic a great deal of bother, as they usually did), and Sunny played in them all apart from a 1–0 win against Hibs when he was injured. It was great, spectacular, Celtic stuff with fast open football and loads of goals. Quinn was of course well to the fore in all this, but Bennett, McMenemy, Somers and Hamilton were all capable of scoring as well and behind them stood the troika, the Holy Trinity, the Porthos, Athos and Aramis of Alexander Dumas's *The Three Musketeers*, the eternal threesome of Young, Loney and Hay with one chronicler, clearly well versed in classical literature comparing them to Aeschylus, Sophocles and Euripides, the three tragedians of 5th-century BC Athens, and a mathematician talking about the cos, sin and tan of trigonometry

Crowds flocked to see them. On 30 September 1905, 35,000 came to Parkhead to see the equally strong-going Airdrie, and the gates were rushed (causing a few unfortunate injuries) when the roar from inside the ground announced the arrival of the Celtic team. They saw a great game, well balanced at 1–1 until Sunny Jim slipped a ball through to McMenemy who ran on and scored the winner to release, "a yell of triumph from over 20,000 throats, and the roaring was maintained and grew in volume on to the close". Young was described as, "the best right-half in the land. If the England game were tomorrow, he would be in", while Loney showed, "robust energy" and Hay (somewhat peculiarly) described as having, "a tireless trot". On the same day, Third Lanark beat Rangers in the Glasgow Cup semi-final to set up a final against Celtic.

The previous Saturday Celtic had beaten Partick Thistle in the Glasgow Cup semi-final very convincingly 4–0 and had earned some praise from *The Glasgow Herald*, (a newspaper not known to dish out excessive praise to anyone other than their beloved Queen's Park). It states that Thistle could make nothing of the Celtic half-back line, "which is quite the best in Scotland at the present time". On the Monday before the Airdrie game, Celtic had beaten Third Lanark 1–0 in the Scottish League in a thriller at Cathkin with, "never a dull minute in the ninety" and they were now the favourites for the Glasgow Cup.

The Glasgow Cup Final was scheduled for 7 October. One would have expected a crowd of close to 50,000 but unfortunately, incessant, typically Glasgow rain, before and during the game cut the attendance to about half that amount. Hampden Park, for all its magnificence, lacked shelter.

The teams were;
Celtic: Adams, Campbell and Orr; Young, Loney and Hay: Bennett, McMenemy, Quinn, Somers and Hamilton.
Third Lanark: Raeside, Barr and McIntosh; Comrie, Sloan and Neilson; Johnstone, Graham, McKenzie, Wilson and Munro.
Referee: Mr J Baillie, St.Bernard's.

The diminished crowd saw a wonderful Celtic performance but a disappointing final in that Third Lanark rarely troubled the Celtic defence, being unable to get past the Celtic midfield line which was, "as usual, irreproachable", and indeed

Thirds were lucky to get off with a 0–3 defeat. The first goal from Jimmy Quinn was hit from 20 yards and (remarkably on a wet day) it smacked into the soaked netting and rebounded out again into the field of play! On the half hour mark, Celtic were 2–0 up with Peter Somers, "the powder monkey" finishing off a nice move which had involved the three Jimmys – Young, McMenemy and Quinn. In the second half, McMenemy scored a third and possibly irrelevant goal, for Thirds were a well beaten side. The Cup was presented, as was the custom in those days, in private after the game, and Sunny thus picked up his second successive Glasgow Cup medal.

As last year however, midwinter was not quite so good for Sunny. A defeat by Rangers on 21 October was disappointing, but not fatal, but the following week when Dundee came to Parkhead, Sunny was badly injured in a clash with a Dundee player (accidental, one presumes) and forced to limp on the right wing in those pre-substitute days. Ironically he scored the third goal in Celtic's 3–1 win, but it was clear that he was badly injured with what looked like ligament damage. In fact he would be out of action until 9 December when Aberdeen came to Parkhead.

His return in fact caused Maley a dilemma, for in his absence, Alec McNair had fitted in very well in his place, and Maley was loath to leave out the earnest McNair. In time of course, Eck McNair would become a legendary right-back, but at the moment Maley could not unseat Donnie "the slasher" McLeod who was playing superbly there, having taken over from Bob Campbell who had been less of a success. The team was in fact going very well – Hearts were still top of the League but Celtic had games in hand – without Young, and even when Young returned, he still didn't look quite fit.

Maley, anxious not to upset either McNair or Young, both of whom he regarded highly, alternated the right-half spot between them for a spell. It was a characteristic of both men that they accepted this situation with equanimity, and neither of them could really feel hard done by. Celtic were, by the end of January, comfortable at the top of the League with victories over Rangers on New Year's Day and Airdrie on 13 January (McNair playing at right-half in both cases) and Hearts, their main rivals having a very bad January as Celtic caught and overtook them.

In the month of February, Young seemed to be the favoured right-half, but it was McNair who was given the nod for the Cup tie against Hearts at Parkhead on 24 February. Whether this was because Young had a slight knock or because Maley felt that McNair, being more defensive minded than the naturally aggressive and forward thrusting Sunny, might be better able to cope with Hearts inside trio, we cannot be sure, but it was McNair who played at right-half in this Cup tie. It attracted a crowd of "International proportions" to Celtic Park. 50,000 were said to be there with another 10,000 still queuing at the inadequate turnstiles as the teams ran out for the 3.45 pm kick-off. This was as late as they dared make it in late February given the situation with the light. The later kick-off was preferred in order to give more people a chance to get from Edinburgh, after they had worked their shifts in the morning.

It was Hearts who won this game. Young could only watch impotently in the pavilion. Even though McMenemy scored first for Celtic, Hearts equalized just after half-time through the great Bobby Walker (sometimes called "Houdini") and then at a critical stage in the second half Alec Menzies scored the winner. Celtic staged a late rally but the game was lost, and Celtic were out of the Scottish Cup. Young might, of course, have said, "I told you so" and blamed team selections, but he realised that such things did not matter. The team that he loved was not going to win the Scottish Cup that year (in fact Hearts would go on to win the trophy for the fourth time), and although Celtic now seemed to be odds on to win the Scottish League, people now began to ask whether there was a hoodoo on the same team winning both the Scottish League and the Scottish Cup in the same year. It was a sore defeat for Celtic.

By this time a change had been detected in areas other than football. The Liberals had won the 1906 General Election. It had not been so much that they had won the Election as that it had been a landslide that had been so significant. Sunny Jim had often been distressed by some of the sights that he had seen in and around Parkhead. In particular the sight of children without shoes, wearing merely stockings on their feet was a sight that appalled the compassionate man from Kilmarnock where there was poverty, yes; but nothing like on the scale or the intensity that there was in Glasgow.

Celtic had of course been formed to try to deal with this problem, and although the lofty ideals had been discarded in favour of making money,

Sunny liked to think that there was still a residue of goodness in Maley and the Board of Directors. It was not unknown for Maley to allow poor children in for nothing on occasion, and on one occasion Young and a few others had seen him bending down to speak to a child in a pram, and thinking that no-one was watching him, dropping a coin into the pram, as if by mistake!

Young himself, however professional he was and as keen to earn money as anyone, realised on occasion with a pang of conscience that, in comparison with many people, he was absurdly wealthy and lucky in his choice of career. His wife and daughter were comfortable. He hoped that with the Liberals now in power, more and more people might now get a better deal out of life. It was not only the Liberals with their kind old Glaswegian Henry Campbell-Bannerman as Prime Minister and these clearly ambitious young men Lloyd George and Winston Churchill, but there was also the new Labour party, looked upon by some (*The Glasgow Herald* in particular!) as dangerous anarchists, but by others as people who were genuinely wanting to make a better society. Sunny had some sympathy with them, and others like Quinn and Loney, with their mining background, were 100% uncompromising supporters of the new Labour party with their charismatic Scotsmen called Ramsay MacDonald and Keir Hardie.

March and the arrival of spring was of course traditionally the time of International matches. Both Young and McNair must have been amused to discover that Maley's dilemma about which of the two of them was the better right-half was in fact one that was shared by the Scottish selectors. McNair was chosen as Scotland's right-half for the game against Wales at Tynecastle on 3 March – a 0-2 defeat which rocked Scotland who didn't normally lose to Wales in those days – and then for the Irish game in Dublin on 17 March (St Patrick's Day!), Young was chosen along with Donnie McLeod and Jimmy Quinn to represent Scotland.

This of course was a great honour for Sunny. It came on the back of a brilliant performance by Young in the 6-0 defeat of Queen's Park which guaranteed the Scottish League Championship for Celtic for the second year in a row. Quinn scored four goals and Hamilton and Bennett one each and the football played against a poor Queen's Park team was truly magnificent and much talked about for years afterwards. It was Celtic's way of apologising to their supporters for their defeat by Hearts in the Scottish Cup, and it all came from the now restored half-back line of Young, Loney and Hay.

The trip to Ireland was a great experience in itself, the team sailing from the Broomielaw on the Friday and returning on the Sunday. Ireland was, at the moment, quieter than it had been for some time and a lot quieter than it would become in the next ten years, but one would be a fool not to detect a certain amount of political tension, particularly on St Patrick's Day where men like Redmond and O'Brien were making speeches about Home Rule, and the Lord Mayor's Parade passed fairly close to Dalymount Park where the International was to be held. The Parade was blamed by some for restricting the attendance to 5,000, but in truth, Ireland was not really a footballing nation, in the sense that Scotland obviously was, in 1906.

The Band of the Cameron Highlanders entertained the crowd with a selection of Scottish and Irish songs but there were also less politically acceptable songs sung unofficially by the crowd. *"The Wearin' O The Green"* for example. Young had of course heard Celtic supporters singing that particular song, but to hear it in Dublin was another matter especially when the lyrics of "They are hanging men and women for the wearing o' the green" were sung with a special earnestness, and *"God Save Ireland"* with all its talk about "gallows trees" and "noble hearted free" was bawled out at full volume. And of course *"My Old Fenian Gun"* was about as explicit as one would get.

Scotland's team was; Rennie (Hibs), McLeod (Celtic) and Hill (Third Lanark); Young (Celtic), Thomson (Hearts) and May (Rangers); Hamilton (Port Glasgow), Walker (Hearts), Quinn (Celtic), Fitchie (Woolwich Arsenal) and Smith (Rangers). The game was a poor one, with Young one of the few real stand out successes for Scotland. Scotland's goal, the only goal of the game, came from the interesting and unusual character called Tommy Fitchie of Woolwich Arsenal who was an amateur and had therefore cheerfully ignored the attempts of his club to stop him going to Dublin. Nevertheless, in spite of the game being a poor one on a pitch which was less than perfect, Young felt delighted that he had played in a winning Scottish team. He learned soon after his return that he had been chosen to go to Stamford Bridge, home of Chelsea in London the next week to play in the League International (for the third year in a row) and he began to nourish hopes of a game for the "big" International against England at Hampden on 7 April.

Alas! Sunny Jim had a poor game against the English League at Stamford Bridge, being accused, along with some others in *The Glasgow Herald* of "shakiness" in the early stages. The same paper however is adamant that the 6–2 defeat was not as bad as it sounds, for the Englishmen were simply better than the Scotsmen at taking their chances in front of goal, and in Colin Veitch of Newcastle United, the English League had someone quite special for he seemed (most unusually) to be able to get the better of Jimmy Quinn. Young's play improved after his uncertain start, and he had a good shot saved near the end, but his overall performance was poor enough to prevent him getting a Scotland cap against England in the "big" International. When the team was announced it was again Andy "the Dadler" Aitken of Newcastle United who was right-half. Indeed the Dadler played brilliantly in Scotland's 2–1 win over England in what was a then world record crowd of 102,471, while Sunny played for Celtic in a friendly match at Alloa in aid of a new grandstand before 2,000!

The 1905–06 season now fizzled out as far as Sunny was concerned. With the League well won and no Scottish Cup Final to look forward to, it was mainly friendly matches in the month of April at Bolton, Bradford and Galashiels where Sunny deliberately scored an own goal to make the score a more respectable 4–2 on the same day (18 April 1906) as the San Francisco earthquake in which about 3,000 people perished.

The first week in May saw a disappointment for Young in two respects. He was injured and could not play in the Glasgow Charity Cup semi-final against Rangers. Even more disappointing was the result a 5–3 win for Rangers in a game universally described as "very exciting" , although Rangers were 5–1 up at one point. Young was able to console himself with the thought that he was not to blame for the loss of two trophies out of four in season 1905–06 – he was not playing in either defeat! And with him on board, they had won the other two!

There followed two tours, such was Maley's ongoing enthusiasm for spreading the word. The first was to the Highlands, beginning in Aberdeen, then Forres, then Inverness before moving slightly further afield to Germany and Austro-Hungary. This time there is no indication of Sunny getting lost as he did in 1904, but there were games played in Hamburg, Leipzig, Berlin and two each in Prague and Budapest. It is a shame that we do not know more about these games – we know that they comfortably beat local opposition, other than Slavia Prague who held them to a 3–3 draw, but there were also two games arranged against English teams who were also on tour at the same time. Celtic beat Southampton 1–0 in Budapest, but we would like to know more about the game played against English Cup Finalists Newcastle United in Prague on 30 May. We know that it ended 2–2 (Alec Bennett in an odd interview several years later said that it had been agreed to draw the game 1–1!) but it might have answered the question of who was the better right-half – The Dadler or Sunny!

Sunny is seen here beside Manager Maley in Leipzig. Observe the poor condition of the pitch, the abdominal protector of goalkeeper Davie Adams and the prevalence of boater hats!

Season 1906–07 was a remarkable one. The club achieved great success, and it was hardly a coincidence that Sunny Jim missed only two games all season (one of them because he was playing for the Scottish League), and it was the season which really marked him out as a Celtic great. It was indeed all the more praiseworthy for Sunny because both Loney and Hay, his natural partners with whom he had a deep empathy, were both out for lengthy periods of the season with a broken arm and a broken collarbone respectively. In spite of all this, it was the season that Celtic achieved the Holy Grail, the Scottish League and Cup Double – the first team to be able to do so. It was also the season in which Celtic could reasonably claim to have been the best in the world, and how one wishes that there could have been a European Cup that season to prove it. In England, Newcastle United (with a team packed full of Scotsmen) won the League and were generally reckoned to have one of their best ever sides. But how would they have got on against Maley's Celtic with the prolific Jimmy Quinn, the mesmeric Jimmy McMenemy and the powerful, driving, thrusting force called Sunny Jim?

The season started with a bang, and it was only in the Glasgow Cup Final on 6 October (which they won) that a goal was conceded! And this was done with a Rangers goalkeeper between the sticks! This extraordinary series of events began before the season started. Davie Adams cut his hand on a goalpost at Ibrox. This was in a benefit match for Finlay Speedie, and Rangers, clearly feeling guilty at having a nail sticking out of their post and ever willing to oblige (Maley and Wilton were great friends and not without cause were Celtic and Rangers called "the Old Firm") lent them their reserve goalkeeper until such time as Adams' hand healed up.

The reserve goalkeeper was called Tommy Sinclair, and he was an old friend and teammate of Alec Bennett and Jimmy McMenemy from their Rutherglen days. In a story that would be rejected as too far fetched by editors of fiction, Sinclair proceeded to keep eight clean sheets in a row, and in each of these games Jimmy Quinn scored at least once at the other end. This was the pure wine of football as Motherwell, Kilmarnock, Morton, Partick Thistle, Hearts, Queen's Park, Third Lanark and Airdrie all failed to breach the Celtic defence. Sinclair played well, but in truth, the half-back line, variously described as "irreproachable", "impregnable", "burglar proof", "unbreachable" and "the Rock of Gibraltar", meant that very seldom were opposing teams able to cross the half-way line!

In the game against Hearts at Parkhead on 15 September, a great performance leading to a 3–0 win with two goals from Davie Hamilton and one fantastic one from Jimmy Quinn, Willie Loney was injured with what turned out to be a broken arm, but he was immediately replaced by Alec McNair, which was scarcely a weakening of the team. Crowds rolled up to Celtic Park to see this Edwardian juggernaut, and in the same way as sixty years later in season 1966–67 it would be Hogmanay before they lost, it was actually New Year's Day 1907 before they lost a game, and even then, there were extremely extenuating circumstances. Sometimes Celtic were called the "Dreadnoughts" after the ships that were very much in the news. It was true, mused Sunny; they dreaded or feared nothing.

Sinclair eventually conceded a goal, two in fact, in the Glasgow Cup Final on 6 October. He was, according to all accounts very upset at this, but his anguish was mitigated by the fact that he also won his first medal that day, for Celtic won 3–2. It was in fact one of the better Glasgow Cup Finals in the opinion of most observers. The game was played at Ibrox and 40,000 were there. Third Lanark actually scored in the first and last minute of the first half, but in between that Willie Orr had scored with a penalty-kick. Thus Celtic 1–2 down at half-time and without Willie Loney and Alec Bennett were up against it, but the makeshift half-back line of Young, McNair and Hay took command.

This time the tactics were slightly different. Willie Loney was an old fashioned centre-half who liked to come forward, Alec McNair was less so. So Alec, not without cause called "the icicle" for his ability to keep cool in difficult situations, stayed back with McLeod and Orr, and allowed Young and Hay to join the attack. This paid dividends in the 70th minute when Sunny scored one for his rare goals for the club in a goalmouth scramble to level the tie, and then ten minutes later with the resurgent Celtic, inspired by Sunny Jim, roaring forward "like waves breaking on the shore", the worthy Peter Somers, a grossly under-rated talent scored the winner, from a Bobby Templeton corner.

Celtic had now won the Glasgow Cup for the third year in a row. When the medals were given out, experienced men (as Young now was) said, "Well, that's anither ane" while Tommy Sinclair gazed in pride at his first ever. His time at Celtic Park was now over, for Davie Adams had now recovered, and he was on his way back to Ibrox or the "land o' nae medals" as Sunny Jim put it. Sinclair's career would get a further boost at the end of the 1906–07 season when he went to Newcastle United and played a few games there at the end of the season to help them win the English League! It was a pity for Sinclair that Adams was so good, for Celtic could certainly have used him.

The teams in the Glasgow Cup Final were;
Celtic: Sinclair, McLeod and Orr; Young, McNair and Hay; Templeton, McMenemy, Quinn, Somers and Hamilton.
Third Lanark: Brownlie, Barr and McGhie; McIntosh, Sloan and Neilson; Cross, McLuckie, Fairfoull, Wilson and Munro.
Referee; J. Lewis, Blackburn.

Bobby Templeton, a close friend of Sunny's had joined the club in summer 1906, and he was another man to win his first medal that day. He was of a wilder disposition than Sunny and had already played for Aston Villa, Newcastle United and Woolwich Arsenal, and indeed was said to have been the unwitting cause of the Ibrox Disaster in 1902 when the crowd swayed to one side to see "the Blue Streak" charging down the wing. He would sadly not stay very long with Celtic, for Maley did not always approve of his behaviour. In later years he would go into partnership with Sunny in the licensing trade in Kilmarnock before his untimely death in 1919.

For a few games in autumn 1906, Sunny found himself temporary captain. Both Willie Orr and James Hay were injured, so the mantle fell on Young. According to some folk, it made no difference for he acted like the captain in any case. He was ideally suited for this job for he was an inspiring leader on the field, and off the field a superb diplomat, able to handle difficult situations and to "have a word" with someone if necessary. He also went out of his way to advise and support fringe players like John Mitchell, Alex "Tug" Wilson and Ned Garry, pointing out that they too were vital members of the team. But he ate, lived and slept for the club. He was a particular friend of McMenemy, Quinn and Loney, but if he "fell out" with anyone – an inevitable occurrence in a football club from time to time – he always made sure that he made his peace with him before the next game. The important thing was the team. One of his more revealing remarks was that "Celtic had eleven captains" – as if everyone was totally involved in the team. There were no passengers.

He had the ear of Maley and suggested various ploys from time to time, but the form of the team made this hardly necessary for the team reached the New Year undefeated with 33 points from 18 games played. Just occasionally Celtic struggled, or more likely, the opposition raised their game. On 24 November for example, neighbours Clyde came to Parkhead and were 2–0 up at Parkhead soon after half-time with one or two Celtic players having off-days or carrying injuries. Sunny (still temporary captain that day) organised the rescue, scoring himself, then earning a penalty which he himself converted to make it 2–2. Even that did not seem enough, for Clyde then scored again, but one last effort from the Young-inspired Celtic team saw Jimmy Quinn squeeze home a late equalizer. Young might have claimed the goal (and thereby scored a hat-trick!) but he did admit that Quinn had touched it on.

1 January 1907 saw another major incident involving Jimmy Quinn when he was sent off at Ibrox by referee Fred Kirkham of Preston for allegedly kicking Hendry of Rangers in the face. Celtic maintained Quinn's innocence, but he was suspended for two months. This was a serious blow for Celtic, because although the play of the team remained good, the supply of goals dried up. Three games were required to dispose of Morton for example in the Scottish Cup in February and it needed a "lucky header" by Jimmy Hay on a heavily sanded, frosty pitch to finish the job.

A postcard of Celtic in 1906-07. Sunny Jim is fourth from the left in the back row

2 March saw Sunny earn his now annual game for the Scottish League against the English League at Ibrox. 50,000 saw an evenly contested 0–0 draw at Ibrox.

Sunny, the only Celtic player in the team, was generally regarded as having had a superb game and he must have felt that this year was surely the one in which he would get his call up for the full Scotland v England International to be held this year at St James' Park, Newcastle. He didn't, as it turned out, and the game was a sterile 1–1 draw with one newspaper report saying, "Oh, for a Young or McMenemy to make a difference!"

In the meantime Celtic took a huge step towards the League and Cup double on 9 March when they beat Rangers 3–0 at Ibrox in the Scottish Cup quarter-final. It was a game full of meaning for Jimmy Quinn in particular. It was Quinn's first day back after his long suspension, but the wise Sunny Jim, realising that Quinn would be targeted by Rangers defender (Hendry did in fact injure him in the first half), sprayed his passes to the other members of the forward line while Quinn, sensing the ploy and aware of the nuances of the situation, acted as a decoy, taking at least one Rangers player with him every time. It was Somers, Hamilton and then Hay who scored the goals. Well over 60,000 attended, said to be the biggest ever attendance at a club match in Scotland even beating the 1904 Scottish Cup Final, and there were probably more than was estimated, for gates were burst open and thousands poured in. But in the last 15 minutes, the Rangers fans "began to skail" with the additional problem of snow encouraging an early departure. They thus left their ground to the Celtic fans who could not believe their luck, but celebrated loudly. They sang *"Erin's Green Valleys"* and threw snowballs on the way home!

Progress was being made to the Scottish League as well with wins over Third Lanark and Queen's Park and a draw against Dundee, but Hibs provided a more difficult problem in the semi-final of the Cup. Goalless draws were ground out at Celtic Park and Easter Road, before everyone wondered what the fuss was about when Celtic suddenly turned it on and devastated Hibs 3–0 with Bobby Templeton in particular earning plaudits. This was on 13 April, and the Cup Final was next week at Hampden against the other Edinburgh team, Hearts.

A great deal was at stake in this game, which became extremely significant in a historical context. Hearts were of course the previous winners of the Scottish Cup and had indeed put Celtic out last year. There was also a little more to the niggle between the two than the normal Edinburgh v Glasgow rivalry. The religious element was glossed over in the Press, but it certainly existed in the minds of some of the Hearts supporters. But there was also the footballing issue of who was the better inside-right, Bobby Walker of Hearts or Jimmy McMenemy of Celtic. And there was of course the speculation of whether Celtic could win both Scottish trophies in the one season. No one else had, and it was widely believed to be impossible, although Aston Villa and Preston North End had done so in England. The Scottish League was virtually won, and Celtic had already beaten Hearts 3–0 this season at Parkhead in September, but a Scottish Cup Final was a different matter altogether. In addition, both teams had won the Scottish Cup four times, and were looking for their fifth.

The teams were;
Celtic: Adams, McLeod and Orr; Young, McNair and Hay; Bennett, McMenemy, Quinn, Somers and Templeton.
Hearts: Allan, Reid and Collins; Philip, McLaren and Henderson; Bauchop, Walker, Axford, Yates and Wombwell.
Referee: D. Philip, Dunfermline.

Both teams were short of their centre-half. Celtic had been without Willie Loney for a large part of the season, and Charlie Thomson, Hearts centre-half called off a day or two before the game.

The kick-off had to be delayed because Hearts' goalkeeper Tommy Allan was delayed in the crowd, which was indeed a huge one with loads of "football specials" having brought passengers from Edinburgh Waverley. A group of them had a huge placard in the shape of a heart with "Don't lose this" and other banners saying "Bobby Walker – the King of Hearts!" with the word "King" scored out and replaced with "Ace". According to *The Evening Citizen*, the reception for Hearts as they ran out was "warmer" than for Celtic.

It was a typical April day. Not particularly cold, and bright and breezy, but with the occasional violent storm of rain. It was on these occasions that one felt that Hampden, for all its size and magnificence, had one fatal flaw and that was that there was no shelter, unless you were one of the very rich fans who could afford to go to the stand. Queen's Park supporters would have no problem but, "the rest of us simply have to get wet", muttered those of an egalitarian persuasion. To be fair to Queen's Park, however, it was not normally in the mindset of Edwardian football clubs or stadium designers to consider the welfare of their spectators!

The game was a good one, but half-time came with no goals. Both sides had had chances, but neither team had as yet exerted any sort of dominance over the other. Ominously for Hearts however, the Celtic forward line had not yet been seen at their best. The feeling was expressed that once Celtic went ahead, they would be very difficult to dislodge.

"Houdini" had not been seen. This was Bobby Walker, Hearts great inside-right. This was because Sunny Jim had said to the rest of the defence, "Leave Walker tae me! You deal wi' the rest, but I'll sort him oot". Sunny was of course not above a few hefty challenges, but he was careful not to push his luck, and in any case, it soon became obvious that Young had his measure, for Walker had no relish for the physical. "Young's display was marked by certain nasty features," said the disapproving *Glasgow Herald* which was by no means a pro-Celtic newspaper. *The Glasgow Observer*, on the other hand, consistently sang the praises of Sunny.

Willie Orr scored with a penalty-kick early in the second half, and then the excellent Peter Somers scored twice from good crosses from Alec Bennett. The game then lapsed into a dead contest with Celtic, having no great wish to further humiliate their opponents and Hearts, dismayed at the early departure of their followers, having nothing to offer, now that

Walker had been neutralised. The Scottish Cup was duly presented after the game in the Hampden library(!), and Sunny now had another medal. This game was significant in that it marked the start of the Hearts trophy famine which lasted 50 years, and also perhaps the start of their intense, depressing and irrational hatred of Celtic which still to this day characterises Hearts fans, and to the dismay of some of their own fans perhaps, explains why pro-Rangers songs and chants can often be heard at Tynecastle.

Chapter Four

But there was more yet in 1907 for Sunny Jim. All the players were given a £10 bonus (a lot of money in 1907) for winning the Cup, but there was still the League championship. The League was indeed won on 24 April in anti-climactic circumstances for Celtic at Meadowside, the home of Partick Thistle before a meagre midweek 4,000 crowd, and the press too obsessed with the visit of the Prince and Princess of Wales to Glasgow to give it much coverage. Celtic took the Scottish Cup with them to show it off, hoping thereby to boost the crowd, but it was a working day. A few enlightened schools took their kids to see the occasion; other children faced a certain belting the next day for taking the day off! Celtic had thus won the "Double". Aston Villa and Preston had done it in England, but this was the first time that it had been done in Scotland. It was in fact a treble because the Glasgow Cup had been won too, but the quadruple was missed when Celtic, surprisingly went down 0–1 to Rangers at Cathkin on 18 May in the final of the Glasgow Charity Cup.

Celtic supporters in the 38,000 crowd at Cathkin were very disappointed, and there seems to be no reason for this defeat, much fumed about by Maley, other than the age-old one of "the serpent of complacency". There were more than a few hints that this might happen for, after Celtic had won the League, there were a number of half-hearted draws, although the Charity Cup semi-final against Queen's Park had seen a fine 6–2 victory. It was simply that Rangers were more "up for it" than Celtic were, and ex-Celt Bob Campbell scored midway through the first half. It was the only goal of the game, and hard though Young tried to inspire the others out of their lethargy on this beautiful summer day, Rangers held out in spite of some intense Celtic pressure, and had one of their rare moments of triumph in a depressing period of their history. But for Celtic it was only three trophies in season 1906–07, not four. Sunny was vexed about that.

Sunny was by now becoming a seasoned tourist of European countries. This year from 1 June until 12 June, Sunny was in Denmark with Celtic, for a light hearted tour of four games. Celtic had no goalkeeper for Davie Adams' mother was very ill. Alec McNair was left behind because he was getting married, and such was the lack of knowledge of the Danes about football that Willie Maley refereed two games. Sunny Jim took his share of the goalkeeping duties, but his friend Bobby Templeton permanently alienated himself from

Maley for giving a virtuoso display of dribbling which Maley described as "silly" and "selfish". Sunny Jim disagreed, thinking that Templeton was brilliant, but Celtic lost that particular game, and relationships between Templeton and Maley were never quite the same again.

CHAPTER FIVE

THE GREATEST SHOW ON EARTH

1907–1910

It was the Barnum and Bailey Circus that first described itself as the "Greatest Show on Earth". Willie Maley was very happy when the same name was given to his team from 1907 onwards. 1907 perhaps suggested that this Celtic team might be the greatest show on earth, 1908 proved it. Not until 1967 would another Celtic team win every competition that they entered, so if 1908 can be mentioned in the same breath as 1967, those of us privileged to have been alive in 1967 and to have enjoyed its glories will have a general idea of how good 1908 was!

It was not that they won every game. Just occasionally at difficult places like Dundee, Hearts or Aberdeen, complacency got the better of them (the 1967 team had a blind spot as well, losing home and away to Dundee United, for example), but the team could always fight back and recover from a setback. They could also win the games that they had to win, the important games, and like 1967, they had great players and a young, talented, manager at the height of his powers, who would become a statesman of the Scottish game.

But perhaps as important as anything else was the psychological attitude. All those who played for Celtic at the time were totally committed to the team, at least as far as the next game was concerned. It remains of course one of Edwardian Scotland's greatest mysteries why Alec Bennett at the end of the 1907–08 season decided that he wanted to jump ship and play for Rangers instead. He played well enough for Rangers, whom his family supported, but his best football was without a doubt played for Celtic. And in any case, while he was with Celtic, (after being dropped for the 1904 Scottish Cup Final, which must have taught him no end of a lesson) there was never the slightest dubiety about his attitude or commitment.

Sunny Jim might have had similar fantasies about other teams. He might have preferred to play for his native Kilmarnock or even go back to Bristol

Rovers, but Celtic was now his home. Loads of people (one thinks of the execrable Maurice Johnston) may have said that, "Celtic are the only team I've ever wanted to play for". Sunny never said that in his early life, but by the time that he had settled down at Parkhead, the love affair with the club had taken root. He got on well with Maley (not always the easiest man to live with), and co-operated well with his captains Willie Orr and Jimmy Hay. He would become captain in his own right in 1911, but before then, he occasionally acted as captain when either or both these men were missing, and sometimes when they weren't, for it was his raucous voice that everyone heard! It is a mark of credit to both Orr and Hay that they never resented Sunny's unofficial captaincy of the team!

Anno Domini was catching up with Willie Orr by 1907, and at the start of season 1907–08 there appeared another Ayrshire man in the left-back position. This was Jamie Weir from Muirkirk, one of the lesser known characters of this great team. He was a sturdy young man whose footballing knowledge and skills were much improved by his travelling to Glasgow on the train with Sunny Jim. Weir, although a quiet, shy, unassuming young man when he first joined the team, had a hidden talent (which was soon discovered and exploited) of being an expert in Burns Recitation. This was a great skill for the Celtic team would, on away trips, regale each other (and other guests in hotels) with renditions of songs and poetry. Maley encouraged this, of course, for he wished Celtic to be a sociable concern as well as the greatest team on earth.

Another man had joined the squad in 1907, and this was Davie McLean from Forfar. He was a fine goalscorer and a good football player, but he was a Presbyterian of a different sort from Sunny. He was an atheist, in fact, and his independence of thought (not many people would admit to being an atheist in 1907) and his generally cussed East Coast background led him to question on occasion the dictatorship of Maley. He had his great moments in Celtic history, as we shall see, but it is possible that Maley made a mistake in being rather too keen to let him go in 1909. But McLean until the end of his long life in 1967 (he enjoyed watching the Lisbon triumph on TV) remained very much his own man.

Of more immediate concern to Sunny Jim, however, in the early part of the 1907–08 season was the injury to Jimmy Hay. This meant that the famous half-back line of Young, Loney and Hay would not be back together for some time (and would be further disrupted by Hay's appendicitis operation later in the season), but it did mean that Young would be captain until such time as Hay returned. Thus to Young went the honour of captaining the side in the first two games of the 1907–08 season, both at home, and both 3–0 victories over Hamilton Accies and Motherwell respectively, and thus he was the first captain in front of the new enclosure on the North Side of the field. This shelter had been built to replace the stand destroyed in the fire of 1904.

In later years it would come to be known as "the Jungle" (believed to be coined after the Second World War from returning soldiers who had served in Burma who likened the weeds to what they had seen in the Far East) and it would last until 1966. Even in its youth, it was an ugly building with a distinct resemblance to a cow shed or a barn, but at least in Sunny's time, it had not yet developed the holes in the roof which characterised it in later times. Nor, as yet, did weeds grow unattended among the cinders.

But crowds do not come to admire stadia. They come to watch football, and Celtic in 1907 were off to their customary good start. But then on 7 September in, ironically, the first game that Young, Loney and Hay were back together again, and in which Young had played outstandingly, he was lamed in the closing stages while making a brave tackle. Celtic won the game, beating Falkirk 3–2, but it meant that Sunny would be out for a few weeks.

Sunny and injury didn't go together very often, and thus he did not cope with the situation very well, always fretting to get back to the action especially when he felt that the team were suffering because of his absence, as seemed to be the case. They drew with Kilmarnock and Airdrie and then horrified their travelling supporters by losing to Aberdeen at Pittodrie, a result which became almost the sole topic of conversation in the North-East of Scotland for many months, and was widely seen as a sign that the new Aberdeen team (only formed in 1903 and already because of their black and gold strips nicknamed "the wasps") had "arrived".

The Airdrie game had repercussions. The referee a Mr J.R. Stark of Airdrie (the fact that he was officiating in a game involving Airdrie did not seem to be a problem on the grounds that he had no known connection with the Airdrieonians club) was considered not to have exercised sufficient control and was suspended. The same game saw disturbances on the Parkhead terraces with cinders (all too readily available) being flung at Mr Stark and the Airdrie players. Celtic were censured and ordered to post warning notices about future misbehaviour.

Sunny of course, being injured, was not involved in any of this, other than as a spectator. Being a law abiding man, he disapproved of lawlessness and thuggery, but he might have been, like the rest of the Celtic party, amazed to discover that the referee for his comeback game against Hibs at Easter Road on 5 October was none other than Mr J.B. Stark of Airdrie, doing his last game before serving his suspension and therefore likely to be in an unforgiving mood for any misdemeanours.

In any case, Hibs v Celtic games in those days tended to be rough. There was a distinct lack of any all-Ireland fraternity, for Hibs still resented the success of the Celtic club which they dated from some 15 years ago, they claimed, when Celtic had pinched some of their players. Celtic would win this game in the end, but at a cost. Celtic, although 2–0 up, began the second half with only 10 men, Jamie Weir having had his nose broken in a clash with a Hibs player which Celtic did not think to be accidental. Then Hibs centre-half John Borthwick, a well built man, charged the slender build of Davie Hamilton, knocking him onto the ground to the delight of the Hibs crowd who had had little to cheer about hitherto.

There was nothing illegal about this in 1907, of course, and no action was taken by Mr Stark. Jimmy Quinn however decided to take the law into his own hands and barged Borthwick in retaliation at the next opportunity. Referee Mr Stark, clearly under pressure, then panicked and sent off Jimmy Quinn to the amazement of the crowd and the Press. This was bad enough, but then Davie Hamilton, the original injured innocent said, "I wish I had a revolver" and was sent packing as well. With things now about to get seriously out of hand, it was up to Celtic's captain and vice-captain Hay and Young to calm everyone down. They were two goals to the good, and the real way to hurt Hibs and their nasty fans was to win the game.

But Celtic with Weir off as well, injured, had only eight men – but one of them was Sunny Jim. Keeping calm, he took control of the game, and although Hibs right-back James Main scored a goal in the tension ridden final stages,

Hibs could not find another, and Celtic won this thoroughly unpleasant game 2–1. Diplomatically, Young shook hands with everyone at the end, and held his tongue, so that that damage was minimised, but Celtic were later fined for failing to keep their players under control.

There were to be further mutterings (of a totally different kind) about Celtic in another context soon. The Glasgow Cup Final against Rangers was played over the next three Saturdays, the first game being a 2–2 draw, the second a 0–0 draw, and the third, eventually, a good win for Celtic. The "mutterings" concerned fixed games and big gates. The temptation for the clubs was huge – crowds of 72,000, 55,000 and 55,000 again were certainly "incentives", but the cynical among the fans, and the other clubs in the Scottish League who thus found their fixture schedules disrupted, had much to feed upon.

Yet a detached analysis more than 100 years later would make one realise how difficult it is to "fix" a game. The sheer amount of people who would have to be "in on it" would surely mean that sooner or later, someone would squeal to the Press. After all, if a player were crooked enough to fix a game in the first place, he would be crooked enough to accept the Edwardian equivalent of "chequebook journalism". In Celtic's case, although Maley tactlessly boasted about the amount of money that could be brought in (Maley had an unhealthy obsession with money on occasion), it is hard to imagine tough, dedicated professionals like Sunny Jim going along with anything crooked, and it is of course possible that two equally balanced teams like Celtic and Rangers could indeed draw games. Some of their League games were draws as well!

That said, there can be no doubt that they pushed their luck with draws in cup games. Next year would see three games required in the Glasgow Cup Final against Third Lanark, and of course, the riot at the Scottish Cup Final in 1909 had its genesis in this widespread, albeit unsubstantiated, belief that both teams were "at it". No evidence however exists to back up any allegation, however, and the jury must remain out, but one would be a fool to deny the possibility. Match fixing and corruption certainly have happened in our modern game, particularly in Europe and notoriously in Italy, in recent years.

In the first game of the Glasgow Cup Final, Rangers were generally reckoned to have been the better team, and the same is true to a lesser extent in the second game, although McMenemy might have settled the issue at the end when he hit the bar. But *The Glasgow Herald* (is it hinting at something?) says that both clubs are, "wallowing in unexpected wealth" thanks to the superiority of the Celtic defence. Jimmy Hay had to play at left-back to cover for the injury to Jamie Weir, and so John Mitchell was brought in at left-half where he played well alongside Young and Loney. Moreover, another after effect of the Hibs game was that, although Quinn was merely admonished (it being generally agreed that the referee had been too zealous), Davie Hamilton was suspended for two months for his desire to possess a firearm. Such was the laudable Edwardian passion for law and order, but it was nevertheless felt that two months was rather severe for Davie's admittedly rather ill chosen words. He had not, after all, committed any act of violence.

For the third game in the Glasgow Cup Final, the Glasgow FA, clearly under pressure, allowed 15 minutes extra-time if necessary. It would indeed have been a serious matter if this game were drawn, and Celtic decided to give the young Davie McLean a run at centre-forward while putting Jimmy Quinn out to his old haunts on the left-wing. Bobby Templeton, Sunny's friend, was still out of favour following his performance on the summer tour of Denmark.

The teams were;
Celtic: Adams, McNair and Hay; Young, Loney and Mitchell: Bennett, McMenemy, McLean, Somers and Quinn.
Rangers: Newbigging, Jackson and Craig; Gordon, May and Galt; Hamilton, Livingstone, Campbell, Kyle and Smith.
Referee: D. Philp, Dunfermline.

This game, like the rest, was a hard fought game, but this time Celtic emerged victorious although Rangers were on top towards the end but unable to force an equalizer that would have brought extra-time. Somers had opened the scoring for Celtic following a defensive error, and then came Davie McLean's greatest moment as the 17-year-old Forfarian scored "a well-judged shot of power" following a delightful Celtic move involving Young, Bennett and McMenemy. The youngster then disappeared under a mass of brawny Celts as Young, Quinn and a few others offered their congratulations. The second half saw a tremendous amount of Rangers pressure, and half way through the half, Kyle pulled one back. But in moments like this, men like Sunny Jim show their value, running about, urging his men on, and not being afraid to tackle and tackle hard. Behind him, Davie Adams had a great game in the Celtic goal, and up front Bennett and McMenemy were always likely to lead a counter-attack. When Mr Philp, who had handled all three games admirably, blew for time, Celtic had won the Glasgow Cup for four years in succession, and Sunny had another medal.

In the meantime Celtic found that their main challengers for the flag were not so much Rangers as less usual ones of Dundee and Falkirk. Celtic had beaten them both 3–2 in successive weeks but they had both strung together a few good results, and it was they who were the most vociferous in their protests about Celtic and Rangers being allowed to postpone Scottish League games in order to fit in three Glasgow Cup Finals.

Celtic kept winning most of their League games in this winter of 1907–08 which seems to have been bedevilled by fog, the only bad game being a 0–1 defeat by Hearts at Tynecastle, in which McLeod is criticised for putting on weight, and the forward line blamed for being ineffective. The last game of 1907 was a 0–0 draw at Airdrie, a game in which Jimmy Hay was out with an illness which looked for all the world as if it were the dreaded appendicitis.

A hundred years later, appendicitis is no laughing matter, but normally a timeous and simple operation will see the patient recovered to health within a few weeks. In Edwardian times, pre-National Health and before anyone possessed any real understanding about surgery, anaesthetics and infections, appendicitis was frequently a killer. In 1902, King Edward VII's coronation had to be delayed to allow him to have an operation. It was not exactly the first ever for this condition, but it was one of the first. Fortunately this operation was a success, but not everyone was as lucky as Edward VII. James "Dun" Hay, however, was one of the lucky ones, but he was out of the side until the middle of March.

All this meant that Sunny was "de facto" captain of the side once again. Supporters joked that it made no difference because he shouted all over the field to all and sundry in any case. What made life difficult for Sunny was of course another injury, this time to Jimmy Quinn, who was also out of the side in the early part of 1908 with a poisoned toe which took a long time for the great man to get over.

Faced with such difficulties, the team needed inspiring leadership, and of course they found it in Sunny Jim. He did one strange thing on 25 January when he deliberately approached Maley and asked not to be picked for the Scottish Cup game against Peebles Rovers (the team won easily 4–0). He chose to go to Brockville to spy on Falkirk v Rangers instead. Perhaps surprisingly Maley agreed. This game was a draw, but Rangers won the replay and thus for the second year in a row, Celtic were fated to play in the Scottish Cup against Rangers at Ibrox.

This time there was a poor crowd of 23,000 caused by two factors. One was the widespread belief that the game would be drawn and there would be another replay, and the other was that Rangers tactlessly doubled the price of admission, alleging that their ground was under reconstruction and that they had tried to get Hampden for the game. This cut little ice either among their own fans or the Celtic fans who saw it as little other than greed.

The game in any case was a disappointing one with defences on top, and for Celtic, Sunny Jim and Alec McNair well on top of the Rangers attackers. Celtic's two goals came from ex-Ranger Willie Kivlichan, the second and winning goal as a result of an appalling mix up in the Rangers defence. Further advance in the Scottish Cup came when Celtic made a rare trip to Kirkcaldy to get the better of Second Division Raith Rovers by 3–0 on a day of appalling wind and rain. The local instrumental band's *"Songs of Ireland"* programme, designed to make the visitors feel at home, was hardly heard in the wind and rain, and a supporter who was fined £1 for being drunk, appealed to the Sheriff that he was a lover of the "Bould Celts" and had his fine reduced to 15 shillings!

By March, Hay was back and the heat was really on for a team going for the grand slam of honours. For a change, Sunny was not chosen for the Scottish League International this year, but he had enough to do with Celtic, as well as, on the domestic front, his wife's imminent giving birth. In 1908, pregnancy was no easy matter any more than appendicitis was, and of course there was Alice Maud (now four and a half) to keep an eye on as well.

On 7 March, although the team won 4–0 against Hibs, Sunny missed a penalty-kick, *The Evening Citizen* describing it thus, "Young completely foozled (sic) the kick, the ball going wide of the mark." Seconds later, with the score still at 1–0 for Celtic, Young was at the other end to clear his line.

He, "came in at the pinch and kicked away from right under the bar, the visitors' claim for a goal being ignored". A week later, even with Quinn away on International duty in Dublin, Celtic beat Partick Thistle 3–0 to consolidate their League challenge.

On 21 March, Celtic had to face the long trip to Aberdeen for a Scottish Cup semi-final at Pittodrie, and the game was tough in every sense of the word. Celtic eventually won through to the Final with a late McMenemy header, but the Aberdeen crowd were not happy, with Young being the target for quite a lot of their abuse. *The Evening Citizen* concedes that the, "football, if not fine, was vigorous" and that on one occasion" Quinn received the attentions of the referee for a charge on McFarlane" (the Aberdeen goalkeeper). The game finished in a chorus of booing, with orange peels and other things being thrown at some of the Celtic players. Nor did it stop there.

Stones were thrown at the horse-drawn carriage which was taking referee Mr Ferguson of Falkirk to the station and a window was shattered, and when the Celtic charabanc was making its way along King Street, it too was the target of stones thrown by the less well-educated of the Granite City. Apparently, Young smiling out of the window did not help, but even after the stones had been thrown, he kept smiling and waving. Not without cause was he called Sunny Jim. *The Aberdeen Press and Journal* denounces with full Presbyterian vigour the miscreants who shamed their city and their team, calls for the magistrates "not to stint" in their punishments and blames it all on the presence of "cheap ale in the environs". There were too, says *The Aberdeen Press and Journal,* "a few ragamuffins and low types from Glasgow", involved.

The following week, Celtic met brutality of a different kind, this time in Dundee. Dundee, with feelings inflamed by the prolonged Glasgow Cup Final of last autumn, and playing with desperation (Celtic would have overtaken them in the League if they had won), defeated Celtic 2–0 but at a cost which even the local press found hard to defend. Jamie Weir, so often very unfortunate with injuries missed most of the first half, and Peter Somers never resumed at half-time. Willie Maley acting as linesman (it was a game without neutral linesmen) was seen to complain to the referee about the brutality of some of the challenges, while Sunny Jim was hacked mercilessly by a particularly nasty character with the unlikely name of Herbert Dainty. Once again as at

Aberdeen, he feigned insouciance and kept telling the Dundee players and fans that, "We play fitba! What dae you play?" and that although Dundee were ahead in the League race, Celtic still had four games in hand.

It was the Thursday (2 April) after that, when Florence gave birth to Irene Beatrice. She was a sturdy healthy girl and everything went well with the birth in his house at 45 Fitchfield Street, Kilmarnock. Once again, as in 1903, his occupation is described as Iron Turner (Journeyman). Does this mean that he was still only a part-time professional football player with Celtic? Or does it perhaps mean that he was a full-time football player, but still considered himself an Iron Turner by profession, on the grounds that he did that job in the summer, and it was the base, as it were, to which he would return once his footballing career was over? It certainly seems strange to modern eyes that one of the best known footballers of the day does not describe himself as a footballer on his daughter's birth certificate! But then again not many other professional football players described themselves as such in 1908.

Two days after Irene's birth, her father was playing in a 2–0 win over Morton at Parkhead before 3,000 people when little over a mile away at Hampden McNair and Quinn were playing in the 1–1 draw for Scotland against England before a crowd of 121,452. Considerably fewer (11,000) were at Hampden the following week to see Celtic take another step towards the League title by beating Queen's Park 2–0. Dundee had now been caught and overtaken, but Falkirk were still one point ahead, but Celtic had three games in hand. One of them however was against Rangers and the other against Falkirk themselves!

But that was put on the back burner for a while, as Saturday 18 April was the Scottish Cup Final against St Mirren. It was the first ever Cup Final for the Paisley men who had delighted their supporters by beating difficult opposition in Motherwell, Third Lanark, Hearts and Kilmarnock to get there. The game was played on a lovely warm spring day, and for Celtic supporters it was a great occasion. It was less so for the Buddies and the neutrals in the 60,000 crowd, for Celtic beat St Mirren 5–1 in one of the more one-sided Cup Finals. Celtic played superbly all through the game and the Paisley men simply could not get past Young, Loney and Hay, as, up front, Bennett scored twice, and Quinn, Somers and Hamilton one each. McMenemy, the only forward who did not score, was the best player on the field.

The teams were;
Celtic: Adams, McNair and Weir; Young, Loney and Hay; Bennett, McMenemy, Quinn, Somers and Hamilton.
St Mirren: Grant, Gordon and White; Key, Robertson and McAvoy; Clements, Cunningham, Wylie, Paton and Anderson.
Referee: Mr J.R.W. Ferguson, Falkirk.

The Cup having been presented by Sir John Ure Primrose, gracious as always, Celtic did not make the mistake of over-celebrating, for League games remained. They made sure that the Scottish Cup was on display on the Monday, though, for viewing by a large holiday Monday crowd which had assembled for the visit of Hearts. The crowd saw a display worthy of Scottish Cup winners and League aspirants as they put Hearts to the sword 6–0 with Jimmy Quinn scoring a hat-trick. Celtic were cheered to the echo by the jubilant crowd as they left the field, they then returned with the Scottish Cup and walked round the cycle track with it, allowing a few youngsters to carry it. Maley, although fearful of the security of the trophy, walked with his players and smiled. Sunny, now with three Scottish Cup medals in his pocket, was a happy man.

This result against Hearts meant that a further two points would win the Championship. Of all places, Saturday's game was to be played at Ibrox against Rangers. It was one of the League games postponed in October to make way for the Glasgow Cup, and now Celtic had the opportunity to win the League at the ground of their greatest rivals. It would also be the fourth League title in a row, and this would equal the record run of Rangers who, of course, had won the title from 1899 until 1902.

40,000 were there, once again in lovely weather. Due respect was paid to the memory of ex-Prime Minister Sir Henry Campbell-Bannerman, an honourable Glaswegian, who had died in midweek, but then there occurred a pretty disgraceful exhibition as Quinn had to go off (to the cheers of the Rangers fans) after 25 minutes with injuries to both thighs and McNair and Hamilton were also injured and forced to play on both wings. But Young, Loney and Hay remained intact, and as important as anything else, did not lose their composure nor their discipline. It would have been the easiest thing in the world to retaliate, for the provocation was severe, but Young rose magnificently above it, and in the 35th minute slipped a ball through to Alec Bennett to score the only goal of the game. Full-time came, and Celtic had completed back-to-back Doubles.

"Even the ranks of Tuscany could scarce forbear to cheer". A few reluctant ripples of applause were heard from some of the Ibrox diehards, and on the Monday *The Glasgow Herald,* a respecter rather than a lover of the Celtic, and usually finding it hard to conceal its bias towards Queen's Park, nevertheless paid tribute to the Celtic team and the Celtic management who had stuck, more or less, with the same squad of players for several years. "Celtic players have done well by the club, but it must not be overlooked that the players have been heartened and nursed as they nowhere else would have been". It was a fine tribute to Maley, and to his players at the same time and reflects the symbiosis of manager and players in a way that was rare at the time. Maley celebrated his 40th birthday on the day of the Ibrox victory. One could hardly imagine a better way of celebrating it!

The Evening Citizen is also full of praise for Celtic, turning classical in its appreciation of the team landing two back-to-back Scottish doubles, by saying that, "even the mighty Hercules himself could scarcely have done more". But it also adds, "It is not perhaps the best thing for the game that such a monopoly of success should favour any one club. There is no remedy, however, except the assertion of superiority by others on the field".

Generally agreed to be the greatest Celtic team until 1967. Sunny is beside Manager Maley on the left of middle row

But there was one piece missing as yet in this unprecedented jigsaw. That was the Glasgow Charity Cup. Normally this trophy was the least valued of the four that Celtic competed for, stuck at the end of the season with the players (theoretically at least) playing as amateurs and all the proceeds going to deserving causes. It was played in May, by which time Glasgow's sporting public had usually turned its attention to cricket, with the Western Union teams like Clydesdale and Poloc regularly attracting crowds of around 2,000. This year was different. For the second year in a row Celtic needed to win the Glasgow Charity Cup, (like the Glasgow Cup a beautiful piece of ornate silver) to complete a grand slam of trophies. Maley had been annoyed at the way they slipped up in 1907. He was determined to do better this year.

But in one important aspect, Maley's persuasive skills (and those of McMenemy and Young) failed. Four years ago in 1904, Alec Bennett had been tapped by Rangers, and did not play in the Scottish Cup Final. Now at last in 1908, Rangers approached him once more and succeeded in landing him. Why he did so, no-one knew in 1908 and no-one knows now either. It cannot have been anything to do with religion, for Sunny Jim, Alec McNair, Jimmy Hay, Davie McLean and others did not seem to let that bother them. It may be that Alec felt he had achieved as much as he could with Celtic, and simply wished to move on to the club that he had supported as a boy. Or it may be that Rangers simply offered him more money!

For whatever reason, he moved on. He was never as good a player for Rangers as he was for Celtic, and he was always well respected at Celtic Park. There was never the cult of hatred that followed Maurice Johnston, for example, for Alec had been a straightforward honest nice guy who gave his all for Celtic when he played for them, and made friends with everyone. In later years, he served in the Scottish Rifles during the Great War, and then became manager of Third Lanark where he had as little success in curbing Tommy McInally's excesses as Willie Maley did!

Bennett was a loss on the Glasgow Charity Cup campaign, but there was a determination in all of this cohesive team that it was not going to be a fatal blow. Without the injured Quinn, they beat a spirited Partick Thistle side on 2 May at Parkhead 3–2 thanks to a questionable penalty duly sunk by Hay, and then a late winner from Willie Loney. Then a week later, Davie McLean scored two as they beat Clyde 2–0 at Parkhead before an enthusiastic crowd of 14,000 in the warm sunshine. On the same day Queen's Park surprised Rangers (and themselves, one imagines) by winning 3–1 at Ibrox in the other semi-final. This caused a problem because Queen's Park were booked on a tour of Denmark, but special permission was granted to postpone the Charity Cup Final until 30 May.

The teams on that roasting hot day were;
Queen's Park: Adam, Young and Fletcher; McAndrew, Murray and Bryce; McLean, Sim, Leckie, McColl and Paul.
Celtic: Adams, McLeod and Weir; Young, Loney and Hay; Moran, McMenemy, Quinn, Somers and Hamilton.
Referee: A. Edward, Cathcart.

34,000 appeared at Hampden, giving a huge boost to the Charity Cup fund and its deserving causes, and they saw a game that was described as rather more "robust" than was desirable. Sunny's direct opponent was the dangerous RS McColl, and this was the key duel in the first half, in which Queen's were marginally the better side. The second half saw no lessening of the heat nor of the grim physical battle, but Celtic gradually assumed command and showed why they had won everything else in Scotland and were generally reckoned to be the best in the world. McMenemy scored, then Quinn, then McMenemy again and Celtic finished well on top with a 3–0 scoreline and their supporters on top of the world. They would not have such a season again until 1967.

The Glasgow Herald, while saying that this particular game was not one of Celtic's best, and naturally disappointed that Queen's Park didn't win, nevertheless states, "For the average club, the creating of a record in its history is no mean feat, but for a club like the Celtic, with a history scintillant with great achievements, the putting of a new record on the book is a huge task. But after failing narrowly in their quest last season, Celtic have now managed to place on record a performance which cannot under present conditions be excelled. Everything they have entered for they have won, and other clubs are barren of honours and of trophies because of the monopoly of the Celtic, a monopoly which is the product of consistent and often brilliant play and level-headed management".

A picture of Hampden believed to be taken during the Glasgow Charity Cup Final of 1908. Observe the strange shape of the stand and the absence of the penalty arc. Celtic are possibly wearing a green top that day. The pitch is in poor condition

Life could not be better for Sunny Jim that summer. There being no foreign tour this year, Sunny worked at his craft of iron turning in Kilmarnock, was seen around the town often with Florence pushing a pram, and talking to whomsoever he met, amiable, genial and garrulous, one would never guess that this man was the driving force of the greatest football team in the world, and also the man that crowds in places like Aberdeen, Edinburgh and Dundee loved to hate!

Season 1908–09 opened in August. It was a strange season, dominated in one way or other by the continuing controversy of drawn football matches and the suspicion of collusion between teams. There was also the issue of whether Celtic could win the Scottish League yet again and make it five years in a row (with star man Alec Bennett now playing for the main opposition) and thus better Rangers' four-in-a-row from 1899 until 1902. For Sunny Jim there was also a remarkable occasion when he proved his versatility and dependability, if there had ever been any doubt about it.

The Glasgow Cup was an unhappy occasion for Celtic for many reasons. In the first place, what should have been three games in fact became seven, once again doing nothing to dispel the rumours of fixing and perhaps explaining the gradual decline in attendances – the three games in the final being watched by 40,000, then 26,000 then 17,000 – very good turnouts still, but perhaps the people of Glasgow beginning to make a point.

Yet Davie McLean in his memoirs published in *The Sporting Post* of Dundee said something else. The first game in the first round was a 4–4 draw against Queen's Park. The game had been a thriller with McMenemy scoring in the 88th minute and Leckie equalizing for Queen's Park in the 89th. At one point Celtic had been two goals up, so it had been a good comeback by the amateurs against the best team in the country, and *The Glasgow Herald* is rightly upbeat about Queen Park's performance. The Celtic dressing room was different. McLean said, "Willie Maley came in and pitched into us in a black rage. There were seven internationalists and they sat there, dumb, and took it. I decided there and then that no one was going to talk to me like that and get away with it".

There were several interesting points about this story, if it is true. One was that Maley clearly was not part of any collusion for this game! Another is that we can now see why the talented McLean was not destined to stay at Celtic after this season, but the other is that here we have men like Young, Hay and McNair being shouted at ("the hairdryer treatment" as it is now called) by their manager, and accepting it meekly.

One wonders what the dressing room was like after the second replay against Third Lanark in the final on Wednesday 28 October. After two draws, the game finished 0–4 to Third Lanark, and the tame second half Celtic display when three goals were conceded really did get the tongues wagging among the distressed supporters that night. Rumours abounded of bonuses not being paid, about associations with illegal bookmakers, about a major dressing room revolt – but it is of course possible that Celtic simply had a bad day, or that Third Lanark, never an easy side to beat, simply had a good day.

One way or other, Celtic now had a major rebuilding job if they were to regain their credibility or the respect of their supporters. They did so remarkably quickly, winning every game in November and December until a surprise defeat by Clyde on Boxing Day. There were reasons for this defeat in that the pitch was covered in snow and barely playable, and also during the game Sunny Jim picked up an injury which prevented his participation in the

New Year's Day game at Ibrox, something that was intensely frustrating to him. Celtic won the game against Rangers comfortably 3–1 but a bad injury to goalkeeper Davie Adams ruled him out as well of the following day's game at Kilmarnock.

This presented Celtic with a dilemma, for they had no reserve goalkeeper. Tommy Sinclair who had done so well a few seasons ago was long gone, and it looked as if Maley was going to have to knock on the door of a junior team, but then Sunny Jim limped up to him and offered his services on the grounds that "ma leg's getting better, and in the goal, ah'll no hae tae run aboot sae much. Forbye, it's Kilmarnock, my ain midden heid!" Maley looked at the irrepressible Sunny, realised that this was the sort of courage and bravery that wins wars and forges Empires, and perhaps against his own better judgement, agreed to accept his services.

Goalkeepers of course did not in 1909 wear different coloured jerseys, and so on the surface it was not all that much of a change, but history records that the experiment was not a success and that Celtic went down 1–3. *The Glasgow Herald* however absolves Young from blame. "The Kilmarnock game brought home to Celtic the risk they take in not having a reserve goalkeeper, even though Young did admirably in this strange position. He did not lose the game, but it was the success of the Kilmarnock halves... in creating opportunities for their own vanguard" What this is clearly saying is that Celtic did not suffer because of Sunny being in goal, but they DID suffer because they missed him at right-half!

The Dundee Courier comes to much the same conclusion. "He saved several shots in good style, his height and reach of arm standing him in good stead", but then points out that he is not the first half-back to stand in for a goalkeeper, for Jim MacAuley did likewise for Dumbarton in 1883, and then in criticising Celtic's severe failings in the game, pays an indirect tribute to Sunny when he says that, "not for a long time have Celtic been so thoroughly outplayed. They could never get hold of the slippery Kilmarnock forwards..." Clearly something was missing from the defence and midfield. It was Sunny Jim Young.

Young's injury did not last long, thankfully, and very soon the team resumed its normal consistent form, with the only one defeat before April being to Rangers on 13 March, a narrow 2–3 reverse at Celtic Park, after which Sunny began to wonder whether the movement of Bennett had really made a difference. But Celtic, though now behind, had games in hand over the other teams in the League race. The problem was that people were now beginning to wonder when they would get them played!

The Scottish Cup had seen few problems from Leith Athletic although the team had unconventional dressing room accommodation in a ballroom there, then Port Glasgow, or even from Airdrie who were well beaten in a tough game at Parkhead in February. This game was characterised by Davie Hamilton's diving header to finish off a lovely cross for Sunny Jim, after which, it was said that the minuscule Davie was carried back to the halfway line by his triumphant team mates!

The semi-final of the Scottish Cup was against Clyde at Celtic Park. Tactlessly, it was drawn 0–0 before a crowd of 40,000. The teams were then, equally tactlessly, allowed to play the replay at Celtic Park again on the following Saturday (not Shawfield on Wednesday as our modern understanding might have expected), and this time 35,000 saw Celtic win 2–0 to set up a final against Rangers on Saturday 10 April. All these replays meant that in the Scottish League, Celtic were now nine games behind the leaders Dundee, but still could win the League when they played their games off! The League table at the end of March 1909 saw Dundee played 32 and 46 points, Rangers 27 and 39 and Celtic 23 and 34. The ball was very much in Celtic's court, but from any point of view, it was a highly unsatisfactory situation.

Rangers were desperate to win the Scottish Cup. While Celtic led a "domesticated existence at their own ground", Rangers took their players to Troon for special training. They had not beaten Celtic in a Scottish Cup Final since 1894, and had lost to Celtic in 1899 and 1904, with the 1904 defeat still rankling, for it had been the springboard to Celtic's virtually unbroken success. The weather was excellent, and it was the Easter weekend.

70,000 saw Young "with a huge capacity for hard work" play in his third successive Scottish Cup Final. First Celtic were ahead, then Rangers made the crucial decision to move Bennett to the centre, and they scored two quick goals to make it seem as if the Cup were heading for Ibrox until Jimmy Quinn (legally) barged the goalkeeper who took evasive action but in so doing stepped over the line. The referee Mr Stark was correct, in the opinion of *The Evening Citizen,* but Rangers were unhappy and a further sour note was struck when Davie Adams was fouled by Tom Gilchrist of Rangers and after the free kick had been awarded, threw the ball at him. The game thus finished 2–2 – a result that was hardly good news for anyone except both clubs concerned who now could get another big "gate" next Saturday.

Rangers then returned to Troon for more training but Saturday 17 April was one of Scottish football's saddest days, as frustration at so many drawn big games boiled over into what can only be described as thuggery. Celtic, to their credit, were aware of a few undercurrents and suggested extra-time or a "play till a finish" if the teams were still level. The authorities said neither yes nor no. They gave the worst possible reply – no reply at all – and the game started with everyone generally unaware of what would happen in the event of a draw.

Gordon scored for Rangers, and then disaster struck Sunny Jim when he suffered a clash of heads with Jimmy Galt and had to leave the field, stunned, to have his head wound stitched. Whether this was an accident or not, no-one can say but the possibility of it being other than an accident cannot be discounted. Whether Galt earned his nickname "dirty Galt" from this incident, again we cannot say, but for Young and Celtic it might have been serious. *The Evening Citizen* is tactful when it says that, "Young's face came into contact with Galt's head, and the Celt had to retire to the pavilion".

The incident occurred about the half hour mark with Rangers 1–0 up, and, as stitching was a complicated and painful operation in 1909, it was half-time before Sunny could resume "wearing a big plaster patch over his left eye". He was still groggy, but being Sunny Jim, was determined to come back. Wiser medical advice would have told him to go home or to hospital, and of course in modern times, a substitute would have been deployed, but Sunny, knowing from the roars of the crowd that Celtic were still behind, told Rab Davis the trainer that the team needed him and returned to an enormous cheer from the Celtic crowd, who were now beginning to despair. Celtic, as always, were re-energised by his presence and redoubled their attacks on the Rangers goal. Eventually with time beginning to slip away, Jimmy Quinn equalised for Celtic, and the game finished 1–1, although Celtic had three corners in the last five minutes, all taken by Jimmy Hay, and from one of them "the ball was all but in the net" in a scramble.

When the final whistle went, some players, particularly the Celtic players and Sunny Jim, were seen to hang around to see if there were to be extra-time, but eventually, the referee, Mr Stark of Airdrie picked up the ball and walked off. *The Dundee Courier* goes as far as to blame the Celtic players for causing the riot by their dilatoriness in vacating the field! The same newspaper then goes on to say that the second replay will be played in Dundee, at Dens Park! As the idiom of the time went "Cannae gie ye it, laddie!" or a more modern idiom would have it, "Dream on!"

Everyone knows what happened after the Celtic players eventually did leave the field. Sunny himself may have been privately happy that there was to be no extra-time for he was still struggling with his head wound, but the Hampden Riot lasted well into the night. What may have been seen as a protest against match-fixing to generate more income became an orgy of violence, with whisky being poured on goalposts and pay boxes to make them burn better! For many weeks letters flooded newspapers demanding the end of football, and everyone seemingly agreed on the necessity to ban alcohol. Neither of these extreme solutions happened, and it might have been an idea for Edwardian Scotland to examine itself in more detail to discover the root causes of such disorder. The players were never in any danger, and no-one seems to have been badly injured, but the stadium was ruined, and the Scottish Cup was withheld – a pity, for it deprived Celtic of their chance of winning the trophy three years in a row, something to this day that they have never done.

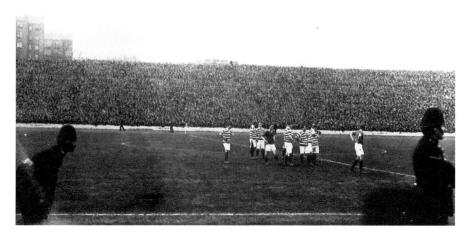

Will there be extra-time? Sunny cannot be identified on this picture. He is probably arguing with the referee about extra-time or perhaps he is taking advantage of a lull in the proceedings to have his head wound addressed

Pay boxes on fire at the Mount Florida end of the ground

The aftermath of this deplorable riot tends to overshadow Celtic's great achievement in winning the Scottish League that season. The fixture backlog meant that Celtic had eight games to play in 12 days before the end of April. (What would have happened if there had been another replay to the doomed Scottish Cup Final?) On Monday 19 April Dundee had played 33 (out of 34) games and had 48 points, Celtic had played 26 and had 39 points. (Rangers, Airdrie and Clyde were all between Dundee and Celtic. Celtic would be reasonably expected to win their games and overtake Dundee, but Dundee with points on the board were the "heirs apparents"). Two points for a win in 1909 meant that Celtic had an advantage, but games had to be played on Monday, Wednesday, Thursday, Saturday, Monday, Wednesday, Thursday, Friday so that the Scottish League could be completed by 30 April, otherwise there would be endless problems with players' contracts etc.

The Scottish League would not budge and extend the season, claiming (not unreasonably) that most of it was Celtic's own fault. Dundee for their part felt that Celtic had an advantage in knowing what they had to do, and Celtic felt equally disadvantaged in their quest for what would be a record-breaking fifth successive League Championship. It was a tall order for any team, but it is in moments like this that Celtic blessed their tireless Ayrshire man called Sunny Jim Young. Loney was out injured, but young Joe Dodds was drafted in as centre-half, and there were other great men like Jimmy McMenemy, Eck McNair and of course the mighty Jimmy Quinn. James Hay was the captain, wise and shrewd, but the leader and the inspiration was Sunny Jim Young whose raucous stentorian bellows would be heard throughout these eight days.

In the event, Sunny, still suffering from his encounter with Jimmy Galt, missed the first of these games against Hearts at Tynecastle, but the team still won 2–1, with Hibs defeat of Rangers that same afternoon seeming to end Rangers' challenge. But Sunny was back for Wednesday's 1–1 draw with Hamilton, then a 5–1 thrashing of Morton, before having to settle for a 0–0 draw in a hard tussle with Airdrie on the Saturday. Dundee won their last game of the season that day against Queen's Park (at Ibrox, Hampden being out of action for some time) and thus they finished with 50 points, and Celtic now had 45 points with four games to play. But four games in five days would not be easy when they had to win three of them. Had they equalled Dundee's points tally, goodness knows what would have happened. A decider, joint champions, goal average?

The Sunday was a key day. Young and some others came into Celtic Park for a shower and to have their legs waxed and to talk to supporters, most of whom were traditionally allowed in on a Sunday to have a look round and a shower, if they wished, in one of Maley's humanitarian ideas. Young was a vital person that day, walking around talking to other players, cheering them up, telling jokes, and saying, "We'll be kent as the team that won the League in a week, if we pu' this aff"! Some of the young supporters, distressingly thin and emaciated in Young's opinion, were given some bread and butter sandwiches and a few black balls, the favourite sweet of the day, and were given free admission passes for the game against Motherwell on the Monday, the only home game that Celtic had left.

A grimly determined Celtic team then beat Motherwell 4–0 on the Monday before a small crowd of about 3,000, then Queen's Park 5–0 at Cathkin on the Wednesday, so that only two points were required. The Queen's Park game caused a few ructions in Dundee, for it was claimed, improbably, that it was a deliberately weakened Queen's Park side that was fielded so that a Glasgow team could win the League! Anyone with the vaguest idea of Glasgow's football dynamics could see that this was rubbish, but people from Edinburgh wrote to Dundee FC inviting them to join in their campaign against "this disgraceful Glasgow monopoly", an indication, perhaps of the deep-seated nature of the Edinburgh inferiority complex and bitterness about Glasgow. The truth was simply that Queen's had many injuries and unavailabilities as, at the end of April, so many of their players were at the "nets" of Poloc or Clydesdale or West of Scotland getting in some practice for the start of the cricket season!

The title might have been won at Easter Road on the Thursday, but on a wet, heavy pitch an exhausted Celtic side could not equalize against a robust Hibs side (whose hatred of Celtic was hardly hidden) and thus it was on Friday 30 April at Douglas Park, Hamilton where the title was to be decided. Defeat would lose it, victory would win it, and a draw would leave Celtic level with Dundee and the Scottish League with a difficult decision to make. Rarely had the Ducal Toon seen such excitement, and *The Glasgow Observer* indulges in a little social analysis when it says, "...probably never more mixed a crowd has lined that enclosure. A survey showed that not only were the collier and the ironworker class present, but the city had sent its representation, nor were these solely Celtic followers – far from it. There were present large numbers from the Barracks, and quite a goodly number of a class who rarely patronise football matches, but who were evidently attracted to the sensational and dramatic finish to the league contest".

The social mix that formed the crowd saw Celtic make one last surge for the League Championship. Young, shrugging off his own exhaustion, covered every inch of the ground saying to himself that, "exhaustion is all in the mind", and once again doing his fair share of shouting in such a way perhaps that a watching Sergeant Major from the Barracks may well have envied him. "Face the ball, Celts" resounded many times round the tight ground. He released Davie Hamilton to score the first goal with a fine well-judged shot, and then could only watch with wonder and awe as the great Napoleon scored the second halfway through the second half. Celtic then should have scored more but were "profligate of chances"(Davie McLean in particular), a situation not helped by Quinn having to play on the wing because of injury. Accies scored a goal almost at the death, but the title was once again Celtic's, and joy was unconfined among the Celtic fans with even the uncommitted realising that in this Celtic team, they had seen something special. *The Dundee Courier* in what seems like a bad attack of sour grapes talks about Celtic's, "unlimited resources"!

One would have expected Sunny Jim and the rest of the Celtic team to collapse thankfully into a chair after all that, but they were playing again the next day! And it was hardly next door! It was in Aberdeen for a Charity Match, then they moved on to Fort William for another such game before returning to Glasgow for the Glasgow Charity Cup. Perhaps their exertions did eventually catch up with them, for although they beat Clyde 2–1 in the semi-final, they lost 2–4 to Rangers in the Final on 15 May.

Hampden still being out of action, Celtic Park was used and a crowd of 25,000 meant that the charities did well, but it was a poor Celtic team with no Quinn, no McMenemy, no Hay, no Somers – all out with an accumulation of injuries. Both teams were on edge and afraid of another riot and it was determined that there would be extra-time and no replay. The victory meant more to Rangers than it did for Celtic, for it was the Ibrox side's first honour for some considerable time. It meant that Celtic finished the season with only one trophy – the breathtakingly won Scottish League. Sunny was disappointed about that, for he still possessed his insatiable appetite for winning honours with Celtic.

Football talk in the summer of 1909 tended to concentrate on the need to rebuild Hampden (Celtic of course would have preferred Hampden NOT to be rebuilt, for it would mean that the Scotland v England Internationals would revert to them) and whether Celtic could possibly make it six League titles in a row. "This is ruining Scottish football" was the cry in the "neutral" press at the time, but the fact was that the Young-inspired Celtic was a sight to behold. No cause was impossible, and there was still in 1909 no visible sign of the great side cracking. The remarkable thing about the Young, Loney and Hay half-back line (now famed far beyond Scotland) was that they didn't always play together, with injuries compelling the introduction of men like John Mitchell and Joe Dodds, who were only marginally inferior.

There was always a ready supply of ammunition to the forward line. The left-wing combination of Peter Somers and Davie Hamilton, although sometimes overshadowed by Quinn and McMenemy, were great players in their own right, and everyone still wondered what on earth Alec Bennett was thinking of when he left that team and the fans who loved him, to play for Rangers who were good, and might even have won trophies in other circumstances, but basically had no answer to the consistent power and thrust of Young, Loney and Hay.

Season 1909–10 opened inconsistently however with a bad defeat at Hibs followed by a failure to beat Motherwell at home and then another defeat at Morton. This of course lead to speculation that the great team was now breaking up, but the reports of the death were premature. The defeat at Greenock led Maley to drop Peter Somers for a spell and to introduce a strong young Fifer by the name of Peter Johnstone. Young sensed a kindred spirit here and the two struck up an understanding which would do Celtic well in future years.

The Glasgow Cup saw Celtic with a bye in the first round, and then a semi-final against Queen's Park at Hampden in late September. It was another insensitive draw and what made matters worse was that both goals were mistakes by the goalkeepers. But the Glasgow FA bowed to pressure and compelled the replay to be played at Parkhead on Wednesday 6 October with extra-time if necessary and the Final scheduled for the Saturday following. It was one of these spells where Celtic simply went into top gear, thrashing Queen's Park 6–1 with Sunny Jim described as, "standing at the centre spraying passes and distributing largesse" to McMenemy and Quinn who each scored hat-tricks.

It being a Wednesday afternoon, only 11,000 were there, but a far larger crowd of 55,000 was recorded as having come to the now partially restored Hampden on the Saturday to see yet another final between Celtic and Rangers. Police were there in massive numbers, lest there be more disorder and letters appeared in *The Glasgow Herald*, fearful of further anarchy and trouble.

The teams were;
Celtic: Adams, McNair and Weir; Young, Loney and Hay; Kivlichan, McMenemy, Quinn, Johnstone and Hamilton.
Rangers: Lock, Law and McKenzie; Gordon, Stark and Galt; Hogg, Gilchrist, Reid, McPherson and Hunter.
Referee: Mr Ibbotson, Derby.

The game was played in a stiff breeze, but it was an otherwise fine day. Rangers were without Alec Bennett, and that would be a vital factor, for the rest of the Rangers forward line made absolutely no impact on the "Holy Trinity" of Young, Loney and Hay, or as they were otherwise known, "Jimmy, Willie and Jimmy" or "Sunny, Obliterator and Dun". There was only one goal in it, a magnificent Jimmy Quinn one, where he took on both Rangers full-backs and the goalkeeper to score, but the Press are united in saying that Celtic were at their magnificent best and that there should have been far more goals. "Against this, Celtic had an almost perfect understanding from goalkeeper to centre-forward" and "the half-backs showed perfect judgement" purrs *The Glasgow Herald* and the game finished with Celtic, even playing against the wind, "bivouacking in Rangers territory".

It was a magnificent victory for all sorts of reasons. It dispelled at a stroke any idea of collusion (a draw had been confidently predicted even in national newspapers that morning), it was magnificent way of making up for last year's Glasgow Cup disgrace against Third Lanark, and it put a stop to any thought of a Rangers revival. But apart from all that, another Glasgow Cup medal in Sunny's cabinet (his fifth) gave him and the rest of the team confidence and heart to take on the rest of Scotland in their quest for the sixth Scottish League title in a row.

By Christmas, Celtic were back on top, having won every game in November and only a torrential downpour on 11 December preventing them beating St Mirren, for on at least two occasions the ball stuck in the mud, and they had to settle for a draw. Peter Johnstone was playing impressively in the forward line, and Jimmy Quinn was scoring goals in quality and quantity, but the whole team was very impressive. Christmas Day saw Sunny walk to the ground, for Celtic were playing at Rugby Park, Kilmarnock. There had been a great deal of rain, and the pitch was a quagmire. Not a lot of great football could be played, but Sunny and his mates simply had to stand in awe at the only goal of the game, scored by Jimmy Quinn, as he rampaged with the ball at his feet from his own half right into the Killie goal. It was like a rather spectacular rugby try, except that the ball wasn't being carried. It was being dribbled and Kilmarnock defenders were simply bouncing off Jimmy.

As 1909 turned into 1910, the country was in the grips of a political crisis. The House of Lords had rejected Lloyd George's "People's Budget" – an unashamed and necessary transfer of money from the rich to the poor – and a General Election had been called over the issue. A "hung" Parliament would result, but the Liberals would be able to continue with the support of Labour and the Irish Nationalists. The future of the House of Lords may have been the issue which dominated the newspapers in early 1910, but there was still enough to read about and talk about in the football.

Trouble was brewing in 1910 for Sunny Jim. Celtic had been making progress towards the Scottish League and Cup throughout January and for some of the time at least, Sunny Jim was virtually in charge of the team. "Dun" Hay was out injured, and for a few weeks in January, Maley wasn't there either, for he had gone to the USA with Director Tom Colgan to investigate the possibility of a tour by Celtic of the USA in either 1910 or 1911 (in fact it would have to wait until 1931!). Victories were recorded over Airdrie, Port Glasgow and Dumbarton, and things were looking very good indeed, and Maley on his return would have felt vindicated in leaving Sunny in charge of the team.

It all changed when Celtic went to St Mirren on 29 January. The game frankly should not have been played for "600 cartloads" (a slight exaggeration, one feels!) of snow had been removed from the Love Street pitch to enable the game to be played. The referee was Tom Dougray of Bellshill, an up and coming referee who would in time become one of the best, but possibly in 1910 still lacking experience. The snow which had wiped out quite a few games in Scotland that day had stopped, but the conditions were treacherous, not helped by the constant throwing of snowballs (sometimes with stones in them) from the crowd.

Celtic played in their change strip of green jerseys and white pants. The first half had been even, with Clements equalizing Jimmy Quinn's goal just before half-time. The tactics of the St Mirren defenders were questionable to put it mildly, and soon after half-time Davie Hamilton was carried off, not to return. Willie Loney was then injured and had to be moved to the wing where his influence on the game was marginal. A fit Willie Loney would almost certainly have prevented Cunningham's goal in the 75th minute, but Celtic were now faced with a hostile crowd, a 1–2 deficit and only really nine fit men.

Young, the captain (for Hay had been out injured for most of January) normally relished this challenge, but when John Mitchell was then injured in a crunching tackle and being treated, anger got the better of him or as modern parlance would have it, Sunny's "anger management skills" were found wanting. No-one will ever know what offensive remarks were said, but Young's version is that he said them to Jimmy McMenemy and not to the referee. The referee however heard them and the clump of players anxiously looking at John Mitchell being treated, was suddenly reduced by one as Sunny Jim was seen to walk off after the referee's finger pointed to the pavilion.

The Daily Record and Mail says, "Nearing the close when the Celts were battling desperately to snatch an equalizing goal, James Young who captained the side came under the notice of the referee and was ordered off. At the time, play was suspended on account of Mitchell being injured. Young, it appears, used language in the hearing of the referee which the Celtic players said was addressed to McMenemy. Young's vocabulary has created no small amusement in the past when interpreted before the SFA, and his latest freak (sic) comes at a time when his club needs him most".

The Glasgow Herald, no great lover of Young at the best of times, chortled, "Young was sent off for allowing his tongue to wag too freely, and with his dismissal, the rest of the play was quieter", meaning perhaps that Celtic now gave up and accepted defeat. The Celtic crowd, a minority but a vocal one at Paisley that day, reacted badly to that turn of events, and only prompt and efficient action from the Paisley police prevented a crowd invasion. As it was, there were a few disturbances after the game. It was a sad day for Celtic, but it was only their first defeat since September and they were still clear at the top in the League. There would however be consequences (far reaching ones) on the playing field from Young's dismissal. It would probably cost Celtic the Scottish Cup.

The Referee Committee of the SFA met on the evening of Wednesday 16 February under the Chairmanship of Mr A.M. Robertson of Queen's Park, and "J. Young, Celtic was suspended until 15 March". This month suspension struck Sunny and the Celtic supporters as harsh, for no violence had been offered, and as he himself said, he was simply talking to McMenemy. But it was a second offence (he had been suspended in 1905) and the SFA were not merciful. Hardly surprisingly, the idea that the SFA was anti-Celtic gained ground once more.

In the event, Sunny missed only two games. It might have been four but Celtic did not play two of them, having so many players playing in the League International on 26 February and the full International against Wales on 5 May (for both of which Young might have been chosen if he had not been suspended) but the two games that he missed for Celtic were Scottish Cup-ties, and one of them was lost.

The first one was against Aberdeen at Celtic Park which Celtic won 2–1, holding off a late and spirited attack from the black and golds. But the second game was the semi-final against Clyde at a packed Shawfield before 38,000 fans. It was a different matter. For Celtic, there were two other complicating factors. One was that Davie Adams, the excellent goalkeeper for all the glory years had taken ill with pneumonia and Celtic, not having a regular deputy, approached the amiable amateur Leigh Richmond Roose, who had played for Wales against Scotland last week at Kilmarnock. He was currently with Sunderland, but they had no objections. The other problem was also a result of the Scotland v Wales game last week, for Jimmy McMenemy had been badly and repeatedly fouled by Welsh defenders who knew no other way to stop him, and was still out injured.

Thus Adams was still ill in bed, and Young and McMenemy sat in the Shawfield stand and watched with horror Celtic's complacent and immature performance against a Clyde side that they had seriously underestimated. Clyde won 3–1, and Celtic without their midfield and forward line generals were simply outplayed in the second half. Roose may have been a Welsh international but he was seriously out of his depth here, but he did gave the Press and the Clyde supporters a laugh when he ran out to shake the hand of the man who had just scored the third goal against him. It was considerably less well received by the Celtic supporters, and one cannot really imagine it going down well with the brooding Sunny Jim.

When Young returned, it was like chalk and cheese, for the team then won their next six League games, unspectacularly but professionally, (although *The Daily Record and Mail* says that their game against Third Lanark on 16 March – Young's first game back – was "simply great") to bring themselves to the cusp of the League title. Other things happened as well – a trip to Ireland to play a charity game, and a seat in the Hampden stand to see the "International" in which Scotland, inspired by Quinn and McMenemy beat England 2–0 – and the League should have been won at Falkirk, the home of their nearest challengers, on 23 April. As it was, Falkirk got the better of them, and thus the League was won in the anti-climactic circumstances of a goalless draw against Hibs on the afternoon of Monday 25 April (Maley's 42nd birthday!) before a miserable crowd of 2,000. Celtic had a few injuries, and were similarly depleted a week later when they lost 0–1 in a depressing Glasgow Charity Cup tie against Third Lanark.

It was a strange and unsatisfactory way of ending a mighty period in Celtic's history, but there had been one great moment on Saturday 30 April when the Scottish League winners met the Scottish Cup winners Dundee at Parkhead. Dundee had beaten Clyde in the Scottish Cup Final (after two draws!) – to date their only success in the Scottish Cup. Both trophies were to be on show and this attracted a crowd of 12,000, but once again the football did not live up to expectations and the game ended 0–0 with both teams and all spectators clearly in need of a rest.

Still, six titles in a row for Celtic and Young. How long could this go on?

Well dressed Celts in 1910, presumably at function to celebrate their six titles in a row. Sunny Jim is third from the left in the back row

CHAPTER SIX

TRANSITION AND CAPTAINCY

1910–1913

Inevitably, this sustained success could not go on. Sooner or later Rangers were likely to fight back, and perhaps the marker was laid down in the Glasgow Cup Final of 8 October 1910 when Rangers defeated Celtic 3–1, and were undeniably the better team. Celtic fought hard, but Rangers were faster to the ball, and their players and fans celebrated in the glorious autumn sunshine a victory over Celtic in a major competition which had been rare over the past few years.

In fact it was no surprise for those who had watched Celtic since August. Sunny's season had got off to a bad start. On the eve of the first game Sunny's mother had died. She had been ill for some time. Sunny had been very close to her in every sense (she lived along with Sunny's father William, in the same street as Sunny and Flora in Titchfield Street, Kilmarnock) and he was very upset. He would have wanted to play in the first game of the season against Airdrie, but Maley felt it was not a good idea. When he returned, Celtic managed to lose three games in a row to Falkirk, Morton and Kilmarnock. Sunny's form was poor. To his credit he did not blame it all on his recent bereavement. It was more the case that he and several others were going through a collective lethargy. The appetite, after such prosperity and plenty, had gone.

The team was changing as well. Peter Somers had gone to Hamilton last season and Peter Johnstone, fine player though he would become, was taking time to find his confidence. Moreover at the start of this season Jamie Weir, finding it difficult to establish his place after his injury, departed to Middlesbrough where he joined up with ex-Celt Donnie McLeod. And still no adequate replacement for Alec Bennett had been found. Willie Kivlichan was good, but he was no Alec Bennett.

In addition, it seemed to quite a lot of supporters that Dodds and Hay were playing in the wrong place. The departure of Weir meant that Jimmy Hay was used as a left-back with Joe Dodds at left-half. There was a certain indication that Hay himself was less than happy with this, and 1910–11 would be his last season before he departed to Newcastle United. Willie Loney struggled with injury for a long time, and Young, Loney and Hay played together for the last time as a half-back line at Rugby Park, Kilmarnock in a 0–1 defeat on 3 September 1910.

Yet Sunny stayed where he was, always Mr Reliable. He had his bad games, but he was never criticised for lack of effort. He had his good games as well. On the Edinburgh Holiday Monday, he was inspirational as Celtic hammered Hibs 4–0 and then a week later on the Glasgow Holiday Monday, he played a fine one-two with McMenemy from a free-kick for Napoleon to crash home an unsaveable shot and earn a draw against Partick Thistle.

But the defeat by Rangers in the Glasgow Cup Final was a sore one to take, and it was some time before the team recovered. But the interesting thing was that the defence did well. It was the forwards who had gone off the boil with McMenemy appearing to have some injury problem which inhibited him, and Quinn was not always scoring the goals. A 0–0 draw with Hearts was depressing, but the 0–1 defeat by Rangers at Parkhead at the end of October seemed to indicate that there was going to be no seventh League title in a row. Quinn was out that day, and Willie Kivlichan had some wretched luck in front of goal.

By this time Young had won for himself another International honour, this time for the Scottish League against England's Southern League at The Den, (then called New Cross) the new home of Millwall. Young had of course played at Millwall's old ground in his Bristol Rovers days. The game took place of Monday 24 October 1910. The ground had been opened a couple of days previously by Lord Kinnaird. Young was "not too successful at half" according to *The Glasgow Herald* as the Scottish League went down 0–1 and he was not considered for the other League game that autumn, against the Irish League a week later.

November saw a 5–0 win over St Mirren, but then a couple of dreary 0–0 draws against Airdrie and Third Lanark before a depressing 0–1 defeat at Dens Park, Dundee, then something of a bogey ground for Celtic. This game was the first recorded case of a Celtic goalkeeper (Davie Adams) wearing a yellow jersey, and a couple of weeks later it became a strong recommendation from the SFA for the goalkeeper to wear a different coloured jersey. Some time later it was compulsory. It was an odd game as well, with no goals scored for 89 minutes, then McFarlane scored one for Dundee before Kivlichan equalized but the referee disallowed it on the grounds that it was time up before he actually scored.

November 1910 was a difficult time for the Liberal Government with a General Election now looking inevitable and a really serious situation developing in Wales in the Rhondda Valley town of Tonypandy. A miners' strike had been accompanied by disorder and rioting, and then the Home Secretary Winston Churchill over-reacted by sending in troops to quell things. It had not exactly helped to calm matters down, and the name "Churchill" was a dirty word in Wales for a long time after that.

December 1910 saw an improvement in Celtic's form with the new half-back line of Young, Loney and Dodds taking charge of the the midfield. Motherwell, Clyde and Kilmarnock were beaten, but then the team could only draw 1–1 with Morton at Cappielow on Christmas Eve. The year closed however with another fine performance against Raith Rovers in their first season in the First Division. Celtic beat them 5–0 and it was all the more impressive in that Loney and Dodds had to call off with flu just before kick-off and were replaced by Tommy McAteer and the ever willing and reliable John Mitchell.

While all this was going on in the month of December the second General Election of the calendar year had been held. It will be recalled that earlier a General Election had produced a hung Parliament, which did not resolve the issue of what to do about the House of Lords. Now, with a new King on the throne, George V having replaced his father Edward VII who had died in May, Asquith the Liberal Prime Minister decided to try again. The result was almost identical, so the Liberals remained in power, supported by Labour and the Irish Nationalists. The whole exercise had achieved very little.

1911 opened with a 1–1 draw at Ibrox, generally admitted to be a fair result, and then Celtic had two good wins over Glasgow opposition in Clyde and Partick Thistle to put them back in the race for the League Championship – for Rangers were also having their bad days – before a disappointing defeat at Aberdeen, a late goal giving the "wasps" a 1–0 win, was followed by a miserable goalless draw against Falkirk. These reverses seemed to rule Celtic out of the race yet again, all the more frustratingly for Sunny because they had seemed to have fought their way back in.

But there was still the Scottish Cup. Celtic had now won the trophy on six occasions, and Sunny himself always felt that he would have added to his own haul of three winners' medals in 1909 but for the Hampden Riot, and in 1910 but for his own suspension and the illness of Davie Adams and the injury to Jimmy McMenemy in the semi-final against Clyde. The Scottish Cup was in any case, in those days, considered of more value than the Scottish League – it certainly had the capacity to engender loads of cash – and Sunny certainly relished the big crowds that the final could attract. It was a shame for Sunny that television was still almost 50 years away, but this did not mean that the Scottish Cup was not a perpetual topic of interest in newspapers and in conversations in pubs, factories, mines, shipyards and school playgrounds (and even staff rooms!).

The first opponents were St Mirren at Parkhead on 28 January. They won 2-0 with goals from Jimmy McMenemy and John Hastie (who, St Mirren claimed, kicked the ball out of their goalkeeper's hands) and Celtic were well in top, even though Quinn was well policed and Kivlichan and Hastie failed to impress. But according to *The Glasgow Herald*, "St Mirren never looked like scoring much less winning... the winners were as usual in defence, much better in fact, seeing that Young was in his most captivating mood, and that McAteer played with a dash and judgement that Loney could not have bettered". Bearing in mind Young's dealings with St Mirren a year ago, it was a particularly rewarding day for him.

Then Galston came to Parkead on 11 February. In a day of Cup surprises – Forfar Athletic for example, beat Falkirk – the paltry 5,000 crowd were appalled at Celtic's inability to finish off the part time amateurs. Jimmy Quinn scored but then in spite of constant pressure, Celtic never scored again with even some supporters turning on the left-wing of Hastie and Hamilton. But at least progress was made and the next round would see last year's conquerors, Clyde at Celtic Park.

The team was indeed going through a period of transition. Two men from Croy had joined Jimmy Quinn in the squad, and what made it complicated was that they were almost namesakes – Tommy McAteer and Andy McAtee.

Tommy was a centre-half who had joined the club from Clyde when the Shawfield side seemed to single him out for blame for having lost the Scottish Cup Final against Dundee in 1910, and Andy was a youngster with a sturdy build "thighs like swelling oak" and "legs like those of a billiard table" who played on the right wing and had an astonishingly powerful shot. Young, as always attentive to fringe players and youngsters, did what he could to encourage them. They were both, he reckoned, worth paying attention to.

As it happened neither McAteer nor McAtee were in the team that played Clyde in the quarter-final, a tie that attracted an astonishing 40,000 to Parkhead on 25 February. In some ways this game was one of Sunny's best games, for Celtic were up against it for long periods. Jimmy Quinn sustained a head injury and was seriously concussed, insisting on playing on when he was clearly disorientated to an alarming extent and not even being able to run straight. He eventually had to go off, and then Willie Loney fractured his wrist before half-time. This left Celtic effectively with nine men, but that did not stop Jimmy McMenemy putting them one up before half-time.

The second half saw Young and Hay at their best. Now playing against the strong breeze, Celtic left Alec McNair to be the sole defender, brought Dodds into centre-half and brought Jimmy Hay forward to left-half instead of left-back. Thus, in the greatest of Celtic traditions, a great half-back line of Young, Dodds and Hay, responding to the massive support of the crowd, took a grip of the game and held Clyde at the half way line. Occasionally the Clyde forwards got past, but not often and when that happened there was "the icicle" Eck McNair to mop up, with even Johnstone and McMenemy playing a heroic defensive part in the last few desperate minutes. But the star of them all was the fair haired, barking, pointing, cajoling Sunny Jim Young, "the wind never got past him that day" who bullied Celtic to an unlikely victory and a place in the semi-final.

His reward was the success of the team – a good day was made even better with the news that Rangers had gone down at Dundee – but he also had another personal reward. He was chosen to play for the Scottish League again, this time against the English League. To his immense pride, he was made captain by the Scottish League management, a strange decision when his club captain Jimmy Hay was in the side. Four Celts, in fact – McNair, Hay, McMenemy and

Young – took part in this honourable draw on 4 March. The game was played at a very congested Ibrox with more people allowed in than the reconstructed stadium could cope with, and Hampden might have been a better choice.

Young is given several good mentions in reports, with the half-back line of Jimmy Young, Alec Raisbeck (of Partick Thistle and enjoying the nickname "Alexander the Great") and Jimmy Hay being singled out for praise. *The Evening Citizen* in a strange sentence says, "All the Scotch half-backs were good and lasted the game till the end". Old friends Bennett and McMenemy teamed up again and were very impressive, thriving on good service from Sunny Jim. But sadly Sunny Jim yet again could not displace Andy Aitken, now with Leicester Fosse, for the "big" International at Goodison Park the following month.

But the Scottish Cup now claimed his attention with Aberdeen drawn at Celtic Park for the semi-final on 11 March. Yet another huge crowd of 50,000 (football was clearly going through a boom) with a large influx of North-East fans assembled to see a classic encounter. Jimmy Quinn scored the only goal of the game, but for the second Cup-tie in a row, Celtic had serious injuries to contend with. Peter Johnstone was badly crippled in the first half and a few other players had knocks and were less than 100% fit, but Young and Tommy McAteer formed an impregnable double centre partnership. *The Evening Citizen* is rather scathing about this game, complaining about a, "want of thrustive (sic) power from the whole Aberdeen forward line, and the Celtic were no better. The game became deadly dull". This was of course a great, albeit indirect, compliment to Sunny, for the game can be as dull as it wants – the important thing is to win!

But even with Celtic's great defending, Aberdeen might have equalized late in the game had it not been for a great save by Davie Adams from Willie Lennie. "Aberdeen's forwards should apologise to their backs" intones *The Evening Citizen* . But for Celtic, Mr Dougray's full-time whistle was greeted with a huge cheer of joy mingled with relief, and the team were through to the Scottish Cup Final to play against Hamilton Accies who had surprised themselves by beating Dundee in the other semi-final.

There were connections between Hamilton Accies and Celtic in that Peter Somers was now at Douglas Park, although by now too old to command a place in the first eleven, and Hamilton's right-winger was J.H. McLaughlin, son of the great John McLaughlin one of Celtic's founding fathers and the man who is given a great deal of credit for his part in founding the Scottish League. McLaughlin senior was now ailing in 1911 and was fated to die a few months later, but his memory was (and remains) still much revered.

"Milo" of *The Evening Times* on Friday 7 April permits himself a certain amount of cynicism about the outcome of this game. He praises Hamilton Accies for what they have achieved so far, but was in the event proved astonishingly prescient when he says, "That Celtic will ultimately win the Cup I cannot doubt, but that they will do so at the first try tomorrow is another matter. A draw will not in the least astonish me". "Milo" was of course a Roman gangster defended by Cicero in the 50s BC in his many ongoing battles with Clodius; perhaps a better Classical nom de plume for *The Evening Times* scribe might have been "Cassandra" or "Teiresias", both with the ability to tell the future with devastating accuracy. The Scottish Cup Final was a 0–0 draw.

It was generally agreed that the first encounter on 8 April at Ibrox (the third successive final that ended in a draw in the first game!) was a poor game with neither side looking likely to score. There had been a long dry spell (a rare event in Glasgow) in spring 1911 and a strong breeze had also militated against good football. Jimmy Hay was quoted in *The Glasgow Observer* as saying, "the dry ground, the light ball, a tricky wind, they were all against good play. I'd like to see a shower or two during the week." Young was ubiquitously diligent, showing no mercy in his tackling, but any chances that he created for the forward line were wasted . Young John Hastie did not enjoy the best of luck. This Cup Final was possibly unique in that the inside-lefts of both Celtic and Hamilton were called Hastie, and of course things were even more complicated in that Celtic's outside-left was called Hamilton!

The Evening Times on the Monday lambasts Celtic for a feckless performance, saying that their namesakes in Glencraig (a small mining village in Fife), the Glencraig Celtic would have given the Glasgow Celtic a run for their money, but exempts Sunny Jim from any criticism, "Young, as of old, saved the situation when danger threatened and frequently did the most needful at the most unexpected moments".

For the replay however a week later, on Easter weekend 15 April, Celtic's Hastie was dropped, Kivlichan was moved from outside-right to inside-left, and young Andy McAtee was given a run on the wing, with the village of Croy ("a hamlet of 70 houses", according to *The Evening Citizen*) thus supplying three men for the Celtic team. Croy needed a boost at that particular time, for only a week previously the Number One Gartmore Pit at Croy had suffered a cave-in and a miner had died and another was seriously injured in one of the many reminders that society was given about the dangers involved in mining for coal. It was also of course a reminder of the cynical indifference of the coal owners to the safety of their men.

The introduction of young McAtee was a winner. Another good thing happened as well in that there had been sporadic, intermittent rain during the week, and then about an hour before the start, an absolute downpour. The pitch would no longer be dry and bumpy. But although the rain had eased before kick-off, the wind hadn't, and the elements seemed to persuade quite a lot of fans not to go, for the crowd was a meagre 25,000 (some sources go as low as 15,000) as distinct from 45,000 a week previously.

The teams were;
Celtic: Adams, McNair and Hay; Young, McAteer and Dodds; McAtee, McMenemy, Quinn, Kivlichan and Hamilton.
Hamilton Accies: J. Watson, Davie and Miller; P. Watson, W. McLaughlin and Eglinton; J.H. McLaughlin, Waugh, Hunter, Hastie and McNeil
Referee: T Dougray, Nitshill.

When the teams came out, something unusual happened in that a rabbit appeared as well and took a bit of catching before the game could start! Was this the Easter bunny? And for whom was it some kind of omen?

Celtic played into the wind and the rain in the first half, and the standard of play was only marginally better than last week as both sides struggled to come to terms with the conditions – totally different from last week, but no easier. But when the teams changed round, Celtic settled down and Young and Dodds came more and more into the game as the Hamilton defence began to wilt at the sheer intensity of the Celtic pressure. The heavy ground was good news for Quinn, for he enjoyed the mud but it was ten minutes from time before he opened the scoring from 20 yards with an "oblique shot" after some good work from Sunny Jim and a dummy from McMenemy. There seemed little chance of a Hamilton recovery, given that they were now against the elements and that the Young-inspired Celtic defence had not yet conceded a goal in the Scottish Cup that season. The songs of the Celtic fans were now beginning to be heard, and Celtic's superiority was confirmed just on time when Tommy McAteer hammered home a shot from a distance.

Tommy thus had his moment of glory, laying the bogey of a year previously when he was unfairly blamed by Clyde supporters and management for gifting the Cup to Dundee. It would be his only triumph. *The Evening Times* praises Celtic for a good performance in awful conditions – Hay complained of being almost blinded by the rain, and Quinn said he could hardly breathe against the wind – and Young is given the compliment of being, "Young, just the old hard-working Young".

It was Celtic's seventh Scottish Cup, and Sunny's fourth winners medal. Baillie James Henderson, Chairman of Rangers, presented the trophy after the game and cheerfully congratulated Celtic on being the first team to win the Scottish Cup without losing a goal. This was not quite true, for Queen's Park had achieved this in the 1870s, and *The Glasgow Herald*, inveterate lovers of Queen's Park, were not slow to point it out, but to do so in 1911 with the team in transition was a tremendous feat, especially as they held out against teams like St Mirren, Clyde and Aberdeen who were able to score goals against other defences. Such was the influence of James Young!

That Sunny was becoming an iconic figure at Parkhead was confirmed by his official appointment as captain in early May. "Dun" Hay had been struggling to get along with Maley for some time. Hay was respected and liked by Maley most of the time, as distinct from Jimmy Young who was loved and adored. It so happened that Newcastle United, then the most famous and most talented side in England with a shrewd Scottish manager called Frank Watt, were interested in acquiring another left-half to replace Peter "the great" McWilliam, (who had been injured while playing for Scotland) and "Dun" went to Newcastle. Like Alec Bennet going to Rangers, Hay left many happy memories behind him, and good player though he was for the Geordies, his best days were for Celtic.

So Sunny thus in 1911 took over the awesome task of captaining Celtic. His first tasks were the Glasgow Charity Cup and then a close season tour of Germany, Austro-Hungary, Switzerland and France. With a weakened team, Celtic beat Third Lanark but then went down 1–2 to Rangers in the Glasgow Charity Cup Final in a game where Jimmy Quinn was repeatedly fouled by Gordon and Galt and had to be taken off in the 65th minute. Sunny was naturally disappointed about that, but then in the tour of Europe, the team won six games and drew two against teams like Dresden, Ferencvaros, MTK and Basle some of whom would make their mark in Europe in years to come.

But Sunny was aware that captaining this mixture of spirited but gauche youngsters on the one hand and gnarled veterans like McMenemy and Quinn on the other would not be easy. But, working in close concert with Maley, he organised social events (including the occasional drunken spree!) to make everyone feel at home in the Celtic party. And no-one was allowed to forget that the season would be starting in August. He loved fondling the Scottish Cup, but he wanted the Scottish League as well next season.

Before the start of the season, however, a very important domestic event occurred on 24 July when Florence gave birth to her third child. This time, Sunny had a son! He would be called James after his father. Alice was now eight, Irene three and now they had a baby brother. Sunny was, as always, a very happy family man, living at 45 Titchfield Street, Kilmarnock and described in the 1911 census as a "football player".

Sunny, now the Captain

If 1910–11 was a season in transition, the next season was even more so, and new captain Young was even more aware of his responsibilities in this regard. In theory at Celtic Park, the Directors picked the team, Maley gave instructions before the game started and at half-time, and the captain was responsible for all that happened on the field during the 90 minutes... but his duties ended there. In practice, it was nothing like that, for Young had the ear of Maley (and to an extent the Directors) and had a large input into everything that went on.

The relationship between Maley and Young was simple. They got on well, no doubt with the occasional spat, and they had the same sort of relationship that Stein and McNeill had in the 1960s. The fact that Young played in the same position of right-half as Maley had a couple of decades earlier helped a great deal. It was an ideal position to captain from – the centre of the field, constantly involved and forever in the thick of things, with Sunny now *ex officio* called upon to act now and again as a peacemaker and a "calmer down" when things tended to get out of hand. He had to be polite to referees, making a dignified protest if necessary, but never lose the place. He was aware that he had done that once or twice in the past.

As a player, as he would cheerfully admit himself, he was not the greatest right-half in the world. He often felt that he deserved more Scottish caps than his solitary one, but was honest enough to see that men like Andy "the Daddler" Aitken were also good. Sunny lacked perhaps the finesse that other right halves did – one thinks of Peter Wilson, Pat Crerand and Bobby Murdoch in later years, or even the much troubled Johnny Gilchrist – but he made up for it all in effort, tirelessness, commitment and enthusiasm for the cause. Not having been born a Celt, he had very soon come to love the club, and appreciated what it meant to so many people. Never was there the slightest hint that he was going to go elsewhere. And before every game as he removed his false teeth to put them in a glass of water, he would reflect how lucky he was.

So now in 1911, he was at the height of his powers. Just short of 30, he was fit enough to have another five or six years ahead of him. The team had peaked perhaps – it was certainly short of what it had been in 1907 and 1908 – but it was up to him and the team which he now led to bring things back to what they once were and restore a few smiles to the faces of the urchins who hung about the pavilion entrance in Janefield Street hoping to catch a glance of great men like Quinn, McMenemy, McNair and the man who would always have time to speak to them, Sunny Jim. He was awarded a benefit at the start of the season – a 0–0 friendly game against Rangers, in which he would get all the proceeds.

Autumn 1911, however, was a bad time for the club, and Sunny must have wondered what he was letting himself in for as captain. Quinn, now 33, was out injured for a long spell and with respect to his successors, he was badly missed as forwards like Nicholl, Brown, Donaldson and Travers all struggled to find consistency and form. Frequent references are found to McMenemy throwing his arms up in despair at the inadequacies of his colleagues, and the slackness in the forward line found its way to the defence as well. The full-back pairing of McNair and Dodds would of course become legendary but it needed time to bed in, Loney came back after injury but was clearly struggling, and Young himself although relishing his new role as skipper, found disturbing comments like, "Sunny Jim takes longer every season to find form" written about him in *The Glasgow Observer*.

The defeat in the first round of the Glasgow Cup to Partick Thistle was particularly spineless, and there were League defeats to Rangers, Motherwell and Hearts as well as a series of depressing draws to teams like Morton, Partick Thistle, Falkirk and Hibs. It was clear from a fairly early stage that there would be no League challenge this year, and Celtic were indeed a team in transition. The bullet simply had to be bit. Young players had to be nursed and coached, and perhaps a few new ones had to be found, and injuries to McMenemy and Quinn did not help.

But there were a few straws in the wind as well. On Thursday 28 September, Maley invited Young to come with him to Dumfries where Celtic reserves (with a couple of experienced men in McMenemy and Hamilton) were playing a friendly for Charity on what was called Rood Fair Day. Maley wanted Young to have a look at "Smith" who would be playing at inside-right. "Smith" in fact was a young Irishman from Clydebank Juniors called Patrick Gallacher.

Young's first impression was that he was far too thin and frail. He might well have recalled Robert Burns comment on the man who did not eat enough haggis:

"His spindle shank a fine whip lash

His nieve a nit

Through bloody field and fire to dash

Oh how unfit!".

But the youngster showed some trickery in Celtic's 6–1 defeat of the local side, and Young agreed with Maley that he should be given another go – but should also be given several good "plates o' kail" and "tatties".

It was after a miserable defeat at Motherwell at the end of November when Maley decided that young Gallacher should get a run in the first team. He called Sunny into his office on Friday 1 December and told him that Gallacher was playing tomorrow at inside-right against St Mirren at Parkhead in place of the ineffective Paddy Travers. The injured Napoleon would be out for a few weeks yet, but Napoleon's opinion of Gallacher was also that Gallacher was good enough. Sunny was to look after the youngster, for the idea was to give him a few games in the team, because the talent was definitely there.

Before the game, Quinn (making his comeback after a prolonged absence since September) and others were heard to make remarks about Maley should be done for manslaughter and that Gallacher's legs were thin enough to have a message tied to them (a reference to the practice of sending messages by pigeon), but Young silenced them with a scowl, then took the trembling young Patsy aside, told him to, "never mind thae c***s", that he was in the team because Maley thought he was good enough " an' I agree wi' im", and that he was to do his best.

Patsy did just that, and Celtic recorded a good 3–1 win in the December wind and the rain with Gallacher described as "tricky... elusive... possessed of no physique... a favourite in his first match...control and passing comparable to McMenemy's... cool artfulness... judgement of a veteran...no superior in the passing of a ball but where does he get the strength to shoot?" in *The Glasgow Observer,* whereas *The Glasgow Herald* contents itself with the observation that "Celtic introduced a new forward...who should go far".

Form now took a turn for the better, and McMenemy was back for the New Year's Day game at Parkhead against Rangers when Quinn scored a hat-trick, hinting at a better 1912 for Celtic, and that there might yet be a flicker in the League championship challenge. But then came more miserable draws against

Clyde, Hearts and St Mirren, and it was soon obvious that the Scottish Cup once again represented Celtic's main chance for glory that season.

The first game in that tournament on 27 January was the visit of the then little known Dunfermline Athletic on their first ever competitive visit to Celtic Park. It was an interesting lesson for Celtic, for Dunfermline, so far from being overawed, led *The Glasgow Herald* to observe that, "a Doonybrook of a game at Celtic Park so upset the Cup holders that they were pleased when the game came to a finish with a goal in their favour and no player incapacitated. Dunfermline Athletic played vigorous football of the old Cambuslang and Cowlairs type, and like Bo'ness some years ago, made Celtic understand that the game is one of many styles, and that the purely scientific is not the one that wins Cups". The journalist is, of course, here being tactful and saying that the enthusiastic Fifers tried to kick Celtic off the park.

Half-time at this game was revealing. Dunfermline departed to the pavilion for their cup of tea, but Maley (as he sometimes did) brought out a kettle or two and made his point to his players on the field, gesticulating, pointing, and clenching his fist to make a point. Then Sunny had his say, clearly telling his men not to rise to provocation, to calm things down and to stop trying to be too clever in midfield, but to punt the ball up the field. The tactics worked, for John Brown, himself a Fifer from Dysart who would have enjoyed scoring against Dunfermline, did just that, and Celtic then with their "long ball game" exhausted the Fifers. It was not the sort of football that Celtic were famous for, but the pragmatic approach was justified by a place in the next round.

East Stirlingshire were the visitors on 10 February. They presented few problems and Celtic won 3–0 on a day on which the news was dominated by the abandonment of the Clyde v Rangers tie at Shawfield because of rioting and pitch invasions when Clyde were 3–1 up. To their credit, Rangers conceded the tie. For Celtic the next round brought a trip to Aberdeen, a team whom they tended to meet often in the Scottish Cup, and the games were usually feisty affairs. It would be a fierce test of Sunny's temperament and his ability to win a game and keep control of his players.

Celtic probably had their biggest away support to date with them in Aberdeen on 24 February. Some travelled with the team on the Friday night, others boarded trains at Buchanan Street from 8.00 onwards, their numbers being augmented by hundreds joining the train at places like Larbert, Perth, Forfar and Stonehaven, all wearing green and white rosettes and favours – a clear sign that Celtic were now a national Scottish institution, no longer a parochial East End of Glasgow outfit. A few, but only a very few travelled by road. The brake clubs were gradually giving up horsepower in favour of motor power, but that was very expensive, unreliable and in any case Aberdeen was just a little too far to go and come back in the same day by any method other than train. There was even a pro-Celtic faction of considerable size in Aberdeen itself. Such had been the success of the spreading of the Celtic gospel from the glory days of a few years ago.

But the green and white favours in the 25,000 crowd were downcast as the game entered its later stages. Not only were the team 2–0 down to a strong Aberdeen side who clearly fancied their first appearance in a Scottish Cup Final, but Celtic had even missed a penalty with the as yet inexperienced Andy McAtee clearly upset by the strange antics of Aberdeen's goalkeeper on the line. Sunny Jim and Peter Johnstone, the wing-halves, were working hard, but the Aberdeen defence was holding firm as Celtic became ever more desperate.

Then with 20 minutes to go, Celtic were awarded another penalty-kick at the Beach End of the tight little Pittodrie enclosure. Andy McAtee must have had the horrors of hell at the thought of missing another one, but Sunny Jim sprinted forward and gave instructions that Quinn should take it, an order that was instantly obeyed in a tribute to Young's captaincy. It was an inspiring decision, but then an eerie silence descended on the ground as the famous, mighty Quinn ran forward and shot. Goalkeeper Andy Greig saved, but could only parry the ball back to Quinn who gratefully scored to put Celtic back into the game.

Now the Celtic faithful took over the ground with their songs and encouragement, and with time running out, young McAtee atoned for his earlier blunder with a fine goal as he picked up a John Brown cross, and Celtic were level. They might even have scored again, but Aberdeen's Greig saved a fierce Peter Johnstone drive, then Donald Colman cleared off the line, and the game finished 2–2 with a replay scheduled for two weeks time at Parkhead, 9 March (not the following Saturday because three Celtic players, McNair, McMenemy and Quinn were playing for Scotland v Wales on 2 March).

The replay attracted a good crowd of 35,000. *The Evening Citizen* puts it rather graphically when it says, "Long before the hour of starting, the Gallowgate and all approaches to the field were one solid mass of camp followers. The weather conditions were well nigh perfect for the chill touch lent by "winter lingering in the lap of spring" gave congenial conditions for players and spectators alike". The game itself was rather an anti-climax after the first Pittodrie game, but Celtic did enough to win, both goals coming from Paddy Travers. Quinn was injured and wrenched his knee, having to play on the left-wing, and Aberdeen put up a fight but failed to break down the fine Celtic defence. Both Celtic goals came at the end of each half, and *The Glasgow Herald* somewhat ungraciously remarked that Celtic had, "little to jubilate upon", whereas *The Evening Citizen* is relieved that, "A pleasing feature was the cleanness of the play despite the spice that was in it". But Celtic were in the semi-final of the Scottish Cup.

Saturday 23 March was a significant day in Celtic football history. While Quinn and McNair were playing for Scotland against England before a six figure crowd at Hampden and drawing 1–1, Celtic had a similar scoreline in yet another game against Aberdeen, this time in a rather insignificant League game at Pittodrie before 5,000. It was important however because this was the first time that Patsy Gallacher and Jimmy McMenemy played together as inside men in the same forward line, Jimmy agreeing to move to inside-left to allow the prodigious Irishman to play at inside-right.

A knee injury to Paddy Travers forced the issue, but it had been obvious for some time that young Gallacher was playing so well in friendly matches and for the reserve XI that he could not really be denied a place. Yet he was hardly good enough to displace Napoleon! Legend has it that the decision was made on the train going to Aberdeen; another story has it that it was decided on a whim in the dressing room, but the most likely version is that Young and Maley discussed the matter at length the week before, McMenemy was then consulted (it was possibly even his own suggestion) and then the trembling young Gallacher, still in awe of such great men, was told that he would be inside-right at Pittodrie as an experiment with Napoleon moving over to inside-left to accommodate him.

The experiment worked well enough with McMenemy scoring from his new inside-left position, and it was decided to keep the new forward line of McAtee, Gallacher, Quinn, McMenemy and Brown for the next game – the far more important Scottish Cup semi-final against Hearts at Ibrox, the game being played there because the SFA had now decided that neutral venues should be used at this late stage of the competition. Clyde awaited the winners.

In spite of a national coal strike (which had begun on 1 March) which cancelled most trains, some 43,000 attended Ibrox at 3.30 pm (paying six old pence for the privilege) on 30 March, and saw a game that was as one-sided as could be imagined. Celtic's inside men ran the show, McAtee was "in merry mood" and "boy" Brown was in great form, but as significant as anything else was the way that Sunny Jim snuffed out yet again Hearts great talisman, Bobby Walker, as he had done so often in the past – the Scottish Cup Final of 1907 for example.

McMenemy scored twice in the first half when Celtic had the wind, but they played just as well in the second half against the breeze and John Brown added another. Long before full-time, the crowd was reduced to half its original amount with the routed and broken "capitalists" (those who lived in Edinburgh) off to discover ways of getting home by means of what few trains there were. Some had even hired omnibuses and charabancs for the day and had travelled the two hour journey by road!

It was now Sunny's job to motivate the players for Saturday's final against Clyde. This was hardly difficult, for they were all on a high following the brilliant performance against Hearts. Clyde were of course near neighbours and friends. They had never won the Scottish Cup but had come close to it two years ago after they had put Celtic out but lost to Dundee at the third attempt. For the first time ever, the managers of the two Scottish Cup Final teams were brothers, for Alec Maley was the manager of Clyde. The third brother of the Maley family, Tom, told *The Weekly News* that he was in no doubt that Celtic would win! Clyde's trainer was incidentally a man called William Struth who would become the manager of Rangers in 1920 following the accidental drowning of William Wilton in a boating accident.

The Evening Citizen in the build-up to the game thinks that it will all depend on how the two half-back lines will fare. "Young, Loney and Johnstone – what they don't know in the art of knocking the other side out of gear is not worth knowing". But the Clyde half-back line of Walker, McAndrew and Collins were, on their day, potentially as good and if they played to their potential, there would be, "not a scintilla of difference between the two lines".

The game was played at Ibrox, the crowd was given as 48,000 but many folk thought that if the game had been played at Hampden (which in any case was closer to the heartlands of both Celtic and Clyde), more people might have attended. The stand which cost two shillings and sixpence (the stand was "all ticket" with tickets available in advance from FA Lumley at 82 Sauchiehall Street or Mr W Wilton, Ibrox) was well populated but there were "gaps in the cheaper parts of the ground" (which cost only sixpence). This perhaps reflected on the amount of Celtic supporters who were miners, and could not afford to attend, given that fact that they had been on strike for over a month. The day was dry, but there was a strong gale (almost as bad as that of 1900 when Celtic played Queen's Park at the same venue) and in these circumstances, *The Daily Record and Mail* is surely correct when it states that the "steadying influence of experienced players was uppermost", whereas *The Weekly News* talks about the qualities of "generalship" with Sunny Jim Young in mind, one imagines.

The teams were;
Celtic: Mulrooney, McNair and Dodds; Young, Loney and Johnstone; McAtee, Gallacher, Quinn, McMenemy and Brown.
Clyde: Grant, Gilligan and Blair; Walker, McAndrew and Collins; Hamilton, Jackson, Morrison, Carmichael and Stevens.
Referee: T. Dougray, Nitshill.

Young won the toss and decided to play with the gale in the first half and towards what is now the Copland Road end of the ground. *The Scotsman* perhaps exaggerates when it says that this decision won Celtic the game but it was a shrewd decision. Young's thinking was that his players would get the benefit of the breeze when they were still fresh, and that in any case, in an hour's time the gale might drop in its intensity. In this, his judgement was correct, for although both teams had problems keeping the ball in play, Celtic were dominant, playing with "relentless intensity" and went in at half-time one goal up thanks to a goal from McMenemy who pounced on the ball "like a cat on a mouse" to score.

But the second half would be difficult. Never would the clarion call of "Face the Ball, Celts" be more relevant as Clyde piled on the pressure. Once again though it was the strength of the Celtic half-back line of Young, Loney and Johnstone which won the day, breaking up Clyde attacks time after time, and in the 61st minute the decision to play Gallacher was vindicated when he was on the spot to net the dropping ball after goalkeeper Grant had got a hand to Brown's header.

There was now no way back for Clyde, and Young simply took control. Almost literally, "the wind did nae get by 'im' that day! *The Scotsman* says more prosaically that, "Young touched his best form". Celtic might have had two penalties, the vociferous claims denied by Tom Dougray, but Dougray was certainly correct in denying Clyde one when the ball hit the hand of Eck McNair. McNair indeed was singled out for his defending, as was goalkeeper John Mulrooney. The game finished with Celtic well on top.

Celtic had now won the Scottish Cup eight times, and Young, McMenemy and Quinn had now each won five Scottish Cup medals. It was a great day for the club and for Sunny Jim. And he was so delighted to see the smile on the face of young Patsy Gallacher. The judgement of the management team in playing him had been vindicated, and *The Weekly News* singled out Andy McAtee by saying that, "not since Bennett have Celtic had such a clever extreme (sic) right-winger as Andrew McAtee." The Scottish Cup was presented to Chairman James Kelly after the game in the Ibrox boardroom.

The Evening Citizen sang the praise of the Celtic team on the Monday after the Cup was won. (The gale was still continuing and led to the cancellation, on the grounds of public safety, of Celtic's game against Raith Rovers that afternoon). Detailing all the honours that the club had won since its foundation in 1888, it says that this current side could be compared with the best of them. After praising their team spirit and their productivity, it goes on to say that "...the mere sight of the green and white jerseys had struck and still strikes something akin to terror into the hearts of a good few teams".

And 1912 wasn't finished yet. While the Titanic was still heading to New York, the Scottish Cup was shown off, draped in green and white ribbons during an unimportant League game on a bright sunny day against Kilmarnock on 13 April and an iconic picture was taken of a small boy with no shoes on among supporters holding the Scottish Cup. There could surely be no more graphic illustration of what Celtic meant to their supporters! By the time that the Glasgow Charity Cup games began in May, the newspapers were still full of questions about how an iceberg could sink such a magnificent and expensive ship. In the circumstances, Sunny Jim was possibly glad to hear that a projected tour of South Africa involving a lengthy sea voyage was cancelled! A shorter and closer one to Denmark was arranged instead.

The Celtic team with the Scottish Cup of 1912. Sunny is beside Manager Maley in the middle row on the right

Supporters with the Scottish Cup. Observe the bugles and the boy with no shoes!

But before that, there was still the Charity Cup. A bye in the first round was followed by a win over Queen's Park in fine weather at Cathkin on 4 May with Gallacher and Quinn scoring the goals in a 2–1 win. The weather was equally kind the following week (11 May) although there was a stronger wind when 25,000 came to Hampden to see the Charity Cup Final between Celtic and Clyde, a game in which Clyde were determined to gain revenge for their Scottish Cup Final defeat. Celtic with Loney injured once again, put Peter Johnstone to centre-half and brought John Mitchell in to left-half, and the teams read:

Celtic: Mulrooney, McNair and Dodds; Young, Johnstone and Mitchell; McAtee, Gallacher, Quinn, McMenemy and Brown.
Clyde: McTurk, Farrell and Blair; Walker, McAndrew and Collins; Hamilton, Jackson, Spiers, Carmichael and Stevens.
Referee: T. Dougray, Nitshill.

There is, of course, the trick question of "Who won the English Cup and never scored a goal?"

Answer Everton, who had a player called Jimmy Never! Sadly it doesn't really work, for Never didn't score a goal, so the question would really have to read "...and Never never scored a goal?". But which team won a Glasgow Charity Cup Final and never scored a goal? Answer Celtic, who won this game by seven corners to nil in a goalless draw, an agreement having been reached before the game that corners would be counted in the event of a draw – a sensible arrangement, surely.

It was in fact not a bad game, although defences were on top with Young grimly determined that he personally would win another Glasgow Charity Cup medal, and that in his first year of captaincy, Celtic would win two Cups. Only in 1905 and 1908 had he won a medal in this particular Cup, and that was not good enough for Sunny. The 7–0 margin in corners however was a fair reflection of Celtic's superiority.

A rare action shot of Sunny Jim in a friendly against
Aston Villa in April 1912

And so it was off to Denmark and Norway for a short tour. The heat was intense, five games were played in eight days, four of which were won and the game that was lost was to the Denmark national side preparing for the 1912 Olympics in Stockholm. This was no disgrace, for Denmark ended up winning the silver medals and losing only to the powerful Great Britain side. Celtic beat the Norwegian Olympic side, Boldklub 93, Drammen and a Danish representative side. Celtic were great ambassadors wherever they went, playing good football and being perfect guests for the sociable Danes and Norwegians. "Man in The Know" in *The Glasgow Observer* describes the Celts as "Schoolmasters". Little wonder that Sunny said when they landed in Hull, "Well boys, I'm prouder than ever to be a Celtic player".

Indeed the future looked bright. The emergence of Patsy Gallacher and to a lesser extent Peter Johnstone meant that Celtic finished 1911–12 as the best team in Scotland. There seemed little to stop them going on to win loads of silverware in 1912–13. Sunny, like the rest of the team knew that this would be Celtic's 25th anniversary, and *The Glasgow Observer* kept making comments about it being a "silver wedding" after 25 years, then Celtic's 25th anniversary should be marked with loads of silver. Sadly, it wouldn't quite work out that way.

For the first time since 1902–03, Celtic did not win either of the major Scottish trophies, Rangers winning the League for the third year in a row and Falkirk (who had been a good team for several years now) winning the Scottish Cup. There were reasons for Celtic's disappointing performances. Quinn and McMenemy were both out injured for long spells, the young right-wing combination of McAtee and Gallacher, good though they were, lacked experience and needed to learn in the hard school of Scottish football, John Brown, that frail Fifer, who had looked so good last year now seemed to have peaked, Peter Johnstone was out for a long spell in the middle of the season, and Sunny Jim himself, who played almost every game, gave disturbing sings of "burn out". He might have benefited from a rest, but Sunny, being Sunny, would not countenance that.

Yet in spite of all that, they pushed Rangers hard in the Glasgow Cup and the Scottish League, remaining in the race until a late stage of the season, lost unluckily in the Scottish Cup to Hearts and had the last laugh in the Charity

Cup. And the team was developing. Unfortunately, Celtic fans, then as now, impatient for success and intolerant of youngsters learning their craft, did not see it that way.

The season started with two draws against Falkirk and Hibs, and by the time that the Glasgow Cup Final came to be played on 12 October, Celtic had lost to Dundee (as they often did at that stage of their history) at Dens Park. They reached the final of the Glasgow competition after a poor draw with Clyde, but then a certain turning on of the style in a 4–0 win in the replay with a goal from Jimmy Quinn which had the "applause still reverberating two minutes later".

No-one could deny the interest in the Celtic v Rangers Glasgow Cup Final. The crowd at Hampden is given as 90,000 but that is uncertain because the exit gates were broken down before the start. Celtic were without goalkeeper Mulrooney (his deputy, young Bobby Boyle made two bad mistakes to give Rangers two soft goals) and McMenemy, whose loss was crucial because the inexperienced Celtic forwards allowed themselves to be caught offside time and time again by a Rangers defence who knew exactly what they were doing. Celtic had led at the interval, but then after an accidental collision with Robertson of Rangers, young McAtee was barracked mercilessly by the Rangers crowd and lacked the experience to deal with it. His play went all to pieces, and hard though Young tried to cheer him up, his contribution was minimal.

It was generally agreed that this was one of Sunny's poorest games. He and McNair were slow, described as "Clydesdales" as distinct from the Rangers "racehorses", and he really needed to get a grip on his forwards to stop them being caught offside. The cause was not helped by an injury to Willie Loney, but Rangers were already 3–1 up at that point.

A certain amount of revenge and self-respect was gained in the League match a fortnight later when Celtic won 3–2 at Parkhead. Young, Dodds and Mitchell were a fine half-back line, and Patsy Gallacher showed Rangers what he could do. Like most young players, though, it did not happen every week, and captain Young was aware that the prodigious talent would have to be nurtured before it could mature.

Sunny had his bad games, but his value to the team was clearly illustrated on 23 November 1912 when he had one of his rare days off, having wrenched his muscle in the previous week's game at Queen's Park. The inexperienced

George Jarvis was played at right-half and, lacking the inspirational clarion calls of their skipper, Celtic went down to a very rare home defeat at the hands of an incredulous Motherwell. A week later, Sunny, against medical advice, came back, but his influence was not enough to bring off a win against Clyde, and Celtic were now three points behind Rangers.

By now a new player had arrived in the forward line. This was left-winger John Browning (for a few games, Celtic played both John Brown and John Browning!) This lad had talent, but he was a challenge of another sort to Young's captaincy. While McAteee and Gallacher needed to be nursed and encouraged, Browning had to be restrained and curbed. Not putting too fine a point on it, he was a bad boy. He would later serve time for match fixing, and was perpetually likely to be involved in fights, but it is to Celtic's (and Young's) credit that they managed to bring out the best in him, even though the rich fruits of the harvest would not be apparent for a year or two yet.

December 1912, a wild, wet rainy month, brought good results for Celtic, and when they beat Rangers 1–0 at Ibrox on New Year's Day through Jimmy Quinn scoring the only goal of the game, they were at the top of the League. Then the following day Young scored his first goal for a long time when he pulled rank on the normal penalty taker Joe Dodds to slide the ball home and make the score 3–0 against Clyde. 1913 was thus well begun.

But there were chinks in the armour. Defeats at difficult away venues like Easter Road and Pittodrie impaired the League challenge with several players notably Quinn suffering from fitness problems, but the season did not really fall apart until a catastrophic defeat by Hearts at Parkhead on 8 March in the quarter-final of the Scottish Cup. An enormous crowd of 70,000 (the turnstiles had to be closed for safety reasons) attended in lovely spring weather, but Celtic made a big mistake in including the manifestly unfit McMenemy, taking the view perhaps that a half-fit McMenemy was better than a fully fit reserve. It was Bobby Walker's day for Hearts, scoring the only goal of the game, and Celtic could not get the equaliser. Two League defeats followed in quick succession and the League challenge season collapsed.

There was a slight rally towards the end of the season, but Celtic lost their third League title in a row, this time to Rangers by four points, something that was all the more distressing, for Celtic had been in a better position for a great part of the season. It was Falkirk's year of winning the Scottish Cup beating Raith Rovers at Celtic Park on a day when the pitch had to be cleared of snow (on 12 April!). Celtic themselves were playing a friendly at Alloa that day, but Sunny stayed at Celtic Park to help Maley and the Directors with the hosting of the Scottish Cup Final, being seen sweeping the pitch in the morning and then changing into his suit to be the perfect diplomat when the teams and the referee arrived. It was a matter of pride for Celtic to do such things well, and Young was prepared to play his part.

There was still time to tweak the tail of the Rangers lion as well before the season ended. The Glasgow Charity Cup gave Celtic the chance to blood a few new players (not unlike what had happened in the case of Sunny Jim himself ten years previously). There was Charlie Shaw the goalkeeper signed from Queen's Park Rangers, Johnny McMaster from Clydebank, Johnny Hill from Dumbarton Harp and Barney Connolly from the same source. Sunny Jim, aware that at least some new players would be needed, went out of his way to encourage them, telling them how important the Glasgow Charity Cup had been in his own development in 1903, and how the supporters could really do with something to cheer them up.

Celtic beat Clyde 1–0 and then Third Lanark 2–1 with Charlie Shaw "an impressive custodian", and Barney Connolly scoring a goal. The opponents in the final were Rangers, and this was the chance to win at least something this season. Celtic won the toss for venue and thus Celtic Park saw a crowd of 35,000 on a blustery, showery day. McMenemy and Quinn were both out injured, and form certainly seemed to favour Rangers. The crowd little realised that they were seeing the first day of the famous Shaw, McNair and Dodds playing together, and indeed the first few minutes might have indicated that they would never play together again!

The teams were;
Celtic: Shaw, McNair and Dodds; Young, Loney and McMaster; McAtee, Gallacher, Connolly, Browning and Hill.
Rangers: Hempsey, Gordon and Ormonde; Brown, Logan and Galt; Paterson, Godwin, Reid, Bowie and Smith.
Referee: J. Bell, Dundee.

The game was a strange one with a few resemblances to the 1904 Scottish Cup Final. Rangers were 2–0 up in the first ten minutes. Willie Reid took advantage of poor Celtic defending and Young was honest enough to admit later that he could have done better. But few could have bettered the way that he now took charge of the situation, organising his team, barking orders, encouraging and exhorting. Before half-time Patsy Gallacher had scored to make the score 2–1.

The second half left the Celtic fans convinced that they now had a worthy successor to Jimmy Quinn in Barney Connolly. He was on hand to put Celtic level soon after the interval, and then later in the second half he scored a goal which was freely compared to those of the great man himself when he picked up a ball from Sunny, beat two Rangers players and crashed home a goal of such brilliance that the applause resounded for a long time. Sadly there would be very few other moments of glory from Barney, but this was enough to win Celtic the Glasgow Charity Cup for the second year in a row and to rescue his club from a barren season.

Thus Celtic finished their 25th year. It was a shame that their "silver" anniversary was characterised with so little silver, yet the record of the club had been glorious with eight Scottish Cups and ten Scottish Leagues. Already at this early stage of the history of this very remarkable club, there was much talk about "tradition" and "Celtic spirit". Sunny Jim was proud to have been a part of this club, and was determined to bring back the glory of a few years ago to the deserving supporters. 1913 was the first year since his arrival a decade previously that the club had not won at least one of the two major Scottish honours. This, he felt, really had to be put right.

Maley and Young would meet once or twice over the summer and discuss things. They were both confident that the team was on the turn. Gallacher, when he came good, he would be very good, McAtee and Browning were fast developing, and Young had liked what he saw of the lantern-jawed, grim faced left-half John McMaster, "of the melancholy countenance" as *The Dundee Courier* described him. And as for Young himself, Maley floated the idea that there might be a job as a trainer for him some time in the future. He was now after all 31. Sunny laughed that idea off, and began to prepare for the coming season.

CHAPTER SEVEN

1913–1914

GLORY ONCE AGAIN, BUT 1914...

Season 1913–14 was one of the best seasons in the history of the club. There was a stuttering start as the team struggled to find form, but following a fine run in late autumn, the team never really looked back. Yet it was a season that indicated above all that the great team of pre-1910 was no longer there. Quinn played only two games, and the team struggled to fill his place before eventually turning up with Jimmy McColl. Loney played three games before going to Motherwell, and McMenemy had a long absence with a broken collarbone from early October. But a new Celtic was emerging, phoenix-like from the ashes of the old.

There was a brilliant goalkeeper in Charlie Shaw. An unlikely looking athlete with his permanent smile and the feeling that he was everyone's favourite uncle, Shaw could be inspirational in goal, radiating confidence and banter. The full-back partnership of McNair and Dodds, after a certain amount of teething problems, had now bedded in, and Peter Johnstone, rugged and determined, became a great centre-half, teaming up well with left-half Johnny McMaster who made up in effort what he lacked in finesse. In that, of course, he resembled Young himself.

In the forward line, Celtic were now well served by two first class wingers in Andy McAtee and Johnny Browning. Good crossers, capable of a fine turn of speed and hard workers, they could both take a goal as well, with McAtee in particular having a devastating shot. And Patsy Gallacher, after an ordinary season in 1912–13 in which his great days were outnumbered by simply good ones, had now developed into a complete player. A wizard of trickery, a great passer and releaser of balls at the right time, an ability to jump and avoid the coarse tackles of desperate defenders, Patsy was now the best player around. Captain Young, always encouraging, told him that. Young did not worry about someone being too big for his boots. Far better to build up, he felt, than to knock him down. "The gem'll dae that quick enough" And of course, McMenemy was still there – as brilliant as ever and after April 1914, the darling of Scotland as well as Celtic.

And there was another constant, and that was the inspirational captain Sunny Jim. Apart from a brief spell at the turn of the year, (he hated being injured) he was always there. Repeatedly passed over for even Scottish League honours as well as full International ones, Sunny was naturally disappointed but sighed philosophically and said "that's fitba" and then turned his 100% concentration on his team. Hurt by the team's (and his own) disappointing form in autumn 1913, he now set about developing this team into medal winners. His experience of the 1907 and 1908 teams had shown him what a good team looked like. He was determined to recreate that. He was, by nature and culture, a winner.

An early indication of what we might expect that season came at the end of August when the good Falkirk team (Scottish Cup holders, of course) were put to the sword 4–0. Patsy Gallacher and Sunny Jim teamed up brilliantly as, "Gallagher (sic) twisted and turned at will, slipped passes and back-heeled in the most tantalising manner" according to *The Evening Times*, and the crowd of 30,000 were ecstatic at such a performance.

Problems, however, began on 13 September, a day of miserable weather with driving rain and a strong wind. Only 6,000 turned up at Parkhead to see Celtic go down to St Mirren thanks to two freakish goals – one an own-goal off Eck McNair and the second a rebound off the post, which came fortuitously to a St Mirren player. Against that, McMenemy missed an open goal, several other forwards had good chances, and in spite of incessant Celtic pressure both with and against the rain, a goal simply would not come, and the referee, Mr Humphrey of Glasgow, was distinctly unwilling to give penalties. According to one report Sunny Jim was heard to bawl at the end "Hey, ref, we should have had nine penalties the day!". Nine was possibly a bit of an exaggeration, but newspaper reports agree that at least three were justified.

Still seething with this injustice, Celtic then went to Hearts on the Monday for the Edinburgh Holiday fixture. Hearts were on a high, having beaten Rangers on the Saturday whereas Celtic made the mistake of carrying luggage from Saturday's game with them. In spite of that, they played well enough to deserve a goal in the honest opinion of *The Scotsman* , but at crucial points, the defence slipped up and the Hearts won 2–0 with Celtic's forwards unable to break down the strong Hearts defence. In the other game that day, Rangers ran riot at Hibs, and Celtic lost ground.

Worse followed on Tuesday 7 October when Celtic went out of the Glasgow Cup, losing 0–1 to Third Lanark at Cathkin in a semi-final replay. Thirds scored after a corner kick through McTavish after a scramble in which the Celtic defence simply failed to get the ball away, and poor Charlie Shaw was unsighted. Then Celtic simply could not get one past Third Lanark's talented goalkeeper Jimmy Brownlie. *The Glasgow Herald* enthuses about what an exciting finish it was, but *The Glasgow Observer* is more judgemental, describing Celtic's forwards, without Quinn and McMenemy as "stingless." It then went on to say, "A scoring centre must be found!"

It was another test of Young's captaincy. He and Maley were aware of the side's deficiencies, and various attempts were made to find scoring centres – George Whitehead on loan from Hearts, red-haired Ebeneezer Owers on loan from Clyde, Irishman Billy Crone who had impressed for the Irish League against their Scottish equivalents – and the one who would eventually solve the problem, Jimmy McColl from St Anthony's.

They all met with moderate success, and "Ebbie" Owers in particular had his moment of glory when he put four goals past Ayr United on the last Saturday of 1913, but Young now marshalled his defence with devastating precision. "Marshall" was perhaps the wrong word, for there was nothing complicated about it. The modern concept of "zonal marking" would have found little favour. The instructions would have been along the lines of "tak a man apiece" ie McNair took the left-winger, Dodds the right-winger, Young himself the inside-left, Johnstone the centre-forward and McMaster the inside-right. If in any doubt about what to do, then "Kick the f***in' thing up the park" or "Pass it back to Charlie", a reference to Charlie Shaw reputed to be the loneliest man in Scottish football, such was the dominance of the Celtic defence.

Being a great character, Charlie Shaw attracted stories like "going home early for his tea", "away to the theatre to see his favourite actress" or "wandering round to the other goal to ask the goalkeeper if he needed a hand". He also earned the nickname of "nothing doing", and even the "Catholic Jew". Maley himself often had that nickname because of his perceived unwillingness to spend money, but now it was given to Charlie in a reference to his reluctance to concede goals. Celtic were occasionally referred to as "ten internationalists and Charlie Shaw", for Charlie was never busy enough to attract the attention of the Scottish selectors.

From the defeat against Third Lanark on 7 October in the Glasgow Cup until a 2–1 win against Raith Rovers at Kirkcaldy on 13 December, the defence of Shaw, McNair and Dodds; Young, Johnstone and McMaster conceded not one single goal! And even that was put down to the malign influence of triskaidekaphobia, for it happened on the 13th in 1913 and it was Celtic's 13th game without losing a goal! In fact it was really a very good goal scored by Jimmy Scott of Raith Rovers, a man fated to perish on the Somme on 1 July 1916. Raith in fact scored first before Browning equalized and Owers notched the winner.

It would be the end of February before Celtic conceded another goal! By this time Celtic were clear at the top, beating Rangers twice, 2–0 at Ibrox and 4–0 at Parkhead on New Year's Day. The Ibrox game saw Andy McAtee make his mark with a wonderful goal after George Whitehead had put Celtic ahead, and Charlie Shaw "psyche" Alec Bennett into missing a penalty by a "dance" on his line, but it was the New Year's Day game at Parkhead that indicated that the balance of power really had shifted to Celtic. It was Sunny Jim himself who scored the first goal in a goalmouth scramble, but then came a great goal just before half-time from McMenemy (only recently recovered from a broken collarbone) before Johnny Browning hit another two. Then poor Alec Bennett managed to miss another penalty-kick to Charlie Shaw, and left the field the picture of misery, jeered and booed by those who used to adore him. No doubt it hurt, but oh, you should have stayed, Alec!

One game in particular in mid-November indicated the popularity of football and Celtic at this time. On a day of incessant rain 17,000 turned up at the inadequate Boghead in Dumbarton (always an intensely Celtic supporting area with local boy Johnny Browning now playing for Celtic) and so great was the crowd that three Dumbarton players could not get in! Some supporters eventually solved the problem for them by breaking down an exit gate so that they got in with about a couple of thousand spectators. The Sons of the Rock had had to start with eight men when the referee Mr Binnie of Falkirk lost patience waiting for them, and the game was played with fans sitting on the wet grass a yard from the touchline, some of them without even bonnets or coats! They were rewarded with a 4–0 win for Celtic.

A fine picture of Celtic in season 1913–14, but look closely at the front row. This picture has in fact been doctored with the heads of two comic characters turning to look at Patsy Gallacher. Sunny Jim is fourth from the left of the second top row

On 3 January, the team went to Firhill to play Partick Thistle. There had been some snow but a sudden thaw rendered the pitch playable, if very slippery, and Sunny was one of three Celtic players (McMenemy and McNair being the others) who suffered injuries, in Young's case a severe groin strain which rendered him unable to run. But Sunny did not "do" injuries and insisted on staying on. Celtic with only eight fit men did well to get a 0–0 draw, but Young would now miss the next three games.

But being captain he was still there, talking to his replacement young Andrew Davidson before the start, appearing in the dressing room at half-time to encourage everyone and to suggest tactical changes to Maley. The team beat Dumbarton, Clyde and then a rare victory at Dundee with Sunny being a mentor rather than a player. It was Sunny's suggestion that Browning should be brought into the centre-forward position that won the day, for Browning scored late in the game to record a victory at what was becoming known as a "hoodoo" ground. There had been a piece of tragic news that day, for just as the team were about to board the train at Buchanan Street, a telegram was delivered to Andy McAtee to say that his father Peter had been killed as he crossed the railway near Croy early that morning on his way to work in the fog. Sunny's diplomatic skills were called for here, for Andy would need careful nurturing when he came back.

Sunny returned from injury at the end of January. His second game back on 31 January saw scenes of disorder at Love Street, Paisley, a place where there had been a bit of history between the clubs. Celtic won the game comfortably 3–0 but in the second half with only three minutes to go Johnny McMaster of Celtic and Fred Sowerby of St Mirren were sent off for fighting by referee Mr Hamilton of Motherwell. Both players should have known better and would in due course be suspended, but as they trooped off to the pavilion, McMaster apparently made a "nasty remark" and Sowerby turned on him again. Sunny sprinted over and shepherded McMaster off.

By this time some intellectually challenged supporters had invaded the field to join in the fun. Sunny appealed to the supporters to get off. As it was Sunny, some of them did so, but not all and Maley now came on to sort the lawless elements out. When they did succeed in clearing the pitch and the remaining three minutes were played out, Maley having done his fair share of apologising to the St Mirren management and the referee, got back to the dressing room to discover that his wallet was missing!

Sunny was involved in a more humorous incident at Forfar on 21 February. Celtic had beaten Clyde to progress to the next round of the Scottish Cup and now they were on new ground at Station Park, home of Forfar, who played in the Northern League. Celtic had offered over £200 (some said £400) to buy the ground rights, but Forfar had laudably refused. Forfar had unearthed a great little player called Alec Troup, who in years to come would win Scottish caps in his career with Dundee and Everton. Frankly, he got the better of Sunny on many occasions and his antics earned the cheers of the large crowd packed into the somewhat primitive Station Park. In a small ground like Station Park, you can of course hear everything that the crowd shout, and Sunny was singled out by a group of yokels who called him "Funny Jim" amidst a few obscenities like "Up yer bum, Jum!" ("Jum" being the local way of saying "Jim"). Even the Celtic supporters, there in large numbers and now relaxed because their team were well on top, were admiring the wiles of Troup, and comparing him with their own Patsy Gallacher.

The game was 5–0 in favour of Celtic and fizzling out towards the end, when Sunny downed Troup in circumstances which a hundred years later would have earned a straight red card. But men were men in 1914, and Troup picked himself up and walked away as referee Mr Mitchell of Falkirk was seen to give Sunny a severe "wigging", pointing clearly to the pavilion behind the goal to indicate that Sunny would be there before everyone else if there were any more of it.

The game finished soon after that, and as the players headed off to the charabanc which would take them to the local Baths where they would change, an elderly lady was seen to approach Sunny with an umbrella, muttering imprecations like, "Foul my Eckie, wid ye, ye durty Gleca bugger!" and swinging her umbrella with aggressive intent at Sunny. This was Troup's mother! Fortunately, the blow was parried, no damage was done, Troup himself was embarrassed by such maternal football hooliganism, and Troup and Young sat beside each other at the dinner after the game at the Queen's Hotel, discussing football.

The Weekly News while eschewing the incident with Sunny and Mrs Troup (the poor lady was in the early stages of dementia, as it later became clear), makes the prediction that Celtic could sign Troup some time in the future, and says that, "Celtic had heard a great deal about Troup – what player of class do they not get to know? – but they scarcely expected their eyes to alight upon another McMenemy in the bud", and says that Patsy Gallacher denied all suggestions that he was going to "lay out Troup" for reasons of jealousy. "He's just a wee lad, like me!" said Patsy.

The following week, something unusual happened in that Celtic lost a game, the first League defeat since 15 September and they conceded their first goal since 13 December. The winners were Falkirk by 1–0 at an overcrowded Brockville, but there were extenuating circumstances in that three Celtic players, Joe Dodds, Jimmy McMenemy and Johnny Browning had remained at home at Celtic Park to play in the Scotland v Wales international. Even at that Celtic had bad luck, for they might have scored near the end in a a game in which both "custodians" were outstanding, Charlie Shaw in particular. This reverse hardly made any difference to Celtic, for they were still six points ahead of Hearts and Rangers.

The quarter-final of the Scottish Cup saw Celtic at Motherwell. Motherwell doubled the admission prices for this game, claiming rather unconvincingly that the prices would, "deter a large crowd and reduce crushing". In fact it was a rather unsubtle piece of profiteering. In spite of this, some 18,000 turned up (some sources give it higher) and they were well rewarded with a thrilling tie which saw Celtic win 3–1. Patsy Gallacher and Jimmy McColl scored for Celtic, then Young marshalled his defence yet again to make sure that no goals were conceded, other than a penalty which is described as "dubious". Then with the score at 2–1 and Motherwell in desperation mounting wave after wave of pressure on the Celtic goal which was "in hot water", Andy McAtee was released by Jimmy McColl to break away at the end and put the issue beyond doubt. *The Evening Citizen* thought that Celtic were lucky but that, "they owe much to little Gallacher", who was now clearly thriving under Young's captaincy.

Celtic were cheered to the echo by their supporters, who frankly did not like Motherwell, for they were perceived to have a strong Orange element in their support. Motherwell had only recently changed their colours from blue to claret and amber, in conscious imitation of Bradford City who had won the English Cup in 1911. They claimed that too many Scottish clubs wore blue, and it was seen as an effort by the Motherwell management to distance themselves from Rangers. Some Celtic supporters had walked from Glasgow, having decided that if they had to pay Motherwell's extortionate prices, they would not be able to afford the train fare. Sunny was impressed by this, and on the charabanc as they passed the cheering supporters, would point out to his team mates, "Look at that! Walkin' a the way fae Glesca! We've tae mak sure that they get guid performances fae us! They deserve it!"

The semi-final was at Ibrox on 28 March against a Third Lanark side who had perhaps peaked too soon after their Glasgow Cup success. They had had a prolonged struggle to get the better of Stevenston United in the previous midweek in the quarter-final and 50,000 saw a very one-sided contest with Celtic scoring twice in the first half through Andy McAtee and Ebeneezer Owers, and then giving nothing away in the second half. "Brigadier" of *The Daily Record and Mail* is disappointed. It reminded him of a tale he once read in *Arabian Nights* when everyone was invited to a banquet and found nothing but empty plates. The guests were then told to "imagine" what the banquet would be like. But "Brigadier" did not have to imagine – for everyone heard - Sunny Jim's stentorian "Shut up the shop, Celtic" bellowed repeatedly all over Ibrox.

Indeed this was the strength of Sunny in this memorable season. Celtic, throughout the ages even up to the present day, have been a team that have enjoyed playing cavalier football. The weakness of this is that goals are conceded far too readily. The historian is often surprised to discover just how many goals the great Lisbon Lion defence of Billy McNeill and Tommy Gemmell actually conceded, and there was of course that awful night in September 1989 against Partizan Belgrade when Celtic played brilliantly, Dziekanowski scored four goals, then a lapse of concentration at the back threw it all away. In 1914, however, Sunny with his iron discipline and concentration, made sure that this did not happen.

His philosophy was that the forwards should be the ball players. McAtee, Gallacher and McMenemy were all skilled football players, and the job of the defence was to kick the ball up the park for them to do the job. He was of the persuasion that football was a simple game, and that defenders should stop the ball from entering their own net. Punts up the field therefore were not to be disdained, "They cannae score fae up there!", he would tell his defenders. "Even if the ba' comes straight back, ye hae time tae get ready for it". It was an astonishingly successful ploy in 1914, for all its simplicity, but then again he had the players to implement it, and the backing of a manager who saw the worth of his inspiring captaincy.

Another defeat of an even more exhausted Third Lanark in midweek on 1 April saw Celtic close in on the League championship, being one point ahead of Rangers but with two games in hand, and then Young was at Hampden on 4 April to see the Scotland v England game which Scottish soldiers would talk and boast about in the trenches in future years. Scotland won 3–1 with McNair and Dodds the full-backs, but the man of the match was undeniably Jimmy McMenemy who teamed up brilliantly with Willie Reid of Rangers to win the game. Of course, Sunny would have loved to have been playing, but he was delighted to see Scotland do so well in a game that would resonate the length and breadth of the British Isles with English newspapers wondering why a Scotsman could have the still slightly treasonous nickname of "Napoleon"!

Celtic then beat Sunny's home town team of Kilmarnock on 8 April. It was a typical 1914 Celtic performance that the supporters had seen all season with Patsy Gallacher scoring in the middle of the first half, and the second half Celtic closing it down with the half-back line of Young. Johnstone and McMaster now freely compared to Young, Loney and Hay of a few years previously with the supporters calling them "the padlock" and even resurrecting the old dicta applied to Willie Loney of "No Road This Way" "The Obliterators" and "Gobbling up everything that came down the middle".

Celtic's glory season was defined in the next four games, three of which were against Hibs. The first was the Scottish Cup Final at Ibrox, called by some the "Irish Cup Final". There was of course in 1914 very much a political dimension to all this, for Irish Home Rule was a hot and topical issue. The Government were determined to give Ireland its much deserved Home Rule, but was being thwarted by the Orange bigots in the North who turned out spurious and bogus nonsense like "Home Rule is Rome Rule". The gathering of the two Scottish teams with strong Irish connections did lead to vigorous support being expressed at Ibrox (of all places!) that day with a strong rendering from both sets of supporters of "God Save Ireland" with all its references to "gallows trees" and "vindictive tyrants" and so on.

Sunny Jim and Alec McNair and a few others of 100% Scottish backgrounds may have been bemused at all this, but they were more aware of the undercurrents between Celtic and Hibs supporters. Hibs and their supporters frankly resented the success of Celtic, and how it was Celtic who now represented the Irish community in Scotland and how Celtic's sustained success had attracted support from the East of Scotland, even from the Protestant population and from those progressive minded people who despised sectarianism and all it stood for. Hibs of course had been slow to abandon their insular "Catholics only" approach and had paid the penalty.

They had had a good team in 1902 when they beat Celtic in the Scottish Cup Final, and in 1903 when they won the Scottish League, but since then, success and Hibs had been strangers, with even in Edinburgh itself, Hearts being clearly the better team.

Thousands arrived from Edinburgh to Glasgow on 11 April on Football Specials, and Ibrox saw serious overcrowding to such an extent that the Hibs team charabanc could hardly get to the ground on time. It was a pity that after such a build-up, the game was a disappointing 0–0 draw, spoiled by a stiff breeze and marked by missed chances by the luckless Ebeneezer Owers who might have put three away. Sunny Jim then rattled the post with a fierce drive from long range – 40 yards according to some accounts – before there was a moment of heart failure and panic for the Celtic defence near the end when Willie Smith of Hibs for once got the better of Eck McNair, but shot wide past a relieved Charlie Shaw.

The replay was scheduled for Thursday 16 April, but before that Celtic had a League game against Queen's Park on the Monday. (Incredibly Hibs also had a game on the Wednesday – the night before the Cup Final replay – against Dumbarton!) Celtic dropped Owers and replaced him with Jimmy McColl who scored twice in the 5–0 defeat of the amateurs who were having a poor season. McColl therefore kept his place for the replay on Thursday night, a game which attracted 40,000 to Ibrox for an early evening kick-off at 5.45 pm.

The teams were;
Celtic: Shaw, McNair and Dodds; Young, Johnstone and McMaster; McAtee, Gallacher, McColl, McMenemy and Browning.
Hibs: Allan, Girdwood and Templeton; Kerr, Paterson and Grosert; Wilson, Fleming, Hendren, Wood and Smith.
Referee: T. Dougray, Barrhead.

Celtic kicked-off facing the strong setting sun and after an initial difficult spell, took complete control with Sunny Jim whose clarion calls of "Come away, boys" and "Get intae that ball" were heard with perfect clarity in the Press Box, as he sprayed passes at will to the excellent forwards. They rounded the

Hibs defence time and time again, and by half-time were three up thanks to two beautiful goals from Jimmy McColl (the second being particularly singled out for praise) and one from Johnny Browning. Browning scored again early in the second half, and although Hibs scored a somewhat fortuitous goal half way through the second half, Celtic remained well on top, showing every sign of easing off and not humiliating their fellow professionals. *The Glasgow Observer*, chortling with delight, says that 8-0 would have been a more appropriate scoreline. Willie Maley was seen to stand up near the end and gesture to referee Tom Dougray that "enough was enough". The Cup was presented by Mr Robertson of Queen's Park and the SFA at the close of the game, and Celtic had now won their ninth Scottish Cup, of which Sunny (and Napoleon) had won six.

The supporters rejoiced long and well into the night, walking back to the east end of the city and their heartlands with their banners and their songs, but Sunny Jim "the Chief of the Clan" in the words of a supporter's poem, had to sternly remind his celebrating players that there were two other trophies still to be won. "Dae ye enjoy seein that?" pointing to the Scottish Cup. "Dae ye want tae see mair? Well, there's still the League and the Charity Cup tae be won, and then we're gaun tae Germany again!".

Two days later on Saturday 18 April Hibs were back in Glasgow to face a Celtic side, full of enthusiasm and needing only a win to secure the Scottish League. "Celtic's ovation was unmistakable, the appearance of the Scottish Cup winners with the Scottish Cup being the signal for resounding cheers", according to *The Evening Citizen* . There is a photograph taken that day of Celtic with the Scottish Cup and Sunny Jim in the middle holding on to the trophy. His fair hair has turned a bit darker, but he is holding on to the trophy in such a way as to dare anyone to take it off him. It is the same grim determination that he had shown all season. On this day before a large, cheering, singing crowd in weather of "dazzling brilliance of the sun" Celtic won comfortably 3–0 against a clearly demoralised and exhausted Hibs team. McMenemy scored the first and the third goals and McColl the second.

This picture was taken on 18 April 1914. Celtic have just won the Scottish cup on the Thursday night and today they will win the Scottish League as well. Sunny has a firm grip on the Scottish Cup

Celtic had now won the Double for the third time, and Rangers' run of three League championships from 1911 until 1913 was now broken. Celtic supporters left Parkhead that afternoon arguing convincingly that their team was the best in the world. They would find *The Evening Citizen* that night congenial reading, "That the Celtic have carried off the National and League honours by sheer merit does not admit of a scintilla of doubt. Throughout the season their form has been magnificently sound and consistent. Flash-in-the-pan displays constitute no part of their curriculum. 'They are a wonderful team' is the common remark of every section of the football public, and perhaps no further eulogy is necessary. Their record is so outstandingly brilliant that to attempt to enlarge in glowing terms upon it savours pretty much of the futility of endeavouring to paint the lily."

Fine poetic stuff for a Saturday night and on the Monday the more august and prosaic *Glasgow Herald* is compelled to agree, conceding that the winners of the Double must be, "brilliant and consistent", and that Celtic were indeed both these things. Credit is paid to management of the club, and Willie Maley is given his place, but the organisation of the team on the field is also a very important component of success. The captain must be enthusiastic, committed, prepared to "die for the cause" and capable of being "infectious in his desire to spread his zeal". This Sunny Jim Young certainly was – and 1914 was not yet finished for Sunny.

In this context we must consider just what a tragedy the events from 1914 to 1918 were. Now obviously a lot of people lost an awful lot in that cataclysm, and one cannot really compare the loss of life with football, but in the context of Scottish football history, we must surely lament the greatest team on earth being deprived of their chance to play in official competition when they were at their prime. No-one in 1914 could have predicted what was about to happen, and in those bright days (those "Sunny" days!) of spring 1914, there was a tremendous spring in the step of Celtic supporters everywhere. Their team was looking virtually unbeatable.

A brilliant cartoon of Sunny Jim with the Scottish Cup of 1914

9 May 1914 saw Celtic at Hampden for the Glasgow Charity Cup semi-final against Queen's Park. The Celtic machine rolled relentlessly on with a 3–0 win, Jimmy McColl scoring twice and Andy McAtee once. Young and Johnstone, however, did not have quite as easy a game as the score would suggest because

they had to deal with, "the dashing runs of A.L. Morton", a young man playing in the centre of the Queen's Park forward line and who would after the war become more famous as Alan Morton, "the wee blue de'il", the legendary left-winger of Rangers.

The final was brought forward to the following Tuesday in view of Celtic's imminent departure on tour to Central Europe, and it was a return to Hampden to take on Third Lanark who had beaten Rangers on corners on Saturday. As it was a Tuesday evening and an unpleasant, rainy, windy night, it was a disappointing crowd of 8,000 which turned up to the shelterless Hampden. It was a pity that so many supporters missed what was a devastating Celtic display.

The teams were;
Celtic: Shaw, McNair and Dodds; Young, Johnstone and McMaster; McAtee, Gallacher, McColl, McMenemy and Browning.
Third Lanark: Brownlie, Lennon and Orr; Rankin, Hannah and Brown; Gibson, Ferguson, Galloway, Smith and Mountford.
Referee: J.W. Vick, Glasgow.

From the time that Sunny Jim hit the bar in the first three minutes, the tie was entirely one-way traffic as Celtic played brilliant football with passes finding the man, the man beating the defender and passing to a colleague. Jimmy Brownlie was arguably the best goalkeeper around at the time (although Celtic supporters talked endlessly about their own "Bonnie Prince Charlie" in the goal) and he deserves credit for keeping the score to 6–0. The defenders all got into the goalscoring mode with Dodds, McMaster and Johnstone all finding the net as well as McColl and a brace from McMenemy.

Celtic had thus won three out of the four available competitions this year, and there could be little doubt that the team had regrouped and that nothing seemed capable of standing between them and saturation success over the next few years. *The Glasgow Observer's* resident poet "J.C.", who, admittedly, seldom reaches the heights of William Wordsworth or Robert Burns, says on this occasion;

What of records they're making and breaking
The fruits of their season's toils
Sure big Sunny's arms are aching
Carrying home the spoils

The team were almost immediately on their way to Europe where an interesting time awaited them. They left St Enoch Station on the following day, Wednesday 13 May at 11.00 am to the skirl of pipes and the cries of good wishes from their adoring support, travelling to London, then Flushing by 7.00 pm on the Thursday, before travelling by sleeper to Dresden on Thursday night, then Vienna on the Friday and Budapest by the Saturday. Interestingly enough Budapest in 1914 is sometimes spelt Buda Pesth, because of course it was a combination of two cities.

On several occasions the diplomatic skills of captain Young were called for! Six games were played, three were won, two were drawn and one lost. On at least two occasions, the referee was not only incompetent but biased as well – one was in Budapest where Celtic were held to a draw by Ferencvaros, and would have won if the referee had given them any decisions at all! Worse happened in Leipzig where Celtic lost 0–1. Herr Hofman the referee stood on the touchline and blew for offside every time Celtic came close. Sunny Jim hit an aimless punt up the field, the goalkeeper and several defenders missed it, the ball went in... and the referee blew for offside! Sunny managed to keep his cool, but only just! Patsy Gallacher added a few more details in an article for *The Sporting Post* years later when he said that the pitch was 180 yards long, the grass was up to one's knees in patches, and when the Germans scored a blatantly offside goal, the referee not only abandoned his stance on the touchline but, "almost kissed the German who scored". There may be a little exaggeration in Patsy's account, but it does seem to have been a rather unsatisfactory game of football!

And then there was the game arranged at short notice and without Celtic's consent against Burnley, the English Cup winners who just happened to be in Budapest at the same time! The proceeds were all for charity, so a team of Celtic's pedigree could hardly refuse such emotional blackmail. It was a tough game played on a bumpy pitch in suffocating heat with a disagreeable character called Jimmy Lindley of Burnley fouling and threatening all the Celtic players with broken legs. Full-time came with the game at 1–1, and the referee ordered extra-time. But the players said that they had had enough and walked off, a riot being narrowly avoided. (Shades of Hampden in 1909!) The Cup was to be played for between Celtic and Burnley in September 1914 at Turf Moor – a game which Celtic won, but the Cup hardly surprisingly did not arrive from Budapest which was on the other side in war-torn Europe!

There were good times as well. The weather was beautiful, the scenery was breathtaking, and the players were treated to concerts and banquets. The Germans were admirable hosts in Berlin, and clearly impressed by Celtic's good football and general sociability with Sunny and others sampling German beer and trying to teach the Germans some Scottish songs. Celtic departed for home in early June with more good memories than bad ones of what had been a generally pleasant tour on the back of an excellent season.

So Sunny returned to Kilmarnock to see Florence and the three children, all now growing and the eldest two who were able to understand, proud of their daddy who was the captain of what was generally agreed to be the greatest football team in the world. Sunny probably had made enough money with Celtic that he didn't need to work in the foundry that summer, but he did so nevertheless, making congenial conversation with his workmates who all enjoyed his company, even the lovers of Kilmarnock and Rangers. One Killie supporter said of Sunny, "I hate the b****** on the field, but he's ma best pal when the game's ower."

Weekends were spent at home with his children and the summer passed pleasantly. The weather was good, and Sunny enjoyed the occasional round of golf and kept training for the new season. He was 32 now, cheerfully accepting the term "veteran", and aware that if he were to stay at the top of his game, he would have to train hard. But he knew where his strength lay – it was his vigour, enthusiasm and commitment. He knew he was not skilful in the sense that McMenemy and Gallacher, or even young McAtee, were but the club needed him no less for that. And what a club it was to belong to! What a man Maley was!

He often speculated on what he would do when his playing days were over. Could he become a trainer, or a coach or a manager? Maybe Maley would retire some day, or (more likely, for Maley loved football and Celtic, and was never likely to contemplate standing aside) would need an assistant? Or Sunny could simply give up the game and just work in the foundry all the time. Or what about doing what so many other football players did, namely run a pub? Yes, that was an idea, for he had now accumulated a nest egg from his football earnings. But in any case, he did not need to think about that for a few years yet. He was still fit and already looking forward to the new season.

The Glasgow Observer tells how he and many other football players were spotted at Prestwick while the Open Championship was being held there. Harry Vardon won his sixth Open Championship, but Sunny gained a special souvenir of a golf ball from Ted Ray, the winner of 1912. Ted Ray was famous for this friendliness and geniality, and of course, Sunny was likewise. Both were overawed in each other's presence, for one was the Open Champion of two years previously and the other was the captain of the football team reckoned by most people to be the best in the world.

He may have noticed in a corner of a newspaper at the end of June that some high ranking Austrian had been shot in Sarajevo. From his travels in Austro-Hungaria he was aware that the Austrians didn't like the Serbs and that the Serbs didn't like them, but like the rest of Britain, he paid little attention to a matter of no real concern to himself. The matter smouldered along throughout July, and it was only when training for the new season got under way in earnest in late July that he noticed that the *Kilmarnock Standard* was beginning to pay more attention to places like Belgrade and Vienna, and that some sort of war had broken out to affect people in Serbia and Budapest.

Sunny was sorry about that, for he had made friends with quite a few people there, and he hated the idea of them picking up a gun and shooting someone they had never met for a cause that nobody seemed to understand. But then with bewildering and stunning speed, the war spread to Germany, Russia, France and within a day or two, Belgium and Great Britain. Suddenly, he was at war with those nice German chaps he had got drunk with two months ago! The Germans and the Austrians had told him that Celtic were the greatest and most famous team on earth, and Maley and he had visibly glowed with appreciation. Now he was expected to shoot them! They were his enemies! It was astonishing!

CHAPTER EIGHT

THE WAR YEARS AT PARKHEAD

1914–1916

The war changed everything. For all the suddenness of its onset, the war within a few weeks changed life in Great Britain radically and in some respects, totally and irreversibly. It has become the habit for history books to imply that the war was inevitable and that everyone knew it was coming sooner or later. Willie Maley himself (hindsight being a wonderful thing for creating delusions) falls into this trap by saying that there were far more men in uniform in Germany and Austria in May 1914 than had been the case previously.

This may have been the case, but it is emphatically not true to say that the war was in any way "planned" or even anticipated. Sunny Jim and his Celtic players as they sailed up the Rhine or drank in a Bierhaus at the end of May would never have dreamed that the two countries would be at war (and a prolonged, bloody and horrible one at that) by the beginning of August. The reader of newspaper files as late as 25 July or 26 will find not the slightest inkling that anyone was preparing for or even thinking of war, and the leader writer of *The Evening Citizen* on 1 July will surely qualify for an award for the least successful prophecy of all time. A few days after the assassination in Sarajevo, the paper reports on some strong anti-Servia (sic) feeling in Vienna and Budapest, but, "this will no doubt spend itself without serious consequences"!

But war came. For all his bellicose nature on the football field, one finds it hard to believe that Sunny would have welcomed this development. Sadly so many young men did and the rush to the colours was remarkable with the predominant emotion being one of excitement at the prospect of an adventure, mingled perhaps with a thrill of patriotism and the expectation of "serving one's country", but with no great fear of what the future would bring. The good weather helped to service such emotions, and euphoria, mingled with war fever, was very definitely in the air.

To a certain extent, this can be explained away by the propaganda of politicians (only a very few like Ramsay MacDonald paused to think) and even the teachings of the Church, which did lamentably and predictably what the politicians asked of it, even if that meant laying aside for a moment the teachings of Jesus Christ. But there was also the undeniable fact that people had poor houses, boring jobs, grim poverty and shocking health conditions with few prospects of any of these things ameliorating in the near future. Life in the Army or Navy suddenly seemed attractive. Better to join up quickly, before the opportunity passed! It might after all, as some people said, be "over by Christmas" or even "before the leaves fall".

Some people wanted football stopped altogether, in that 22 fit young men would be better employed chasing Germans out of Belgium rather than kicking a ball around a football field on a Saturday afternoon. Fortunately that view never prevailed, for the counter argument was of course that football and other entertainments were good for morale on the home front. Indeed the theatre and the infant cinema (with Charlie Chaplin and Douglas Fairbanks) flourished during the years of the conflict, and so too did football, albeit with a few major alterations to its structure. For Celtic supporters during the Great War, football was a wonderful antidote to the horrors that surrounded them in other areas of life.

The main alteration was that full-time professional football was not allowed. Part-time earnings were tolerated but normally a man could play professional football only if he had a full-time job in war related work. This might even include having to do a half-day shift down a mine or in a factory or a shipyard on the Saturday morning. It was no uncommon sight to see a player take the field with dirty legs, having worked in the pit in the morning and not having had time to wash!

For Sunny this meant that whether he was a professional footballer or an Iron Turner before 1914, he was certainly an Iron Turner in a Kilmarnock foundry now. Like the rest of the Celtic team at this early stage of the war he managed to resist the siren calls of the military, and of course conscription would not be an issue until 1916. Maley, for all his patriotism (he was of course the son of a soldier) was very careful, using his wide circle of contacts in the "village" that Glasgow was (and is), to ensure that his fine team of 1914 stayed where it was, working in jobs like mining, shipbuilding or ironworks that were "untouchable" by the military, and comparatively exempt from the emotional and moral blackmail of the young ladies with their white feathers. Celtic players, Maley insisted, were "doing their bit", and more or less every home game at Parkhead would see some sort of recruiting campaign, whether it be a military demonstration with flags and parades of soldiers, or merely a few posters telling young men that their mothers and girlfriends would be proud of them in uniform.

The Scottish Football Association more or less shut up shop for the duration of the war as far as actually playing was concerned. This meant that there would be no Scotland Internationals, and no Scottish Cup – something that Sunny was annoyed about, for his desire for medals was as insatiable as ever. Indeed there seems no logical reason for this because travel restrictions were minimal, at least in the early stages of the war. The English Cup continued until 1915 before it was suspended. But the Scottish League continued throughout, albeit with severe restrictions about midweek games lest they encouraged players themselves or their supporters to absent themselves from their vital war work. For the first season at least there would be League Internationals against their English and Irish equivalents, until problems of transport and logistics of getting men off their work rendered such fixtures impracticable.

The Glasgow and the Glasgow Charity Cups would continue as normal, for there was no travel problem there, and the games provided a great deal of welcome relief to the war weary, the anxious and those who happened to be on leave from the services, or indeed those English soldiers doing their basic training in Scotland or even civilians whose job obliged them to be billeted on the Clyde. Both the Glasgow tournaments took on a new lease of life, as the attendances would confirm.

It would be wrong to assume that wartime football was not taken seriously, as some books imply. Nothing could be further from the truth, because it was all the more vital to take people's minds off the horrors going on elsewhere. People did have money, for unemployment virtually disappeared and everyone had a job with overtime available. Soldiers were, contrary to what they said and believed, well paid. The economy in fact boomed, and being able to afford to go to football was not a problem.

Transport was more of an issue, for trains were notoriously unreliable, and it was not unknown for loudspeaker announcements to be made asking for anyone who had ever refereed a football match at any level to step forward for the official had been delayed. Young boys got their chance earlier than normal, and often Sunny would find himself lining up against a team of young, fresh faced lads, totally different from the gnarled professionals of last season who were now either in France or unable, through logistic reasons or work commitments, to be there. Sometimes the opposite was the case as far as age was concerned with some men playing well into their 40s, and long past the age when a dignified retirement would have been in order.

War having been declared on 4 August, the season started as planned some eleven days later on Saturday 15 August. The weather was fair, (unlike the foul weather which accompanied the Celtic Sports the previous week) and Hearts chose this day to declare open their new stand, the building which is still there today. The crowd was an excellent 20,000. Celtic had a fair representation, but Hearts fans were in the majority and Celtic seemed to be unduly upset by the barracking of a Hearts support which has always had a "thing" about Celtic. The forwards in particular had an off day, McColl missed a penalty, Hearts scored twice and Celtic simply failed to deliver a reply, being described charitably by *The Evening Citizen* as, "rather unlucky" and suffering from, "poor finishing".

It was a chastening experience, considering that it was the same Celtic side which had finished last season so triumphantly, but it was also part of a pattern of Celtic's success in these glory years. A poor start with people asking whether or not Celtic were finished, and captain Young finding that he had critics, but then a regrouping in the winter, a rally and a gradual wearing down of the opposition to finish triumphant yet again.

Indeed in many ways, season 1914–15 was all about Hearts. They placed their Tynecastle stadium at the disposal of the military, their players famously decided to enlist virtually en masse for the war, (a brave if foolish decision commemorated to this day on the War Memorial at Haymarket Station), and it was Hearts who provided the significant opposition to Celtic that year. It was also a year in which they began their melancholy tradition of throwing away League titles that they should have won. In more recent times they have "blown up" on at least three occasions and "fizzled out" on others. In 1959 they lost to Celtic on the last day of the season, and thus 19 April 1959 became the famous day when Celtic won the League for Rangers! In 1965 they needed only to avoid a 0–2 defeat to Kilmarnock at Tynecastle, yet 2–0 for Killie was the score! And of course, a man called Albert Kidd played his glorious part in Celtic history at Dens Park in 1986. In 1998, they lasted the pace admirably against both Celtic and Rangers, until folding miserably with a few games to go. 2006 was a similarly good performance against Celtic until the somewhat predictable "heroic failure".

1915 was different, in that they were relentlessly pursued and worn down by Celtic who simply kept winning their games in the confident hope that their opponents would buckle and crack under the pressure. As in 1968 (when Rangers were the rivals) psychological pressure plays a huge part in football, and it was precisely in this regard that Celtic landed lucky in their inspirational figure Jimmy Young. War or peace made no difference - every game to Sunny Jim was a game to be won. There could be little doubt about his mental toughness.

Following a 3–3 draw with St Mirren on 29 August (the same day as the newspapers reported the German capture and sacking of the lovely Belgian town on Louvain), on 1 September, Celtic had a piece of unfinished business to attend to in Lancashire, playing for the now ludicrously named Budapest Cup! It will be remembered that on tour, the cup winners of England and Scotland played a nasty game which ended 1–1, and both teams refused to play extra-time. After prolonged discussion the teams agreed to play later in Britain, and Burnley won the toss for venue.

Thus Celtic travelled to Turf Moor for the game on 1 September. Sunny and the rest of the Celts were impressed by the sheer numbers of young men in military uniform with kitbags and kilts on the way to join their regiments in Aldershot or Gloucester. The British Army had of course already been in the field at Mons and within a few days would be fighting desperately to save Paris, and already news of casualties were trickling back. The predominant mood at this time, however, was still optimism. Paris would be saved, Germany would agree a truce, Belgium and Serbia would be evacuated of enemy troops, and the war might indeed be over by Christmas!

14,000 were at Turf Moor to see the game in beautiful sunny weather. It continued in the same unpleasant, rough vein as it had begun in Budapest with Celtic reduced to ten men after half an hour. Peter Johnstone was sidelined and Jimmy McMenemy showed his versatility by taking over as centre-half. Once again, though, Sunny roused his men and goals were scored in the second half by Jimmy McColl and Patsy Gallacher before Burnley pulled one back with a late penalty. Celtic could thus claim to be the best team in Britain and indeed Europe (few would argue!) but, of course there was no Cup! It was now well behind enemy lines. Its recovery should, of course, have been a clause in the Treaty of Versailles in 1919 but Lloyd George and "Tiger" Clemenceau let Celtic down badly, and according to James Handley's *The Celtic Story*, the trophy went to, "a professional Middle-European wrestler who won it in a raffle run on behalf of the Austrian Red Cross Fund during the war". Sunny was thus annoyed at not getting another Cup for his beloved Celtic, but there were more pressing matters to deal with.

12 September saw the result which was said with retrospect to have "caused consternation in the trenches". One says "with retrospect" because the trenches had hardly been dug by September 1914, but there can be little doubt that the 2–0 win by Clyde over Celtic in the Glasgow Cup made everyone sit up and take notice. McNair, McMaster and Johnstone were all out with injuries, and in addition Charlie Shaw chose this game to have a horror – misjudging one harmless lob for the first goal, and dropping the ball at the foot of an opponent for the second. 20,000 at Shawfield looked on in horror, but even then the cause was not yet lost, and if a Young free-kick had gone in instead of grazing the post after a deflection, things might have been different for Celtic. As it was, Celtic's poor run in the Glasgow Cup continued, and it was now five years since they had won that trophy.

Further disappointments came Celtic's way in October with a draw at Kirkcaldy against Raith Rovers on the Holiday Monday and a very disappointing defeat to Ayr United at Somerset Park, a defeat all the more galling because the only goal of the game was scored by a young Celtic player currently on loan to Ayr. This was Joe Cassidy who would of course become a Celtic legend in the years after the war. On the day before (9

October) Antwerp had fallen to the advancing Germans, something that was a great blow to the war effort, however much the newspapers tried to talk about "heroic resistance" and "successful evacuation". If people hadn't realised it before, this war would certainly not be "over by Christmas".

The fans however saw something that they never expected to see and that was the return of Jimmy Quinn who had been out of the team for some considerable time with various problems in his knees. Sadly he would not last long in the team before injury finally ruled him out, but he did, in spite of looking "fleshy, slow and cumbersome" win one game for them with a last minute goal against Hamilton Accies on 24 October.

Hallowe'en 1914 saw the visit of Rangers, a team who were struggling, and today Celtic beat them 2–1 to the delight of their fans in the 40,000 crowd, quite a few of them in khaki. Everyone was exhorted to "join up" by a recruiting campaign (which, as we have said, was normal at that stage of the war) with the emphasis on how well you would look in a uniform and detailed information about what the Germans were doing in Belgium. With a view to influencing the Celtic support, presumably, the ill treatment of nuns and the desecration of Roman Catholic cathedrals and monasteries was highlighted and exaggerated. It was a close fought game but Patsy Gallacher scored the decider when Rangers goalkeeper, the Englishman Herbert Lock, could only parry a fierce Quinn drive.

Thus Celtic began the winter months four points behind Hearts and it would stay that way for the rest of 1914 with both teams winning their games, and Celtic gradually recovering from their poor start. Signs of the times were evident however at Rugby Park, Kilmarnock on 7 November when wounded soldiers from Dunlop House Hospital were introduced to the crowd at half-time and given a warm reception. A tournament called the War Relief Fund Shield was played for with Celtic losing narrowly to Rangers in mid December, while in the League they won all their games, sometimes with a bit of luck and often by the odd goal.

Sunny Jim with Patsy Gallacher

Celtic beat Third Lanark 1-0 in mid November in spite of Sunny shooting a penalty straight at the goalkeeper, while he was singled out by the Airdrie crowd for booing the week before Christmas because of his perceived hard tackling of the Airdrie forwards. He loved that sort of thing, of course, but he would hardly have enjoyed the conditions at Pittodrie on 5 December when the game finished in torrential rain and a fierce wind with the crowd having gone home as there was no shelter from the elements. Celtic however won 1-0, helped by the fact that the black and golds finished with only eight fit men. "Nae a day for a wasp tae be oot in!" they said in the Granite City, for Aberdeen were then nicknamed "the wasps"!

At that time, the campaign against professional football was at its height. The Lord Mayor of Cardiff, for example, claimed (improbably) that he was moved to tears by the sight of so many young men going to watch football matches when they should have been enlisting for the conflict, and such "column dodgers" and "lead swingers" were contrasted with the noble bearing of King George V who had donned military uniform to visit the soldiers in France. Pompous letters from nom de plumes like "Magna est Veritas" (the truth is great) filled newspapers equating professional football players with men who would steal their companions' rations and run away in battle. The campaign to have all footballers in the colours, it would have to be said, was not attended by any great logic!

One wonders whether this campaign had any effect on Sunny to encourage him to join up. He was "safe" enough in his job at the foundry in Kilmarnock, where he helped to make equipment for cannons and other military hardware, one assumes. He was also emphatically not the sort of man whom one would have expected to be cat-called in the street for cowardice! He was in every sense a big man, well known and well loved. But he was not really a military man. He would have been a first rate Sergeant Major with his loud voice and his air of expecting to be obeyed, but like most well adjusted men, he had few desires to kill anyone. Besides he was happy at home with his wife and three children. He did not want to see them bereft of a father, and there was also his love of his football and his club. He felt (and he was right) that he did as much for the war effort in his job in Kilmarnock and in terms of morale by playing for Celtic as he would have done in some trench in France.

But as far as Sunny was concerned, the big tragic event at that time was the death of his old friend and colleague Peter Somers. Peter caught a chill at the beginning of November 1914, but this was merely the symptom of some other problem (undiagnosed diabetes possibly) and he had to undergo an operation in the St Andrews Nursing Home in Renfrew Street, Glasgow for the amputation of his left foot and part of his lower left leg. Poor Peter never recovered from the operation and the cause of death was given as "gangrene". Peter was only 36, left a widow and young family and was, at the time of his death, a Director of Hamilton Academical FC as well as owning a "wine and spirit" business. The Glasgow Herald says that, "the standard of Celtic forward play was never higher in standard than in the years that he was with the club".

Sunny was distraught. Peter "the powder monkey" had always been a great character at Celtic soirees and social events. He could play the piano, sing, do impressions, and Sunny recalled him with affection for the way that he had made him feel welcome when he joined the club. Peter had died on Friday 27 November, the team with black arm bands played at Dumbarton on the Saturday winning 4–1 ("Let's win it for Peter" said Sunny) and then, led by Maley, they attended the funeral at the West Cemetery, Westhall Road, Hamilton on the Monday. The weather was foul, but more or less every club in Scotland was represented with Sunny Jim as the captain of Celtic one of the chief mourners. He did his best to comfort Jeannie Somers, the widow, but that was no easy task. She was destined to survive her husband by only a few years.

Having won 11 League games in a row, Celtic opened 1915 with a bad performance, losing 1–2 to Rangers at Ibrox. The New Year celebrations, normally excessive and extreme in George Square and other places in Glasgow, may have been muted this year because of the war, but the enthusiasm of the 45,000 crowd at Ibrox was in no way diminished with the Celtic crowd outshouting their Rangers counterparts even in a losing cause. The conditions were damp but playable, and Sunny Jim made one of his rare mistakes in slipping at the wrong time when Paterson was about to cross for Bowie to score the first goal. Johnny Browning equalized before half-time, but then it was Alec McNair's error which allowed Tommy Cairns "tireless Tommy" (as he became known) to pass to Willie Reid to score Rangers' winner.

Against that, Gallacher and McColl both came close towards the end as Celtic pressed, but it was not to be. Celtic, though disappointed with the result, felt that they had done well enough. "The game was controlled by the losers" said *The Evening Times*. Sunny Jim, putting his hand up to admit his error, then rallied his troops to ensure that there would be no more errors and that Celtic, being Celtic, would fight back. Indeed they did. Clyde, Kilmarnock and Falkirk were defeated and Partick Thistle hammered in a spectacular 6–1 rout, so that Celtic soon made up the two dropped points on New Year's Day. By the time that Hearts arrived at Parkhead on 30 January, the gap was four points, the same as it had been before the New Year. The Hearts game would be a significant one, it was felt.

Those who had campaigned for the stopping of professional football would have thrown their arms up in despair, one imagines, when they discovered that 55,000 appeared at Parkhead! It would have been a big crowd in peace time, but it was an enormous crowd in the circumstances given the unreliability of wartime transport and the undeniable fact that most of the crowd would have worked a half-shift in their wartime jobs in the morning. On the other hand, war, as we have said, brought a certain amount of prosperity (an uncomfortable truism, perhaps) with unemployment virtually a thing of the past and everyone being well paid for their hard work in the munitions and other industries. *The Glasgow Observer* estimates that about 10,000 of the 55,000 were in khaki, an improbably high proportion perhaps but there can be little doubt that anyone on leave with even the slightest interest in football would have made his way to Parkhead that fine, dry afternoon.

Hearts, of course, who had last won the Scottish League in 1897, felt that this could be their year, and they enjoyed a certain amount of neutral support in view of the much stated intention of so many of their men to enlist. In the absence of the Scottish Cup this season, this game was looked upon as the biggest game of the season – "something between an international and a Cup Final", and the result would be much looked forward to in the trenches, for Maley was always very conscientious about despatching telegrams of results to regimental headquarters for distribution to the men.

The game was a good one but Hearts were "fortunate in effecting a draw" according to *The Glasgow Herald,* and Celtic would have won but for a, "pronounced weakness at goal". As it was, the 1–1 draw (Hearts scoring soon after the start, and Celtic at a similar stage of the second half) suited Hearts for it retained the four point differential. Young and Maley in their after match discussion were both in uncomfortable agreement that the said "pronounced weakness at goal" was due to the now ageing and injury-weakened Jimmy Quinn, now in his 37th year. Jimmy was simply now too slow, and it was a shame that his career ended with this game.

All this meant however meant that Celtic had eleven games to play, as did Hearts, and four points (two for a win in 1915) to make up, and they didn't have them to face again that season. All that one can do in these circumstances is to win one's own games and hope that sufficient psychological pressure can be put on the opponents to make them crack. In more modern times, some older supporters will recall the similar scenario of 1968 when Rangers were ahead soon after New Year. All that Stein's men could do was win their own games, spectacularly if possible, and make Rangers crack. Four impressive away wins at St Johnstone, Dundee United, Hearts and Aberdeen made Rangers do just that. 1915 was the forerunner of that season, but this time it was the consistent, dynamic, dominating Sunny Jim that broke the Tynecastle men from a distance.

Help came from an unexpected source on 20 February. As Celtic were limping to an unimpressive 1–0 win over Dumbarton at Parkhead, Rangers (having a very poor season up to now) beat Hearts 4–3 in a thriller at Tynecastle. Indeed it was a more impressive victory for Rangers than it appeared, for they were 4–0 up until "laxity" at the end almost allowed Hearts a draw. More good news came the following week when Hibs took another point off Hearts at Easter Road, while at Firhill, Celtic beat Partick Thistle 2–0. It was a game which followed the familiar pattern of last season – first half goals from Jimmy McColl and a Joe Dodds penalty, then the half-back line of Young, Johnstone and McMaster taking control. This year, however, the imagery in the newspapers was all about "digging in" and "manning the guard posts"!

Seven games remained as winter reluctantly gave way to spring, and Britain planned its mad scheme on Gallipoli and the Dardanelles. 6 March saw both teams win – Hearts 4–1 over Dumbarton and Celtic 5–1 over Hibs. 13 March was a good day for Celtic without them kicking a ball! By prior agreement, they had already played their League game against Dundee earlier in the season, and arranged a friendly against the Irish side, Glentoran. They won that one 3–0, but by full-time, the telegraph had already buzzed to the Press Box that Hearts could only draw at Airdrie, and thus Celtic, if they won their game in hand, could equal Hearts.

20 March, a less happy day, saw Celtic again idle as far as the League was concerned, for Celtic Park was in use for a Scottish League international and four Celtic players (not Young who was now at 33 too old for representative honours) played in the 1–4 defeat to the English League. Meanwhile at Tynecastle, Hearts beat Partick Thistle 3–1. Saturday 27 March saw Glasgow suffer a heavy fall of snow shortly after half-time but this did not prevent Celtic beat Raith Rovers 3–1, but annoyingly in Edinburgh Hearts beat Clyde 2–0. Thus at the end of March, Hearts were still at the top with three games to play and had 60 points, whereas Celtic with five games left had 56. The advantage still lay with the Edinburgh men, who had the decided advantage of having points on the board. Celtic (two points for a win in 1915) could of course equal them, but they had not yet played their games.

It does not seem to have been made clear what would happen in the event of the teams having the same points. A play-off in wartime circumstances did not seem to be likely, and there was no talk about goal average or goal difference. Probably the title would have been shared as had happened in 1891, the first year of the competition, but Young realised that if goal average were to be implemented, the side that lost the fewer goals would have the advantage. Celtic's defence, though not as niggardly as last year, nevertheless was better than Hearts' rearguard, and he was determined to keep it that way. But all he could do was take one game at a time, win it and hope that the news from elsewhere would be favourable. As it turned out, Hearts had three away games – at Aberdeen, Morton and St Mirren whereas Celtic's next four game were inside Glasgow, where they would be well supported, and at Motherwell where the cries of encouragement would be no less.

It was at Aberdeen on 3 April that Hearts began to crack. A feckless performance led to a 0–0 draw (and Aberdeen should have won!) while Celtic took a grip of things by beating Airdrie 3–0 at Parkhead with goals from McColl, Browning and McMenemy. Celtic then played again on the Holiday Monday and now playing confidently and assuredly dished out another 3–0 defeat, this time to Queen's Park at Hampden. Young was outstanding and Celtic were now only one point behind with a game in hand. He was very aware, though, that the League was not yet won, and the shouting at his men continued even as they left the field at Hampden that evening. "Still three games tae play!"

If Hearts cracked at Aberdeen, they then broke comprehensively in two at Morton on 10 April while Celtic defeated Aberdeen at Parkhead. It was a typical Celtic performance – an early goal, through McMenemy this time, then an iron grip with the half-back line giving nothing away, while Hearts had a miserable time at Greenock, losing to a Morton side which contained Stanley Seymour who would become a legend with Newcastle United after the war. Two points would do it now for Celtic and they duly came on 17 April before a good crowd of 20,000 at Cathkin against Third Lanark.

It was like pre-war days with long queues at the turnstiles, a happy Celtic crowd and a 4–0 victory with some tremendous football being played. Two goals were scored in each half, and the news that Hearts had lost yet again was now irrelevant. Celtic in the 25 year history of the Scottish League had been the champions 12 times, and Sunny had been involved in eight of them.

In some ways, this was his best Championship. The circumstances were unreal, and the team had been behind at a very late stage of the campaign, but had rallied and pulled off an unlikely victory. It had been achieved by basic football common sense of defending well, especially when ahead. There were good players in the team, very good players, but even they needed to be nurtured and encouraged and told to believe in themselves. Sunny Jim made sure there was no failing of confidence, either collective or individual.

It is often argued that football was not important in 1915. There were more important things going on, yes, in France and the Dardanelles, but that did not mean that Celtic's triumph was not much appreciated by their many supporters, especially because so many of them were now far from home. The story of German soldiers shouting across No Man's Land to Scottish soldiers, "Hey Jock, Celtic won the League!" may not necessarily be entirely fanciful, for so many Germans would remember Celtic from their tour of last year, and the name Celtic was even in 1915 known throughout the world. If one can believe that "Tommy" and "Fritz" played football on Christmas Day against each other, we can believe that German soldiers knew all about the mighty Glasgow Celtic!

It remains a pity that the SFA decided not to contest the Scottish Cup during the war seasons, but there was still the Glasgow Charity Cup, and then the closest thing that one could get to a representative game in the war – the game for the Belgian Refugee Fund between the Scottish League Champions and the Rest of the Scottish League.

Celtic's passage to the final of the Glasgow Charity Cup was undistinguished but professional – a 2–1 win over Queen's Park at Hampden and then corners required to get the better of Partick Thistle at Firhill to set up a final against Rangers at Ibrox on 8 May. By this time the war really did impinge on football and came very close to home, for this was the day after the sinking off the Irish coast of the Lusitania by the Germans with over 1,000 lives, mainly Americans and many of them children, lost.

Thus the 40,000 crowd were both stunned and angry, and not at each other! A shipbuilding community like Glasgow took the sinking of the Cunard liner very badly. It was indeed an example of Hun barbarism at its worst, and the recruiting speech before the game was listened to with something approaching reverence and a loud cheer rose at the end of what was said, followed by prolonged clapping.

The teams were;
Rangers: Hempsey, Craig and Muir; Gordon, Pursell and Hendry; Duncan, Cunningham, Reid, Cairns and Paterson.
Celtic: Shaw, McNair and McGregor; Young, Johnstone and Dodds; McAtee, Gallacher, McColl, McMenemy and Browning.
Referee: J. Stevenson, Motherwell.

Celtic were without John McMaster, and it was his replacement at left-half Joe Dodds who scored the first goal with a drive from 20 yards. But then, with tackles flying in recklessly, Patsy Gallacher was taken off injured and stayed off until half-time. With Celtic reduced to ten men, Rangers scored twice and Celtic turned round 1–2 down, but crucially, Patsy Gallacher came on to a huge cheer from the Celtic fans in the crowd.

This game now saw another kind of captaincy from Young. Celtic had to come from behind. It was vital to keep composure and not to react to the coarse challenges from Gordon and Hendry. Tirelessly, Young ran around the park, belying his age, shouting, gesticulating and exhorting until they got their reward. Johnny "Smiler" Browning scored within the last ten minutes and then with two minutes left a Celtic cavalry charge saw the ball bobbing about the Rangers penalty area and coming to the ever ready head of Jimmy "Napoleon" McMenemy who promptly disappeared under the congratulations of his team mates. Celtic had now won this trophy for four years in a row and Sunny now had his seventh Glasgow Charity Cup medal.

If there were the slightest doubt that Celtic were the best team in Scotland or that Young was a great captain of the side, it was dispelled the following week when Jimmy McColl in the aftermath of a shoulder charge on the goalkeeper scored the only goal of the game for Celtic against the Rest of the Scottish League at Hampden in the game for the Belgian Refugees. 50,000 were there in fine summer weather (albeit with a hefty breeze), and the season thus ended on a high note. Lord Provost Dunlop was in attendance and appealed for the crowd to join the Territorial Army, at least, if they could not enlist in the colours. Sunny may have considered this as an option but war or no war, he was on a high and could hardly wait for next season for more honours. He had been an ever-present in the Celtic side that season, and it had shown!

Celtic v Rest of the Scottish League. Celtic are playing in their green tops, whereas the Rest of the Scottish League are playing in the Queen's Park strip of black and white hoops. Sunny is next to the army officer in the front row

Yet his appearance that day for Celtic showed another side of his character as well, for on Wednesday 12 May, his father William Young had died the the age of 73 having been ill for some time with carcinoma of the liver. He had lived at 57 West Woodstock Street, Kilmarnock and was described as a Warehouseman. He had faced his last few months with courage, and Sunny Jim often felt that he inherited his father's courage. Certainly his father was very proud of Sunny and indeed all his family. He had attended quite a few of Celtic's games when his son was playing.

Conscription was not yet in force, although such had been the losses in the early months of the war that it was already being contemplated. Sunny hoped that his job as an Iron Turner (a vital, skilled one) would keep him out of the forces, but he also knew that a job at home was no easy number either. There were long hours – usually 5 am to 5 pm – and this left little time for seeing his family, let alone training, and the standard of football, naturally, slipped. In the summer of 1915 he was 33 years old, and pace was now becoming even more of a problem than it had been before.

Yet his love of football and his love of the club kept him going. Indeed season 1915–16 would present even more challenges to Sunny and his captaincy. The first problem concerned one of Celtic's greatest servants and a particular friend of Sunny's, Alec McNair. On 9 August 1915 in Stenhousemuir, Mary McNair, Alec's wife died of a Cardiac Valve disease. She was only 28 and left a young family for Alec to bring up on his own. Alec, described as a "Grate Fitter" was naturally devastated, and would be out of Celtic's side for some time while he tried to pick up the pieces of his life. When he did come back, he had a very poor time of it, gifting goals and generally finding it difficult to concentrate on his football.

Yet Alec was not called "the icicle" for nothing, and he had the maximum support from two quarters to help him through his problems. His family (Mary's father was still alive) rallied to help him with the children, and the other source of support came from Celtic Park. Maley and Young both realised that Alec was far too good a player to be allowed to go to ruin, and that he needed a great deal of help. Such help meant little other than being there for him, being prepared to listen to him if he wanted to talk about things, but without overdoing it and smothering the poor, vulnerable and exhausted Alec. Sunny made the valid point that football was therapeutic, that the Parkhead crowd loved him, and that Mary's family would certainly want him to continue his football if it were to help him in his grief. Alec, for his part, agreed and, magnanimously, made the valid point that he, in 1915, was hardly the only person that was suffering.

More suffering came Celtic's way soon. September and October 1915 were of course the time of the Battle of Loos. Although by no means the wholesale carnage of the Somme in 1916 or the horrendous mud of Passchendale in 1917, this battle saw a huge loss of life, including in one week in early October the brother of Joe Dodds and the brother of Jimmy McMenemy. The game approaching was the Glasgow Cup Final against Rangers, and the dilemma was whether to play them. Maley consulted Young (as he increasingly did on team matters) and they decided to visit both McMenemy and Dodds at their homes and talk to them. The answer was an emphatic "Yes", a brave decision by both men, but also a tribute the great team spirit that abounded at Celtic Park in these days. Once more, Young stressed the beneficial aspect of playing for Celtic with that huge crowd cheering them on.

Up to that point, Celtic had started the season with the able Tom McGregor taking McNair's place, and they had continued the way they left off at the end of the previous season with good wins and a reluctance to concede goals. A difficult game was at Cappielow on 11 September when Celtic won 1–0 against a good Morton side, and the only goal of the game was scored early by no less a person than Sunny Jim himself, thus scoring his first goal since New Year's Day 1914. *The Glasgow Herald* is distinctly catty about this Celtic performance, stating, "…that Celtic were fortunate to score as they did is apparent to those who have a proper appreciation of Bradford as a goalkeeper and Young as a goalscorer". Young himself on the other hand stated emphatically, "Two points for the Cellic (sic)… I'm a prood, prood man."

The first big game of the season was of course the Glasgow Cup Final on 9 October, the game in which Dodds and McMenemy played in spite of recent family bereavements. Any feeling that wartime football was irrelevant was dispelled by the presence of 70,000 at Hampden that day, of whom 25,000 were said to be either soldiers or sailors in full military uniform, many of them English or Irish servicemen (or men from the Dominions like Australia, South Africa or Canada) training in Glasgow or the surrounding district and keen to see a Celtic v Rangers game.

The teams were;
Celtic: Shaw, McNair and Dodds; Young, Johnstone and McMaster; McAtee, Gallacher, McColl, McMenemy and Browning.
Rangers: Lock, Craig and Muir; Gordon, Pursell and Bowie; Duncan, Cunningham, Reid, Cairns and Paterson.
Referee: A. Allan, Glasgow.

It was an astonishing game, won 2–1 by Celtic, but the verdict was given by Rangers supporters as they left the ground with half an hour left to play, so completely in command were Celtic – and yet the the score was only 2–1! Celtic fans in the 1963 Scottish Cup Final would do a similar walkout, but on that occasion the team was 0–3 down and totally out of it. Here, with only one goal in it, it was the stranglehold of Young, Johnstone and McMaster in midfield which guaranteed that Rangers were unlikely to score. Gallacher scored for Celtic, then Paterson equalized, but after Browning, "with the Rangers defence in a fankle" scored Celtic's second in the 30th minute, the game degenerated into one way traffic, "a huge disappointment for the neutrals" and "one goal did not represent the disparity".

If Sunny had been a "prood, prood man" after his goal at Morton, he must have been even more so as the Glasgow Cup was presented at the City Chambers a few days later. Not only had his team outclassed Rangers, but he had personally played his part in rallying the bereaved McNair, Dodds and McMenemy, nurturing the young and inexperienced Gallacher and McColl and taming the potentially wild Browning. And his half-back line of the three tough guys – Young, Johnstone and McMaster, although lacking the sophistication on Young, Loney and Hay of the previous decade, were nevertheless as effective as their predecessors were in taking a grip of the midfield. Young was of course the link. He was also delighted that Celtic had returned to winning ways as far as the Glasgow Cup was concerned, (they had last won it in 1909) and he had now won his sixth medal in that competition.

And yet he was aware that it was difficult to be really happy in the year of 1915 when there was so much suffering, and no real indication of when it was all going to end. Conscription was now inevitable, and although there was still a certain amount, in fact a great deal, of jingoism and patriotism around, the truth could not really be disguised that the people of Great Britain were in for a long fight, and that although the war was not being lost, it was certainly not being won either, as the casualty lists every morning in every newspaper would clearly indicate.

Football continued to be the opium of the masses, but it was a haphazard business sometimes. Celtic beat Hamilton, but then unaccountably went down to St Mirren at home. Alec McNair was loose with a pass to allow the Buddies to score, then during an intense period of Celtic pressure, Joe Dodds missed a penalty, and then in the last minute with even Charlie Shaw joining in the attack to get that elusive equalizer, the Celtic defence was left exposed and St Mirren got a second. Worse came the following week on 30 October when Rangers got revenge for their Glasgow Cup defeat with Alec McNair having another shocker, Gallacher and McMenemy missing easy chances, Gallacher fluffing a penalty and McMenemy and McAtee getting injured.

"That's fitba" the philosophers would claim, but it meant that Celtic had lost ground in their quest for their third successive League title. They beat Aberdeen 3–1 in early November thanks to an inspirational Young-driven late rally after Alec McNair had given away yet another goal, but then Young injured his hand at his work and was unavailable for three games. He resented that because he said that, "Ye dinnae play fitba' wi yer hand", but the problem was that he couldn't work with an injured hand in the foundry, and therefore, in accordance with wartime regulations, he was not allowed to play football either.

The first game he missed was at Tynecastle and he thus had to sit in the stand and watch an abject performance as the team went down 0–2 to a Hearts side who listed two of their men as Private Martin and Private Wilson. This was a clear dig at the Celtic side, and was picked up by the nastier elements in the home crowd who shouted things like "war dodgers" at the Celtic players. There was a pointed recruiting drive at half-time, led by the band of the Royal Scots, a particularly poignant choice, for so many of that Edinburgh based regiment had lost their lives in the Quintinshill railway disaster of May of that year. It was a painful defeat for the Celtic side, but defeat would soon become an alien concept for Celtic!

Sunny was still out for two mundane victories over Kilmarnock at home and Raith Rovers away before he returned in early December. Suddenly with the return of their inspirational captain, Celtic took off with four first class victories before the turn of the year – 6–2 over Queen's Park, 4–0 over Ayr, 4–0 over Partick Thistle and 6–0 over Airdrie. The weather was terrible with loads of rain, and the mood of depression was hardly helped by the news (or the lack of it) from the front where, more than ever, stalemate seemed the order of the day. But once again, Celtic provided some sort of relief for their fans who continued to turn out and support them in good numbers. Celtic thus finished the year of 1915 at the top of the table, ahead of Hearts and Rangers, although Rangers could equal them if they won their games in hand.

"Seldom does one find such unevenly matched teams finish level" is the verdict of *The Glasgow Herald* of the New Year's Day game at Parkhead in which Celtic were so much better than Rangers, but simply could not get the winning goal. The game was played in heavy rain throughout, and the crowd was thus reduced to just 40,000. Celtic scored first through McColl, then Cunningham took advantage of a McMaster miskick to level the scoring. Celtic went 2–1 up through a fine shot by McAtee from the wing and looked very comfortable until Alec McNair made another mistake, this time scoring an own goal from a Duncan cross. Sunny took a share of the blame for this goal, for he shouted, "Ahent ye, Alick" which made McNair think that a Rangers forward was closer than he actually was. McNair decided to concede a corner but unfortunately the ball was travelling too fast and skidded into the net past Charlie Shaw.

All this happened within the first half hour, and in the second half, Celtic now playing against the wind and the rain could not get the ball past Johnny Hempsey in the Rangers goal, and the game stayed at 2–2. This was a disappointment, an injustice perhaps, but it would be the last disappointment until April, for Celtic won every game until then, often spectacularly so, and conceding very few goals. For a while it looked as if Rangers might match them, but by the beginning of March, they had been "psyched out" by the consistent excellence of Young's Celtic. 6–0 over Dumbarton, 5–0 over St Mirren, 5–1 over Hamilton and 4–0 away wins at Third Lanark and Aberdeen meant that no-one could live with this Celtic team.

Once again, we find *The Glasgow Observer* purring with pleasure about this great side with all sorts of hyperbole like "stupendous" and "dazzling" and headlines like "This is the stuff to give the troops" used more than once. There was of course a real point behind all this, because never has there been a time when good news was more needed. Glasgow itself was all agog with the sentencing of John McLean and a few others under the Defence of the Realm Act for "sedition", a trumped up charge for expressing their opposition to the war. Celtic fans, by no means unsympathetic to the "gentle dominie", and increasingly beginning to wonder (to put it mildly) about the purpose of this war, were "soothed in their distress and anxiety" by the performances of their team, led as always by their genial manager and captain, Maley and Young, both of whom represented some kind of stability in a distinctly uncertain world.

Yet the circumstances in which they won the Scottish League were unusual to put it mildly. It could only have happened in wartime. The game at Motherwell on 25 March was postponed because of a heavy fall of snow. Normally in wartime every effort was made to play a game even in slightly unsuitable conditions, but in this case, the referee had no option, for Fir Park was under about a foot of snow. This presented a problem, for games, under war regulations, could only be played on Saturdays or Holiday Mondays, for midweek games might have an adverse effect on war production. Moreover, the League had to be finished by the end of April.

The Holiday Monday (24 April) was already occupied with a game against Third Lanark, and Sunday football was of course still out of the question in Presbyterian Scotland, so there was no real alternative but to play two games on one day. *The Weekly News*, a newspaper which was based in Dundee but sometimes finds it hard to hide its love and admiration for Celtic, thinks that the idea will be for Celtic, "to draft in a few of the men on loan to provincial clubs, and with a leavening of this, meet Raith Rovers and then motor down to Motherwell"

Other teams had played two games on the one Saturday before, but what made 15 April 1916 different was that Celtic won both games, and in doing so, actually won the Scottish League! Contrary to the prediction of *The Weekly News* the only team selection change was at centre-forward where O'Kane was replaced by Cassidy. A further peculiarity was that both of these men were called "Joe" and both had the nickname "trooper" applied to them! And if all that were not enough, Celtic also, in the course of the first game, beat the Scottish League record for the amount of goals scored in a season!

Raith Rovers were smashed or "whacked" (as they said in 1916) 6–0 in the first game with a 3.15 kick-off. The game finished at about 5.00 pm. Celtic did not even bother to change and trooped into a waiting charabanc. (*The Weekly News* says "taxi" and *The Evening Times* talks vaguely about a "fleet of taxicabs", recalling the imagery used in the early weeks of the war when the "taxis" were deployed to take French poilus to the Battle of the Marne from Paris in 1914.) Whatever method of transport, whether horse-driven or motorised, it conveyed them to Motherwell for a 6.00 kick-off.

The Evening Times has a hint of understatement in its headline of "Celtic's Busy Day". *The Daily Record and Mail* clearly believes that all this is too much work for one writer, because "Grampian" reports the Raith Rovers game, then "Clydebridge" the Motherwell game, and "Clydebridge" waxes poetic about the game when he said that, "it commenced amid the slanting rays of the setting sun and concluded under the pale moonlight". Maley and his old friend and adversary John "Sailor" Hunter, now manager of Motherwell after his heroic playing career with Liverpool and Dundee, agreed with the referee that no matter how dark, the game would be finished. There would be no "appeals against the light". That's what they did in cricket!

There was perhaps a cup of tea awaiting for Celtic at Fir Park, but there would have been no more than that. Motherwell had also played that afternoon (losing 0–3 to Ayr United) and were generous enough to allow their supporters to see two games for one admission charge. The game finished by "pale moonlight" as "Clydebridge" put it, and the players did not even have a half-time interval, simply changing over at half-time, and one could imagine that the pace slackened just a little in the second half. Yet there seemed no stopping Young's Celts. Indeed, "Clydebridge" singles out Motherwell's goalkeeper Rundell for praise for keeping the score down. Celtic won 3–1 with goals from McMenemy, Browning and a penalty from Joe Dodds. Thus Celtic appear to be the only team in world history to win two games in one day and win the League in so doing.

It was indeed a rather odd way to win the League, but that in no way lessened the celebrations or the joy that it gave the supporters both home and abroad, with the newspapers, even those with no particular love of the Celtic, acknowledging their deserved success. Sunny's ability to be a winner shone through once again. Celtic had won three League titles in a row, and Sunny was confident that more were forthcoming. Once again, no doubt, he cursed the SFA for cancelling the Scottish Cup, for he felt (not entirely without cause) that Celtic would have won it. They had succeeded in almost paralysing most of the opposition in other competitions. And they did it without the injured Peter Johnstone!

The Glasgow Charity Cup was played in the month of May. This was allowed because it was technically amateur football, as all players were traditionally expected to play for nothing and the proceeds all went to charity. It was played with Celtic supporters rather mystified by the goings on in Ireland where there had been some sort of rebellion at the Post Office in Sackville Street, Dublin on Easter Monday. The leaders were in early May being summarily executed in a way which even some Liberal and Labour MPs in the House of Commons were upset about, saying that executing a man without trial was "not British" and smacked of "Hunnish justice". Celtic supporters, who of course could only read the very biased accounts in the British press, were confused.

They were not confused however by what was happening in the pitch. Celtic had received a bye into the semi-final, and thus Rangers came to Celtic Park on Saturday 6 May. 30,000 appeared on a day of downpours with the newspapers full of a renewed German offensive on Verdun and a strange story from Dublin about how one of the Irish rebels Joseph Plunkett had been allowed to marry his girlfriend Grace Gifford in Kilmainham Gaol (*The Glasgow Herald* erroneously says Richmond Barracks) before being executed. Rangers had recruited Stanley Seymour from Morton, and had brought back Alec Bennett in a desperate effort to stem the relentless tide of Celtic success, but the game was as one-sided as the 3–0 scoreline suggests. Sunny Jim had one of his best ever games for the club, putting the shackles on Rangers' danger man Tommy Cairns – often called "tireless Tommy" for his energy but today "he never got a kick o' the ba'"- and scoring himself the second goal. The other goals came from McMenemy and McAtee, and rarely had Celtic supporters left Parkhead as happy as they did that day.

The final was scheduled for the following Saturday, but before that there was a certain piece of football nostalgia as Young, Loney and Hay came together to play for a Celtic XI against an Ayrshire XI in a light hearted game for charity at Saltcoats. A young Matt Smith who would after the war go on to be a Kilmarnock legend was thus able to boast to his fellow soldiers in Mesopotamia in 1918 that he had scored a goal against Young, Loney and Hay! Matt was the grandfather of Gordon Smith, of Kilmarnock and Rangers fame.

26,000 came to Hampden to see the Glasgow Charity Cup Final on 13 May. Once again the weather was disagreeable, and once again the Celtic supporters, at least, were disturbed by news of what was happening in Dublin. Stories of the Scotsman from Edinburgh being shot in a chair because he was so badly wounded that he couldn't stand to face the firing squad may or may not have been true – surely too fanciful for belief? - but certainly the order from General John Greenfel Maxwell prohibiting political meetings and the night time curfew that had been imposed throughout Dublin seemed to sit ill with a country that was fighting a war for the freedom of Belgium and Serbia.

The football however took people's mind off such considerations.

The teams were;
Celtic: Shaw, McNair and Dodds; Young, Johnstone and McMaster; McAtee, Gallacher, O'Kane, McMenemy and Browning.
Partick Thistle: Neil, Adams and Bulloch; Morrison, Hamilton and McMullan; Honeyman, Ramsay, Whittle, McTavish and Branscombe.
Referee: A Allan, Glasgow.

Sunny Jim had clearly caught the goal scoring bug for he scored again today, and this time it was a brilliant effort from long range on the 30th minute. Then Patsy Gallacher beat everyone in a mazy run and scored a second to put Celtic 2–0 up at half-time. The shutters then came down in the second half, the play was described as "insipid and uninteresting" as Young, Johnstone and McMaster saw more silver for Celtic. It was their fifth successive Glasgow Charity Cup and Young's eighth medal in that competition.

Celtic had thus emulated 1908 in that they had won every competition entered (sadly, of course, there was no Scottish Cup) and it was a shame that the last game of the season against the Rest of the Scottish League was lost. It was a narrow 0–1 defeat, with the goal coming from Jocky Simpson of Falkirk very late in the game. 50,000 folk however paid their money for the War Relief Fund and enjoyed the game, with Celtic praised for the sporting behaviour and described as the "better-knit" eleven.

Thus finished another season for Celtic. Summer 1916 was the time of the indecisive naval Battle of Jutland, and the wait for the "push" in France. The

French were beginning to crack at Verdun and a British offensive was required further north. Soldiers were given leave in late May and June so that they would be in tiptop condition for the "push" when it did come. It came on 1 July, and it was very soon obvious that it was less than a total success. Indeed it was a colossal military disaster, and became known as the Battle of the Somme.

Sunny, like everyone else, was aware of all this going on, but continued his work in the foundry and looked forward to the new football season. Sometimes however, he wondered about the war. Perhaps John McLean and Ramsay MacDonald may have had a point? But he, Sunny Jim, was 34 and still fit and raring to go. Could Celtic win everything this year again, and could they win four League Championships in a row? They would have to do so, Sunny reckoned, without Peter Johnstone who had now "joined the sodgers" and was in the Argyll and Sutherland Highlanders. He did not however reckon on the fact that they would have to do without Sunny Jim himself. Summer 1916 was as good as it was going to get, as far as football was concerned, for Sunny Jim Young.

CHAPTER NINE

1916 – 1922

THE POST CELTIC YEARS

Summer 1916 was of course dominated by the Somme offensive which began on 1 July. It turned out to be the greatest military disaster in British history, but of course it was not portrayed like that at the time – nor indeed for many years after. The newspapers were all enthusiastic about the "push" and headlines like "hit 'em for six", "Huns in headlong race back to Berlin" and "hitting Huns all round" were prevalent, whereas in other parts of the same newspapers, the appalling numbers of casualties and death notices gave a more realistic and considerably more sombre picture.

Sunny Jim and other footballers may have wondered if they were to be conscripted or not. Sunny was 34, possibly a trifle too old, although a "comb out" was threatened even of what had previously been looked upon as reserved occupations like iron turning. In the meantime all he could do was wait and see. He still of course had to try his best to keep fit for the football season, which would start as usual in August.

His family were of course now growing up. What they felt about their illustrious father is not known, but probably at that age, it did not matter too much that their father was captain of the great Celtic team. He was just their dad. Florence or Flora or Flo, as she was called, was a faithful wife, totally devoted to her husband, as he was to her. Perhaps by now she had begun to understand the broad Ayrshire accent!

The new football season began on 19 August at Love Street. The crowd was 15,000, showing yet again the appetite for wartime football, and Celtic began more or less where they had finished the season before. They beat the Buddies 5–1, but Young was seen to be limping near the end of game with a knee injury. It was a bad one (although there are no precise details about what it actually was) and much to his disgust, one feels, Young was compelled to miss the next game against Hibs at Parkhead. From his seat on the pavilion balcony, however, he watched a 3–1 victory – a victory tarnished a little by the news that Johnny McMaster had been called up to the Army Service Corps, in spite of him being slightly deaf!

In more normal times, perhaps, and with a less fanatical and obsessive player, it would have been an idea to rest his knee for a few weeks, but he turned out for the next three League games as the team beat Ayr United, Airdrie and Motherwell. By the time that Rangers came to Parkhead for the Glasgow Cup semi-final on 23 September, the other two members of the half-back line, Peter Johnstone and John McMaster were listed as "Private Johnstone" and "Private McMaster". Peter Johnstone in fact travelled all night from his base in Southern England to play in this game, such was the team spirit at Parkhead. Peter and 50,000 fans were rewarded with a 3–0 victory, all goals coming in the last quarter of an hour.

The journey of Johnstone from Southern England in wartime was typical of the ability of Maley and Young to persuade people to go the extra mile (or in this case many miles!) for the club. The pair of them believed (and their lives proved it) that the club was of so much importance to so many people "now scattered on many a shore" (as the words of a supporters' song put it) that every effort had to be made by everyone to produce the best results. Jimmy Gordon, the captain of Rangers, a tough uncompromising character and himself a good player, and (off the field) a good friend of Sunny has to admire what Celtic can do, writing in the *Weekly News,* "New players...in a few short months become affected by the Celtic atmosphere and they form part of a very smoothly running machine, and proceed to do their bit in the way of creating more and greater club records". This was in the context of how men like Peter Johnstone, Jimmy McColl and Johnny McMaster had slipped seamlessly over the past few years into the Celtic club and produced the goods.

Sunny was looking forward to the Glasgow Cup Final, but first on 30 September 1916 was the visit of Hearts. This game was fated to be Sunny's last game for the club. What seems to have happened is that he should have given his knee more of a rest after the St Mirren game, but ignoring medical advice, he went out to play, this time damaging his knee irretrievably. Maley always talked about the damage occurring in that "game at Paisley", and he was probably right, but it was certainly the Hearts game in which Sunny hobbled off for the last time. Celtic won the game 1–0 with a goal from Johnny Browning.

Painful times now beckoned for Sunny, painful in both senses with a long time of hospital visits before an unsuccessful operation in February 1917, but painful also in the sense that he could not play his beloved game for his beloved team. By the end of the season, Sunny, now walking with a stick, announced his retirement from the game. Probably at his age he would have had to retire in any case sooner or later (although a large amount of players played on until their 40s in wartime circumstances) but the injury left him with no option.

The one good thing that this injury did was that it saved Sunny from any chance of being called up to the colours. This possibly would have been unlikely anyway given his essential job, but aged 35 in January 1917 and walking with a permanent limp meant that he was saved from the slaughter. (Some of his colleagues were less lucky, notably Peter Johnstone who fell at Aras in 1917, and Donnie "Slasher" McLeod who had joined Middlesbrough in 1908 and was killed in Flanders in October 1917.) We are told laconically by *The Weekly News* of 3 March 1917 that, "Jimmy Young (Celtic) has now left hospital after three months treatment." The announcement of his retiral from the game came a few weeks later.

"Man In The Know" in *The Glasgow Observer* is delighted to meet Sunny in May 1917 when Celtic beat Rangers 2–0 in the semi-final of the Glasgow Charity Cup. "No one was more delighted with the result that our friend Young who came up from Kilmarnock with the sunniest of smiles, but, I regret to say, the stiffest of legs. Poor Young is now finished with football, his knee-joint is quite ruined, and far from showing us any of these acrobatic stunts, those marvellous head swishes or back-heel overhead returns (sic), the old Celt will never be able to walk properly again. He will be a "stiffy" for life, but I undertand he will be able to carry on as a fully qualified engineer or fitter, so his financial future is assured. It is a sad ending to the 14 years faithful service at Parkhead, and I feel certain the directors will give the club following an opportunity to prove thay have not forgotten the part the sunny one has helped to pile up rewards galore". The "sunny one" was back the following week to see them at Hampden beat Queen's Park 1–0 to win the final of the Glasgow Charity Cup for the sixth year in a row!

Sunny and son, taken about 1916

We are now less sure of what exactly he did, but presumably, whenever he was well enough to do so, he returned, as "Man In The Know" predicted, to the foundry to work for the duration of the war which finished, of course, on 11 November 1918. He then went into a partnership with his old friend Bobby Templeton to run a pub (called the Royal bar or sometimes the Royal Hotel) in Duke Street, Kilmarnock. Some sources say that it was in George Street that the pub was situated. It is possible that they ran two pubs. Templeton had been in the licensing trade for several years, and what probably happened is that some time after the end of the war, Templeton had approached Sunny with a view to joining him.

They had parted company in the footballing sense when Templeton left Celtic Park in 1907 but Templeton had not gone far. Apart from a very brief time with Fulham, Templeton played for Kilmarnock, and the two remained friends. In fact, Maley may well have made a mistake in letting Templeton go, for he was twice capped for Scotland while with Kilmarnock, playing with distinction in the Scotland team that beat England in "Jimmy Quinn's" international of 1910 and also in the creditable 1–1 draw of 1912. But Maley blamed Templeton (unfairly and disproportionately) for the loss of the Glasgow Charity Cup Final in 1907, which prevented Celtic winning a grand slam of trophies that year, the offence being compounded by more Templeton indiscretions on and off the field on the tour of Denmark a few weeks later.

Young and Templeton were indeed in many respects similar characters. Both were very sociable and friendly with an ideal disposition for running a bar. Sunny's injury would not have prevented him pouring and serving beer, and he would have been a fund of stories for his clientele, whether they supported Celtic, Rangers, Kilmarnock or anyone else.

Both Templeton and Young had been great footballers, the difference being that Templeton had been more of a soldier of fortune and more "gallus", perhaps, as witnessed by his entry into a lion's cage one night. This happened in August 1908 after he had played a game for Kilmarnock against Celtic. Celtic had won 5–1, but the two friends Young and Templeton and some others then went off to see the Bostock and Wombwell's menagerie of animals in New City Road, Glasgow. For a bet, Templeton went into the cage, twisted the tail of the lion and then came our again to be awarded a gold medal for bravery by the delighted proprietors, who naturally saw advertising advantages in newspaper headlines of, "Scotland International and Lion!"

Sunny did not lack courage, but drew the line at confronting lions. And once Sunny had found his spiritual home at Celtic Park, he stayed there. Maley did not like Templeton's showing off very much ("a silly, selfish display" he described Templeton's performance in the 1907 Glasgow Charity Cup Final) and perhaps distrusted him, whereas Maley and Sunny had a tremendous mutual respect for each other.

Templeton had more flair and class, but Sunny won more medals. Templeton was an accomplished singer, as distinct from Sunny who was merely an enthusiastic one (both were fervent fans of Robert Burns), and he was well known on the local stage as an artiste in operas and concerts. It was always said that Templeton, known as the "Blue Streak" was indirectly responsible for the Ibrox disaster of 1902 in that the crowd all leaned forward at one time to see him pick up a cross ball and charge down the left-wing.

On Wednesday 4 January 1918, Sunny Jim was granted a benefit match. 25,000 turned up to see a game nominally involving Celtic and the Scottish League, but with guest players allowed on both sides, because so many players (like McMenemy and Gallacher) would be unavailable because of essential war work. The crowd was an astonishing one, given that it was a working day for most of Glasgow and can be put into perspective by the knowledge that only 12,000 were at Shawfield the previous day to see Clyde play Celtic in a League match. The game itself was a disappointing 0–0 draw on a hard pitch, but Sunny earned the colossal amount of £1,000.

The teams were;
Celtic: Shaw, McNair and Dodds; McStay, Cringan and Hamill; Aitken (Queen's Park), Rankin (Motherwell); Clark (St Mirren); Bauchop (Bradford City) and Browning.
League Select: Lawrence (Newcastle), Templeton (Hibs) and Taylor (Burnley); Cuggy (Sunderland), Dixon (Rangers) and Walls (St Mirren); Simpson (Falkirk), Holley (Sunderland), Thornley (Manchester City) Wilson (Sheffield Wednesday) and Morton (Queen's Park).
Referee: A. Allan, Glasgow.

The linesmen were Sunny's old tea mates Willie Loney and Jimmy Quinn, and the pavilion was full of people who had played with him, and one or two of an earlier vintage like James McLaren, "the Auld General". When he appeared to have his photograph taken with the players, wearing a bonnet and leaning heavily on a stick, he was given a great reception by a crowd who recognised a truly great Celt.

This is a picture of Sunny's benefit in January 1918. Sunny is barely recognisable with his bonnet and stick

Almost two years later, and with the war now over for about a year, Sunny was dealt a terrible blow. Tragically on the morning of Sunday 2 November 1919, Bobby Templeton collapsed and died "while pulling in his boots" at his home in Grange Knowe, Kilmarnock. He was only 40 and died of a heart seizure. This was a shock to all Kilmarnock and to Sunny Jim in particular who thus became the sole licensee of the Royal Hotel in Duke Street.

Sunny had always been a great local Kilmarnock character, but now he was even more so. His family was growing up, and he remained a great family man, worshipped by his two daughters and one son, and greatly loved by his faithful Florence. He still followed football with a passion, being frequently seen at Rugby Park or Celtic Park (often with Bobby Templeton until the latter's death) where he was always made very welcome. Celtic won the League in 1917, 1919 and 1922, whereas Killie delighted their supporters by winning the Scottish Cup in the first full season after the war, beating Albion Rovers at Hampden before a crowd which some sources give as 95,000.

Limping around Kilmarnock, and behind the bar, Sunny was very aware that his injuries were mild in comparison with so many others. The soldiers started to come back soon after the Armistice, and the trickle became a flood all through 1919. These were hard times, not really the triumph that had been expected, ("If that was a victory, I wouldn't have liked to see a defeat" was a common refrain in 1919) and for those who avoided death and injury in the war, there was also the Spanish flu which raged through all of Europe in 1918 and 1919. In comparison with all this, Sunny knew that he was lucky to get off with a badly injured knee, sustained in playing a game that he loved.

He would always talk to anyone about football. He was particularly willing to talk to newspapers. *The Weekly News,* for example, sent a man to interview him and describes Sunny as "cheery" and "likeable", and tells how he would regale his clientele with stories of Maley, McMenemy, Gallacher, Scottish Cup Finals, the time he got lost in Germany, the time they won the League by playing eight games in 12 days and the other time when they won the League by winning two games on the one day! He would also tell of his trips to England and Europe, adding no doubt a few spicy details for the benefit of his customers. He would even boast that, limp or no limp, he could still dance, run about, and would jokingly say after a Celtic defeat that he was expecting a phone call from Willie Maley about a come-back. He was a larger than life character, with a welcome smile for everyone and a great ability (so vital in the licensing trade) of remembering people's faces and names.

He retained friendship with many of his old colleagues. McLeod and Johnstone were killed in the war, Mulrooney, Somers and Templeton died of illness but the others were still alive and well with McMenemy winning a Scottish cap in 1920 and a Scottish Cup medal as late as 1921 (with Partick Thistle). McNair kept going strong until 1925 and Patsy Gallacher was still playing for Falkirk a good few years after that. And of course Willie Maley remained the boss, even though the team now won fewer honours with the balance of power now clearly swinging to Rangers. There were those who said this was because Celtic lacked an inspirational figure on the field like Sunny Jim had been. Indeed the loss of the Scottish League to Rangers in 1918 was ascribed to just that.

On Monday 4 September 1922 two of his friends from Darvel, Joseph Deans and Andrew Shearer appeared in the pub and invited him to come with them to do some rabbit shooting at a spot near Darvel. They had just been in town buying some ammunition, and the invitation was a tempting one. Sunny was a good shot. Making arrangements for someone to run the bar for the rest of the day, Sunny agreed to go. Very few people in 1922 owned a motor car, but Deans had a motor cycle and sidecar. Sunny was offered the chance to go in the sidecar, but said he'd prefer to travel on the pillion behind Deans, allowing Shearer to travel in the sidecar.

They were travelling along the road to Darvel and reached the Wellington Bridge between Kilmarnock and Hurlford at about 2.00 pm. At this spot the road narrowed. Possibly they were travelling a little too fast (it is possible that Deans may have had a drink at Sunny's pub before he left, although there was no charge to this effect, and indeed the court of inquiry three weeks later decreed that it was a total accident) and maybe the driver of the Kilmarnock Corporation tramcar heading to Kilmarnock was similarly travelling too fast, but for whatever reason, they collided. Deans claimed he was trying to avoid other traffic and did not see the tramcar until it was too late. Shearer in the sidecar was badly shaken, but Deans and Young were thrown off the motor bike. Deans landed in the grass which cushioned the blow and his injuries were minimised, but Sunny was less lucky, hitting the hard ground and injuring his head and his chest.

At first the injuries did not seem to be too serious. Sunny was stunned for a spell but when he regained consciousness, complained of severe pains in his chest. As a precaution, he was taken to Kilmarnock Infirmary, but when the distressed Florence came to see him, he was able to reassure her that he would be better by the morning. This was about 4.00 pm, but unfortunately he had sustained some very serious internal injuries in his chest, and passed away shortly after 6.00 pm.

The news spread like wildfire throughout Kilmarnock, and very soon, folk had gathered at street corners to console each other and to talk about their loss. Joseph Deans was allowed home to Darvel later than night, but his wife kept quiet about Sunny for some time, until he himself was well enough to hear the awful news.

When the news reached Glasgow, there was a certain poignancy about what else was going on that day. Willie Maley had found a young man with prodigious talent (almost as good as Patsy Gallacher) but little self-discipline whom he had decided to sell to Third Lanark. This was Tommy McInally.

The manager of Third Lanark at that time was no less a person than Alec Bennett, right-winger of the great Celtic side of 1907 and 1908, and it may be that Maley and Bennett were together discussing business when they heard the news.

Maley was absolutely shattered by this news. It may be that he had a hankering for Sunny to be his successor, eventually, and indeed occasionally by a Freudian slip, he was known to spell Young's nickname as "Sonny" rather than "Sunny". He was a man who did not cope with grief very well (after the death of John Thomson a decade later, he showed clear signs of clinical depression) and it is no coincidence that the fortunes of Celtic took a distinct dip after the events of 4 September 1922.

The Evening Times of the following day pays a wholesome tribute to Sunny Jim. It says that, "his good qualities were not recognised as they might have been" in a reference to his comparative lack of International caps, and sums up his contribution to Celtic by saying that, "surely never was a club better served than Celtic by Sunny Jim". The funeral was held on Wednesday 6 September. The service was performed by Andrew Aitken (by sheer coincidence the name of the man who had kept Sunny out of the Scotland team on so many occasions) of the Grange United Free Church after the cortege had wound its way from 10 Hill Street where the family now lived. *The Kilmarnock Herald* has this impressive account of his funeral.

"Amidst many manifestations of grief and sorrow, his remains were interred in the New Cemetery, Kilmarnock on Wednesday afternoon. The funeral was public and took place from the deceased's house in Hill Street. It was attended by a large number of relatives and friends, including many prominent businessmen, and also many noted football players, amongst whom were J. McMenemy, P. Gallacher, A. Bennett, J. Dodds and A. McNair. Mr Malley (sic) the popular director of Celtic Football Club was also present. The wreaths sent were so many that a special carriage was requisitioned to carry them. The coffin was an oak one. The streets through which the cortege had to pass on its way to the cemetery were densely populated ; in fact the whole adult population of the town seemed to have turned out to pay their last tribute of respect to one who for many years had been the darling of the football public. As the sad procession slowly wended its way through the streets, hats and caps were doffed reverently and one heard expressions of the deepest sorrow and regret that the career of "Sunny Jim" had been brought to an end in such a sad and tragic manner. In addition to the mourners, a large crowd assembled at the graveside, where a short burial service was conducted."

Sunny's gravestone in Grassyards Cemetery, Kilmarnock

The journalist of *The Weekly News* describes Sunny as, "the best known Celtic player on any provincial ground during the long period of his connection with the Green and Whites" and goes on to say, "A cheery likeable chap was Jimmy Young. His bark was always worse than his bite, and many a young player who started his career just a little afraid of the tall, strapping half-back grew to admire him. He dearly loved a "baur" *(an Ayrshire word for a joke)* and many tales he would tell of his peccadilloes when touring with the Celts and even on some of their home jaunts. To hear "Sunny" and Bobby Templeton try to outdo each other in the story telling line was a treat. And now they are both gone and Kilmarnock is the poorer for the loss of two of her most gifted footballers.

Like Jimmy Quinn "Sunny" used to visit Parkhead very frequently. Always when there was something big on you found the two of them hob-nobbing in front of the pavilion. Young will be missed. The last time I saw him he was in a most cheery mood on account of an improvement of his injured leg. 'See that?' he said, 'I can do a bit of a step dance with the old chap yet' and he did a few steps of a jig on the floor of his establishment in Kilmarnock. Yes, he was a cheery soul."

"Man In The Know" in *The Glasgow Observer* says, "His wonderful individuality made him a world celebrity and many jokes and stories centre round his cheery name. Nobody ever thought of calling him Young. 'Sunny' he was, and 'Sunny' he will remain." He then goes on to tell two possibly apocryphal stories about Sunny. One was when he scored two own goals in a benefit match in which Willie Loney was playing in goal, and the other was when the ball disappeared over the North enclosure roof one day into Janefield Street and was taking a while to come back. There not apparently being a replacement ball, Sunny's loud booming voice was heard all over Parkhead "Ach, never mind the ba'. Get oan wi' the gemme".

The flags were at half mast when Raith Rovers came to Celtic Park on 9 September (a game which marked, incidentally, the debut for the Kirkcaldy side of Alec James, future Wembley Wizard and stalwart of Arsenal, renowned for his baggy pants). It was the second home game in a row that there had been signs of mourning at Celtic Park, for two weeks previously, the flags at Parkhead had similarly been lowered for Michael Collins, the Irish freedom fighter, killed by republicans in an ambush in the Irish Civil War.

In Sunny Jim Young, there perished one of Celtic's greatest sons. As to how good he was, we can argue, but the general consensus seems to have been that, although he was not the greatest ever player in the technical sense, and certainly inferior to at least four subsequent Celtic right-halves in Peter Wilson, Bobby Evans, Pat Crerand and Bobby Murdoch, his contribution to the sustained success of the Celtic side of that time was truly immense and indeed pivotal and axiomatic. He was the *sine qua non*. Only in one season from 1903 until 1916 did Celtic fail to win either the Scottish League or the Scottish Cup – and that was 1912–13 when there was at least a sting in the tail with the Glasgow Charity Cup. But even during that season Sunny was working hard to develop the prodigious talent of Patsy Gallacher, and to a lesser extent Andy McAtee.

Thus Sunny won nine Scottish League medals, six Scottish Cup medals, six Glasgow Cup medals and eight Glasgow Charity Cup medals, a total exceeded only by his friend, the gifted Jimmy McMenemy. But success cannot be counted in medals alone. There was also the psychological and propaganda effect that he had on the rest of the team with his ability to encourage and develop others. For so long, Sunny Jim Young was Celtic on the field. Even before he became captain officially in 1911, he was influential in his taking command of the situation and barking out orders. The real captains Willie Orr and James Hay were tolerant of his doing so, realising that he was simply that kind of a man.

On the International front, his tally of one Scottish cap and six Scottish League appearances seems meagre, but it is probably a fair reflection on his ability. He never let Scotland or the Scottish League down, but we must also remember that he lived in a golden age of Scottish football when Scotland beat England more often than not, there were many rivals for the spot and the normal choice for right-half was Andy "the Daddler" Aitken, the star of the mighty Newcastle United team which dominated English football almost to the extent that Celtic dominated the Scottish scene. Nevertheless, the fact that Sunny never ever represented Scotland in a full International against England was a source of great disappointment to him. Yet he never moaned about it, and always wholeheartedly supported Scotland.

The fact that he personified Celtic for so long and yet was a Protestant (nominally, at least) is a matter of little concern or interest to us a century later, and yet at the time, it possibly was significant. The Celtic club, young but ambitious, owed its strength to its support, largely (but not exclusively) culled from the Irish community. There were those among their support who felt prickly and insecure of their status and there probably would have been a faction who would have welcomed a "Catholics only" policy, as indeed Hibs had – to their cost - for a spell.

But visionary men like Maley and Kelly would have no truck with this inward-looking nonsense, and from an early stage, people of all religions and denominations were welcome. Sunny's religious origins were never an issue, he and others like Jimmy Hay and Alec McNair were welcomed. The spin-off was that Celtic could now attract supporters from all over Scotland from every religion, and as relevantly, men like McMenemy and Quinn, of Scottish birth but undeniable Irish roots, could become heroes of Scotland. Quinn, for example, was the hero of Scotland in 1910 when Scotland beat England at Hampden, and McMenemy was likewise in 1914.

Sunny Jim Young – Celtic Legend

Sunny Jim Young could not have been a better example of the developing Scottishness of Celtic. The fact that he was so all-pervasive, ubiquitous and prominent, on and off the field, took the edge off the arguments of the bigots who sneered at Celtic for being Irish. The ground had been cut from under their feet, in the same way that Jock Stein would do in the late 1960s.

Perhaps it is relevant to consider Celtic before and after Sunny. Before 1903, Celtic were a good, but not necessarily great team. Rangers, for example, had just won the Scottish League for four seasons in a row. Celtic had won the Scottish League in 1893, 1894, 1896 and 1898 but had failed to do so since, and the Scottish Cup had been won in 1892, 1899 and 1900. The record was good but not great. And then after Sunny's retirement and death, we find a decline in Celtic's performances. There were many great players like Patsy Gallacher, Jimmy McGrory and Jimmy Delaney but the League was won on only four occasions in the twenty year period between the two wars, and the Scottish Cup (slightly more often) six times. This was not the dominance of the pre-Great War era. It is hard to imagine Rangers, even with all their fine players like Alan Morton, Tommy Cairns and Bob McPhail managing to get such a stranglehold on Scottish football, if Sunny Jim had still been around. It was only the arrival of Jock Stein in 1965 that changed things – and how!

Historians talk highly of Young's contribution to the club, but sometimes in less than glowingly encomiastic terms. James Handley's *The Celtic Story*, literary and romantic on occasion, talks of Young, Loney and Hay in terms of the Three Musketeers of Alexander Dumas – "the Porthos, Athos and Aramis of the football field", but when talking of Young himself contents itself with saying things like "J.S. (sic) Young has been remarkable for his sustained play", and the highly acclaimed *Glory And The Dream* by Tom Campbell and Pat Woods in its Stuff of Legend section on great players include men like McNair, Quinn and Gallacher – but not Sunny Jim. In the narrative section of the book, Young is described as "strong and totally reliable".

Willie Maley on the other hand in *The Story of The Celtic*, a highly personalised and idiosyncratic account which is prone to mistakes – he thinks for example that Sunny never played again after the game in Paisley on the opening day of the 1916–17 season, whereas it was against Hearts that he bowed out – says, "Celtic have never had a more whole-hearted player. He was a half-back of the rugged type, but there was class in his ruggedness, whilst for stamina he stood in the front rank. His enthusiasm inclined him sometimes to excesses, but a kinder-hearted fellow never wore a Celtic jersey...In time he became captain of Celtic, and a splendid one he made. A player of dauntless courage, he served Celtic faithfully and ably for many seasons".

But the *locus classicus* of Sunny Jim must be *An Alphabet of the Celts* by Eugene MacBride, Martin O'Connor and George Sheridan says, "Who then on grass was the greatest of the Celts? The question seems otiose and the answer obvious. First is Patsy Gallacher, second Jimmy Quinn, third Jimmy McGrory. In fact the truth is Parkhead's forgotten man: Sunny Jim Young. Sunny was the greatest Celt ever. See Matthew 7.16 (By their fruit you will recognise them)".

The closest modern parallel to Sunny Jim is Roy Aitken. There are indeed similarities – obvious ones that they both came from Ayrshire, played in (more or less) the same position, and more subtle ones that neither were what one would have called brilliant players, but they did inspire Celtic to success. Both had a commanding presence, and both were dedicated family men. Roy had more International recognition, but Sunny had more sustained success with Celtic. Both had their "moments" with referees and could dish out the raw meat if required, but both were totally committed to the cause. Roy played in a team that was not quite so good as Sunny's and had quite a few barren seasons. Roy also had a slightly thinner skin than Sunny and was driven out of Parkhead in early 1990 by a combination of boos from the less intelligent of the Celtic fans (who had very short memories) and the ill-informed attacks of one journalist in particular who, frankly, did not like him. Roy then played for Newcastle United, St Mirren and Aberdeen, but not as well as he did for Celtic. Sunny, on the other hand, was a one-team man from his arrival in 1903 until his injury in 1916.

Sunny's tragic early death is curiously not commemorated by Celtic supporters as much as one would expect. This is in total contrast to John Thomson, for example. The circumstances are of course totally different. John was a lot younger and "was killed in action" as it were on that awful day of 5 September 1931. But John's death is commemorated by local Fife supporters clubs (on a cold day in February 2013, Neil Lennon brought the Celtic team to hear a graveside oration from a local supporter called Mark Cameron) and his grave is frequently visited by supporters and adorned with Celtic scarves and favours. Perhaps the grave of Sunny Jim Young should be similarly feted.

In recent years the Celtic Graves Society has done a great deal in finding graves of old Celts and doing a massive job in cemeteries like Dalbeth and others. One of their ceremonies was in the Kilmarnock Cemetery in Grassyards Road for Johnny Doyle and it was from there that some of us were taken to "see Sunny Jim", as it was put! The grave is well kept, but maybe should be better highlighted, and it would be nice if one of the local supporters clubs could take on this task. In terms of Celtic history, Sunny Jim was a mighty man, and deserves to be better commemorated.

Celtic's history is of course full of men who died long before their time – John Thomson, Tommy Burns, Peter Somers, Dan Doyle, Peter Scarff, Bertie Thomson, Donnie McLeod, Peter Johnstone, Johnny Doyle and many others, whose relatives I apologise to for omitting, but Sunny is a particularly tragic case, for he might have, in time, become a great backroom team man for Celtic. He retained the love and the ear of Maley, and might have been Maley's assistant manager or even successor. He certainly retained his love and passion for both football and Celtic until that awful day of 4 September 1922.

A minor mystery surrounds the repeated statements in newspapers around the time of his death that he was the "brother-in-law" of Alick Smith of Rangers. This seems unlikely, for there is no known connection between Smith and Florence, nor does Smith seem to have been married to any of Sunny's sisters. Alexander Smith (commonly known as "Cutty") died in Darvel, a "lace manufacturer" in November 1954 at the age of 79 and his widow is given as Isabella Allison Spiers, again with no known connection to the Young family. It may be that the word "brother-in-law" is a vague one here, and that what is meant is "distant relative by marriage".

Young and Smith of course often played against each other. They were doughty competitors and both fine players with any family connection going out the window for the duration of the ninety minutes. But, as with everyone else, once the game was over, Young became genial, courteous and generous to everyone, opponents, referees and all. Playing for the opposition was never a bar to friendship as far as Sunny was concened.

Florence re-married less than a year later on 6 June 1923 to a man from Saltcoats, a blacksmith called Crighton Burns. Ironically perhaps it was in St Mary's RC Church in Saltcoats and they were married according to, "the Form of the Roman Catholic Church" and Florence is described as a Licensed Bar Keeper. It looks as if Florence kept on the Royal Hotel after Sunny died. Poor Florence herself died at the age of 48 of womb cancer on 27 October 1931 at her home of 37 Irvine Road, Kilmarnock. There is a certain indication that the family of Alice, Irene and James were not 100% in favour of this marriage (this is by no means uncommon, of course!) because the gravestone of Sunny and Florence, erected by the family, pointedly makes no mention of Florence's marriage to Crighton Burns.

Alice had already married John Callaghan, an Engineers Fitter on 18 April 1923 in Kilmarnock (again in a Roman Catholic Church), Irene being the bridesmaid and witness. Irene herself of "Cramond" Grange View, Kilmarnock on 20 June 1932 married a motor mechanic called Robert Cochrane in Glasgow, with James Young, her brother, being the best man. James himself married Elizabeth Beaton, a few days after D-Day on 15 June 1944.

James's marriage seems to have been childless, and he died in 1990. Poor Alice was not fated to live long, dying in 1936 but not before she had four children. Irene on the other hand lived until 1983 but only seems to have had one child. Sunny thus had five grandchildren. It is a pity none of them ever met their illustrious grandfather, for he was some man!

A hundred years is of course a long time ago, and it is hardly surprising if the name Sunny Jim does not mean very much to the current generation of Celtic supporters. Most will have heard the name, but will not know many details. McGrory and Quinn are of course better known, but they were great goalscorers, and Gallacher is still referred to as the greatest player who ever lived. (My father said frequently in any discussion about Puskas or Pele, "Look I ken a thing or twa aboot fitba! I saw Patsy Gallacher!"). Sunny Jim deserves at least a place in the massive pantheon of Celtic heroes. This book has been an attempt to do that.

"One fine big Celtic boy would play without the money
Parkhead's endless inspiration, salute Jim, the genial Sunny!"

STATISTICS

Appearances for Celtic;

Scottish League 392 – nine winner's medals viz. 1904–05, 1905–06, 1906–07, 1907–08, 1908–09, 1909–10, 1913–14, 1914–15, 1915–16 (he may have won a medal in 1917 as well, but he played only 5 games)

Scottish Cup 51 – six winner's medals viz. 1903–04, 1906–07, 1907–08, 1910–11, 1911–12, 1913–14

Glasgow Cup 39 – six winner's medals viz. 1904–05, 1905–06, 1906–7, 1907–08, 1909–10, 1915–16

Glasgow Charity Cup 31 – eight winner's medals viz. 1902–03, 1904–05, 1907–08, 1911–12, 1912–13, 1913–14, 1914–15, 1915–16

Appearances for Scotland;

Ireland 1 - 1906
English League 5 - 1904, 1905, 1906, 1907, 1911
Southern League 1 - 1910

Appearances for Bristol Rovers;

Southern League 19
English Cup 3
Gloucestershire Cup 3 - one winner's medal 1903

Appearances for Barrow;

Lancashire League 6

ND - #0281 - 270225 - C0 - 234/156/13 - PB - 9781780913124 - Gloss Lamination